THE
𝕱ootball 𝕮imes
North of Scotland
Football Review
2023

Researched & Compiled by
Niall Harkiss

K & N Publishing © 2023

ISBN 978-1-7391375-4-0
niall.harkiss@kandnconcepts.co.uk
twitter @NiallFH @TheFitbaTimes
www.tainpost.co.uk/review

TABLE OF CONTENTS

SO NEAR YET SO FAR FOR CHAMPIONS BRECHIN CITY

Two late goals decided the fate of this year's Scottish Highland Football League championship as Brechin City edged nearest rivals Buckie Thistle on the final day of the season.

The Glebe Park have established themselves as a force to be reckoned with in the Highland League ever since their relegation in 2021, dropping out of the national leagues for the first time in 67 years.

A tightly contested race between the Hedgemen and Buckie saw both sides go into the final week of the season in a head-to-head meeting at Buckie. The hosts, ahead by one point, only had to avoid defeat.

With no goals to speak of in the first half of a tense affair at Victoria Park, it was substitute Ewan Loudon who eventually broke the deadlock in the 87th minute, before marksman Grady McGrath put the game to bed with a second

in injury time.

Brechin had secured their first Highland League title – their first senior championship honour in 18 years.

For Buckie it was a repeat of the misery they experienced in the season prior, losing out on the final day to then champions, Fraserburgh.

Entering the last fifteen minutes of the match, the game was poised to go either way, but Brechin looked the most likely to score.

And that they did with three minutes of normal times remaining when Loudon broke clear of the defence and

SCOTTISH HIGHLAND FOOTBALL LEAGUE 2022-23

		Pl	W	D	L	F	A	GD	Pts	PPG
1	Brechin City	34	28	5	1	101	16	+85	89	2.62
2	Buckie Thistle	34	28	3	3	92	26	+66	87	2.56
3	Brora Rangers	34	26	2	6	116	32	+84	80	2.35
4	Formartine	34	23	5	6	81	31	+50	74	2.18
5	Fraserburgh	34	21	8	5	91	31	+60	71	2.09
6	Inverurie Locos	34	14	8	12	63	57	+6	50	1.47
7	Nairn County	34	12	10	12	51	63	-12	46	1.35
8	Huntly	34	13	6	15	44	49	-5	45	1.32
9	Rothes	34	12	8	14	64	60	+4	44	1.29
10	Banks o' Dee	34	19	6	9	98	49	+49	39	1.15
11	Forres Mech	34	10	6	18	57	60	-3	36	1.06
12	Turriff United	34	11	3	20	56	76	-20	36	1.06
13	Clachnacuddin	34	10	4	20	44	76	-32	34	1.00
14	Lossiemouth	34	8	3	23	38	83	-45	27	0.79
15	Keith	34	7	6	21	38	87	-49	27	0.79
16	Wick Academy	34	7	5	22	34	100	-66	26	0.76
17	Deveronvale	34	6	6	22	48	90	-42	24	0.71
18	Strathspey Th	34	2	4	28	24	154	-130	10	0.29

Brechin City became Highland Football League champions for the first time after two late goals sealed victory against closest rivals Buckie Thistle. Photo: Graham Youngson

fired a right-foot shot into the bottom corner.

The goal sparked a short pitch invasion as sections of a 750-strong City support who had traveled north for the game struggled to hide their jubilation.

Buckie threw everything at an equaliser in the dying minutes of the game, but it was Brechin who had the final say when McGrath finished well after receiving the ball from Botti Biabi five minutes into stoppage time.

Celebrations had to be short as City faced the immediate prospect of a pyramid play-off meeting with Lowland League winners Spartans on April 29th.

The first leg, which took place in Edinburgh, ended in disaster as City found themselves down to ten men and a goal down going into the home leg one week later.

Back at Glebe Park, a thriller 3-2 win saw the play-off end all square, sending the fate of both sides to a penalty shoot-out. The winner would go on to meet Club 42, Albion Rovers, with a place in SPFL League Two at stake.

In the end though, the opportunity was not to be for Brechin, as they lost the shoot-out 4-3.

It was a tragic end to a memorable season for the Glebe Park side, who will scarcely have enjoyed such dominance throughout a season, albeit with no reward of promotion at the end of it.

Such was their success, it is not surprising that manager Andy Kirk was snapped up by Premiership side St Johnstone in November 2023 to assist former Brechin advisor Craig Levein in the dugout.

Grady McGrath, who joined Brechin in the summer of 2022 after netting a barrage of goals with Midlands junior side Dundee East Craigie, ran away with the top scorer's spot in the Highland League, netting 35 goals in all competiions, including 29 league goals in 34 games.

The striker was undoubtedly the breakout name in the league throughout 2022-23, and along with his City comrades, has helped to establish Brechin as a force within "Highland" football circles, and a club we should all be ready to get used to thinking about when it comes to honours.

There is little doubt that Banks o' Dee had the most jekyl and hyde of campaigns in 2022-23.

Hit with a 24 point deduction after being found to have played an ineligible player on multiple ocassions, the Aberdeenshire side found themselves rooted to the bottom of the table – albeit temporarily – instead of competing at the top half of the table, as some believed they may have been.

In the end they finished in 10th place with 39 points. Had they not had the deduction, they would have achieved a 6th place finish.

On the park, they impressed as the newest addition to the senior ranks, having graduated from the ranks of the North Region juniors in place of long standing member Fort William after their "relegation" to the North Caledonian League in 2022.

The Spain Park side's fortunes had firmly turned around by April, when they secured their first senior honour, as winners of the Highland League Cup with a 1-0 victory over Inverurie Locos.

Third placed Brora Rangers saw their title hopes drift away with early-season defeats to Brechin City and Formartine before manager Craig Campbell left the club in January. Defeats under new boss Ally MacDonald in March, to Banks o' Dee and Buckie Thistle, ended any hopes of catching the leading pair.

Despite their results, the Cattachs were nothing if not prolific in front of goal, with the Macrae namesakes, Jordan and Andrew, grabbing 31 and 30 goals, respectively.

In fourth, Formartine United were ultimately undone by their results against the top three. Finalists in the Aberdeenshire Cup, they enjoyed their best form in the first half of the campaign. The high point of their season was arguably their third round meeting with Stenhousemuir in the Scottish Cup, having earlier eliminated East Stirlingshire and Carnoustie Panmure in earlier rounds.

Former champions Fraserburgh will feel they should have made a better fist of their title defence after finishing in fifth place – but the season did end with some silverware in the cabinet, collecting the Aberdeenshire Cup with a win over Formartine United in November. A good showing in the Scottish Cup also ended with a third round defeat at the hands of SPFL championship side, Arbroath.

Disappointment for Inverurie Locos in the Highland League Cup final was the punctuating point for the Railwaymen after they finished sixth in the table. Early exits in the other cup competitions spelled out a disappointing campaign overall, falling short of being able to match the top sides on the park in the league.

A surprise seventh place for Nairn County, enjoying their first full season under the management of Steven Mackay, was made possibly in part by the inspired signing of Inverness Caledonian Thistle legend Ross Tokely. The arrival of the 44 year old defender coincided with an upturn in fortunes that saw County embark on a run which saw lose just once to title contenders Buckie Thistle between October and February.

Just 21 points separated the sides in 8th (Huntly) and 17th place (Deveronvale), with bottom placed Strathspey Thistle cut adrift at the bottom of the table, fourteen points behind their closest rival.

Unlike season 2021-22, none of the Tier 6 league winners were eligible for promotion due to licensing restrictions, and as such the Jags were spared the concern of a relegation play-off match.

In the lower ranks of Tier 6, the north half of the pyramid's three division – the North Caledonian League, the North Region Junior Premier League and the East Region Midlands League – produced no licensed winners.

In the North Caley, Loch Ness, who joined the league in 2020, won their first ever league championship – which was also their first ever trophy in the division – when they were named champions after a 13-team campaign which was the longest the league has seen since the 1980s.

Manager Shane Carling has worked hard to build a squad of players who have been playing all year round – as members of the Inverness & District amateur league during the summer and the North Caledonian League during the winter.

The unique merging of interests has been mirrored by other clubs in the north, such as Clachnacuddin and Inverness Athletic, who also enter amateur combinations in the Inverness & District league, and Fort William, who as well as playing in the North Caledonian League, also play as members of the North West Highland AFA.

For Loch Ness, their ascendence to

The North Caledonian League saw a new champion crowned with Loch Ness lifting the championship trophy for 2022-23. It was their first senior honour. Photo: David Jefferson

the title came at the expense of last season's champions Invergordon, who were denied a treble having also won the association's two cup competitions.

The reward for the Fortrose-based side was a place in the 2023-24 Scottish Cup.

NORTH CALEDONIAN LEAGUE 2022-23

		P	W	D	L	F	A	GD	Pts	PPG
1	Loch Ness	24	20	2	2	101	28	+73	62	2.58
2	Invergordon	24	19	1	4	75	24	+51	58	2.42
3	Fort William	24	15	0	9	79	46	+33	45	1.88
4	St Duthus	24	14	2	8	63	49	+14	44	1.83
5	Orkney	24	12	6	6	57	35	+22	42	1.75
6	Golspie Suth	24	13	3	8	56	48	+8	42	1.75
7	Inverness Ath	24	13	1	10	50	45	+5	40	1.67
8	Halkirk United	24	10	2	12	53	56	-3	32	1.33
9	Alness United	24	10	1	13	69	63	+6	31	1.29
10	Clach A	24	9	0	15	50	64	-14	27	1.13
11	Nairn County A	24	5	1	18	33	73	-40	16	0.67
12	Thurso	24	4	3	17	38	70	-32	15	0.63
13	Bonar Bridge	24	1	0	23	20	143	-123	3	0.13

It is the second time the winners of the North Caledonian League have been granted a place in the preliminary round of Scotland's national cup competition – irrespective of their license held.

Join top of the goalscoring charts in the North Caledonian League was former Forres Mechanics man Allan MacPhee, who since joining Loch Ness, has becomed a potent striker, netting no fewer than 31 goals in 26 matches during 2022-23.

Just as impressive was Invergordon's Ben Kelly, with 31 goals in 28 games. The Black Isle based player caught the eye of Steven Mackay at Nairn and has since secured a move to Station Park for the 2023-24 campaign.

Returning to the North Caledonian League for the first time since 1985 was Fort William, having been relegated from the Highland League after failing to compete in the Tier 6 pyramid playoff at the end of the 2021-22 season.

The Claggan Park side finished in third place, falling well short of the points needed for an immediate "try" at securing promotion via the pyramid playoff.

The Lochaber side remain one of only two teams in the North Caley who are eligible for promotion, the other being Golspie Sutherland.

Further east, Culter undoubted dominance of the North Region junior scene was cemented with a

NORTH REGION JUNIOR PREMIER LEAGUE 2022-23

		Pl	W	D	L	F	A	GD	Pts	PPG
1	Culter	26	24	1	1	90	17	+73	73	2.81
2	Hermes	26	20	5	1	94	16	+78	65	2.50
3	Dyce	26	14	7	5	52	29	+23	49	1.88
4	Stonehaven	26	13	6	7	44	29	+15	45	1.73
5	Bridge of Don Th	26	12	6	8	57	35	+22	42	1.62
6	Stoneywood PV	26	12	4	10	47	50	-3	40	1.54
7	East End	26	11	5	10	52	40	+12	38	1.46
8	Ellon United	26	10	4	12	41	50	-9	34	1.31
9	Mon Roselea	26	9	6	11	42	49	-7	33	1.27
10	Maud	26	7	3	16	30	60	-30	24	0.92
11	Colony Park	26	6	5	15	28	69	-41	23	0.88
12	Nairn St Ninian	26	5	5	16	38	71	-33	20	0.77
13	Ban. St Ternan*	26	3	3	20	23	76	-53	9	0.58
14	Dufftown*	26	3	6	17	22	69	-47	8	0.46

quadruple trophy haul, including the Premier League title.

Adding to their success, they also won the Grill League Cup, North Regional Cup and the all-Premier, McLeman Cup.

Lee Youngson's side were uncompromising throughout a campaign which saw them defeated just once in league competition, by close rivals Hermes, dropping a total of just five points across 26 games. The Aberdeenshire side's only other tastes of defeat came in the Quest Engineering Cup, falling at the first hurdle against Stoneywood-Parkvale, and an ousting from the Scottish Junior Cup via penalty-shoot against Stonehaven.

With 47 goals in 41 appearances, ex-Brechin Victoria striker Cammy Fraser terrorised goalkeepers and defences throughout the campaign and the striker, who lives in the Aberdeen area for work, has extended his stay with the Crombie Park club into 2023-24.

The 2022-23 season saw the last of the 14-team format for the top tier, with Banchory St Ternan and Dufftown relegated to the Championship, and Montrose Roselea transferring to the East Region.

Adding to the misery of St Ternan and Dufftown, both sides were handed point deductions for fielding ineligible players. A total of three was deducted from St Ternan for one

NRJFA President John Carroll presents the Premier League trophy to club captain Ritchie Petrie. Photo: Culter FC

instance, while Dufftown were dealt with more harshly with a seven point penalty for several instances.

In the recently restructured second tier of the North Region JFA, Sunnybank emerged as winners of a sixteen team Championship, and have joined five

NORTH REGION JUNIOR CHAMPIONSHIP 2022-23

		Pl	W	D	L	F	A	GD	Pts	PPG
1	Sunnybank	30	23	4	3	80	23	+57	73	2.43
2	Fraserburgh Utd	30	21	3	6	85	38	+47	66	2.20
3	Rothie Rovers	30	20	5	5	76	27	+49	65	2.17
4	Buchanhaven H	30	19	4	7	65	39	+26	61	2.03
5	Newmachar Utd	30	19	3	8	71	38	+33	60	2.00
6	Forres Thistle	30	18	5	7	60	31	+29	59	1.97
7	Banks o' Dee JFC	30	15	4	11	85	53	+32	49	1.63
8	Islavale	30	15	1	14	47	51	-4	43	1.43
9	Longside	30	10	7	13	57	52	+5	37	1.23
10	Burghead Th	30	9	6	15	40	65	-25	33	1.10
11	Glentanar	30	10	1	19	43	66	-23	31	1.03
12	Deveronside	30	8	4	18	42	74	-32	28	0.93
13	Aberdeen Uni	30	9	4	17	53	72	-19	25	0.83
14	Cruden Bay	30	5	5	20	31	65	-34	20	0.67
15	Lossiemouth Utd	30	5	4	21	33	93	-60	13	0.43
16	New Elgin	30	3	2	25	24	105	-81	11	0.37

other teams who have been promoted to a new sixteen team Premier League for 2023-24.

Now in its second season since its inauguration as a participating league in the North football pyramid, the East Region Midlands Football League produced little in the way of shocks.

Carnoustie Panmure, who were crowned the first winners of the league in 2022, retained the title after 36 games, with three points to spare over closest rivals Broughty Athletic.

The Gowfers sauntered over the finish line, despite stuttering defeats to Downfield and Lochee United on the way, but even with several games in hand at an early stage, they met expectation in retaining this season's championship.

It was a double-winning season for the Laing Park side this time around too, winning the East Region League Cup with a penalty-shoot out win over Broughty Athletic after an entertaining 3-3 draw.

Experienced forward Dale Reid was the standout man for Carnoustie again, netted 56 times during the campaign, only narrowly bettering his 2021-22 total of 54 to record an astonishing 100 goals in just two seasons.

The former Montrose man put further smiles on Gowfers fans' faces by signing a two-year contract extension in January.

Carnoustie Panmure's season ended with the news that manager Phil McGurie would be stepping down from his role to focus on "connecting with the community and building youth links off it."

Within the Midlands League, the only two SFA licensed clubs, Lochee United and Tayport, had tepid campaigns. United had the better chance in the latter stages to mount a challenge, but ultimately defeats to Scone Thistle, North End and Broughty Athletic in March and April saw them finish eight points behind the leaders.

Dundee based sides Broughty Athletic,

Carnoustie Panmure manager Phil McGuire stepped down from his role after the two-time league winners secured the East Region League Cup.   Photo: Carnoustie Panmure Facebook

EAST REGION MIDLANDS FOOTBALL LEAGUE 2022-23

		P	W	D	L	F	A	GD	Pts	PPG
1	Carnoustie Pan.	36	28	4	4	131	33	+98	88	2.44
2	Broughty Ath	36	27	4	5	121	34	+87	85	2.36
3	Downfield	36	26	4	6	104	41	+63	82	2.28
4	Lochee United	36	25	6	5	112	45	+67	81	2.25
5	North End	36	24	4	8	97	43	+54	76	2.11
6	East Craigie	36	23	6	7	94	44	+50	75	2.08
7	Kirrie Thistle	36	20	9	7	102	65	+37	69	1.92
8	Tayport	36	19	3	14	74	58	+16	60	1.67
9	Letham	36	15	8	13	64	56	+8	53	1.47
10	Arbroath Vics	36	12	7	17	57	73	-16	43	1.19
11	Forfar United	36	12	6	18	61	95	-34	42	1.17
12	Dundee Violet	36	11	6	19	65	102	-37	39	1.08
13	Coupar Angus	36	10	5	21	58	91	-33	35	0.97
14	Scone Thistle	36	10	5	21	50	96	-46	35	0.97
15	St James	36	8	7	21	47	99	-52	31	0.86
16	Blairgowrie	36	7	4	25	48	114	-66	25	0.69
17	Lochee Harp	36	5	5	26	57	108	-51	20	0.56
18	Brechin Vics	36	4	7	25	36	94	-58	19	0.53
19	Forfar West End	36	5	2	29	36	123	-87	17	0.47

Downfield, North End and East Craigie mounted the closest challenges – as well as Lochee United – and all finished in the top six.

For 2023-24, the league faces an increase in size with the introduction of Montrose Roselea, who have successfully negotiated a transfer from the North Region to the East.

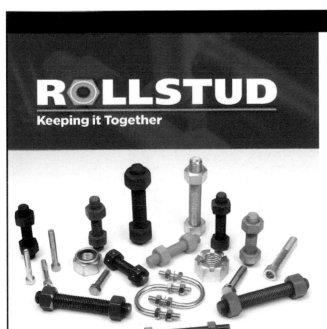

North Region Premier League contenders Dyce go in front against Maud.

Photo: Dyce FC

Highland League runners-up Buckie Thistle celebrate a late winner.

Photo: Alan Robertson

Wick Academy's Ross Allan and Lochee United's Gary Sutherland lock horns during a Scottish Cup meeting between the Highland League and Midlands League sides. Photo: Melanie Roger

East Region Midlands Football League champions Carnoustie Panmure celebrate winning the league championship for a second time. Photo: Carnoustie Panmure Facebook

PLAYING SQUAD & STATISTICS 2022/23

BANKS O' DEE F.C.
Spain Park, Aberdeen

	Age	LEAGUE		CUPS		ALL	
		Apps	Goals	Apps	Goals	Apps	Goals
ALEXANDER, Max	33	1 (5)	0	-	-	1 (5)	0
ALLAN, Neale	35	9 (7)	0	2	0	11 (7)	0
ANDERSON, Jevan	23	1	0	1	0	2	0
ANTONIAZZI, Chris	23	8	4	1 (1)	1	9 (1)	5
ARMSTRONG, Rob	34	19 (6)	5	3 (3)	0	22 (9)	5
CROSBIE, Lewis	22	8 (9)	4	2 (1)	2	10 (10)	6
DAVIDSON, Ramsay	18	7	0	1	0	8	0
GAULD, Neil	36	13 (11)	11	3 (3)	4	16 (14)	15
GILMOUR, Mark	25	28 (2)	10	7	1	35 (2)	11
HENDERSON, Jack	28	14 (10)	8	2 (4)	1	16 (14)	9
KELLY, Darryn	35	26 (1)	2	6	0	32 (1)	2
LAWRIE, Dean	35	13	0	2	0	15	0
LAWSON, Paul	39	5 (2)	0	2	0	7 (2)	0
LEWECKI, Kacper	20	26 (1)	1	4 (3)	0	30 (4)	1
MACASKILL, Craig	28	4 (4)	1	-	-	4 (4)	1
MACLEOD, Hamish	23	17 (6)	6	5 (1)	0	22 (7)	6
MACLEOD, Lachie	25	24 (7)	19	5 (1)	3	29 (8)	22
PHILIPSON, Michael	25	14 (5)	2	2	0	16 (5)	2
ROBERTSON, Matthew	32	(1)	0	1	0	1 (1)	0
ROTHNIE, Charlie	18	(1)	0	-	-	(1)	0
SALMON, Ross (GK)	30	14	0	2	0	16	0
SELBIE, Jason	18	4	0	2	0	6	0
SHEARER, Andy (GK)	40	20 (1)	0	5	0	25 (1)	0
STARK, Alasdair	25	29	0	7	0	36	0
WALLACE, Matthew	25	11 (14)	1	2 (1)	0	13 (15)	1
WATSON, Magnus	21	19 (5)	9	2 (4)	1	21 (9)	10
WILLOX, Kyle	25	1	0	-	-	1	0
WINTON, Kane	29	26	13	6	2	32	15
YOUNG, Marc	34	13	1	2 (1)	0	15 (1)	1

MATCH RESULTS 2022/23

Date	Opponent	Comp	Score	Scorers
Jul 23	Nairn County (H)	LGE	1-1	Winton
Jul 27	Fraserburgh (A)	AC R1	0-1	
Jul 30	Inverurie Locos (A)	LGE	1-1	Watson
Aug 6	Huntly (H)	LGE	5-2	Gilmour, Winton (2), Henderson, Armstrong
Aug 13	Brora Rangers (A)	LGE	0-3	
Aug 20	Keith (H)	LGE	8-0	Armstrong, Winton, Gauld, Gilmour (3), Watson, L Macleod
Aug 24	Turriff United (A)	LGE	1-1	Henderson
Aug 27	Clachnacuddin (H)	LGE	2-1	Gauld, Gilmour
Sep 3	Wick Academy (A)	LGE	8-0	Winton (3), L Macleod, Armstrong, Gauld (3)
Sep 17	Turriff United (H)	SC R1	4-0	Gauld, Winton, L Macleod, Crosbie
Sep 24	Forres Mechanics (H)	LGE	2-0	Young, Henderson
Oct 5	Deveronvale (H)	LGE	2-0	Henderson (2)
Oct 8	Buckie Thistle (A)	LGE	2-2	L Macleod, Kelly
Oct 11	Fraserburgh (A)	AS R1	3-3	Gauld (3)
Oct 14	Fraserburgh (H)	LGE	1-1	Crosbie
Nov 2	Rothes (A)	LGE	0-2	
Nov 5	Strathspey Thistle (A)	LGE	7-0	H MacLeod, Winton, Henderson, Kelly, Watson, Gauld
Nov 12	Brora Rangers (A)	HLC R1	3-3	Gilmour, L Macleod (2)
Nov 19	Inverurie Locos (H)	LGE	3-4	Gauld, L Macleod, H MacLeod
Nov 26	Huntly (A)	LGE	2-0	Winton, L Macleod
Dec 3	Forres Mechanics (H)	HLC QF	3-2	Winton, Crosbie, Henderson
Dec 23	Brechin City (A)	LGE	4-4	L Macleod, Crosbie, Philipson, MacAskill
Dec 30	Brechin City (H)	LGE	1-4	Armstrong
Jan 7	Nairn County (A)	LGE	0-3	
Jan 14	Turriff United (H)	LGE	2-0	Watson, H MacLeod
Jan 28	Wick Academy (H)	LGE	6-0	L Macleod, Watson (2), Henderson, H MacLeod (2)
Feb 4	Rothes (H)	LGE	2-0	Watson, L Macleod
Feb 11	Forres Mechanics (A)	LGE	2-1	Watson, L Macleod
Feb 18	Formartine United (H)	LGE	2-3	Gilmour, Winton
Feb 22	Lossiemouth (A)	LGE	2-1	Gauld (2)
Feb 25	Deveronvale (A)	LGE	4-1	Antoniazzi, Crosbie (2), L Macleod
Mar 4	Buckie Thistle (A)	HLC SF	1-1	Antoniazzi
Mar 11	Buckie Thistle (H)	LGE	1-3	L Macleod
Mar 18	Fraserburgh (A)	LGE	3-0	Gauld, L Macleod, Watson
Mar 22	Formartine United (A)	LGE	0-2	
Mar 25	Brora Rangers (H)	LGE	4-3	H MacLeod, L Macleod (2), Wallace
Mar 29	Clachnacuddin (A)	LGE	1-3	Lewecki
Apr 1	Lossiemouth (H)	LGE	7-0	L Macleod (2), Henderson, Philipson, Gilmour, Antoniazzi, Gauld
Apr 8	Inverurie Locos (A)	HLC F	1-0	Watson
Apr 15	Strathspey Thistle (H)	LGE	9-1	L Macleod, Antoniazzi (2), Winton (2), Gilmour (3), Armstrong
Apr 22	Keith (A)	LGE	3-2	L Macleod (2), Winton

BRECHIN CITY F.C.
Glebe Park, Brechin

	Age	LEAGUE		CUPS		ALL	
		Apps	Goals	Apps	Goals	Apps	Goals
ARNOTT, Aaron	20	5 (5)	1	1 (2)	0	6 (7)	1
BAIN, Jamie	32	27	3	5 (2)	0	32 (2)	3
BIABI, Botti	27	19 (5)	9	5	4	24 (5)	13
COONEY, Nathan	21	24 (3)	0	7 (1)	0	31 (4)	0
CRUICKSHANK, Michael	31	15 (4)	1	5 (1)	0	20 (5)	1
DAVIDSON, Iain	39	1 (1)	0	(1)	0	1 (2)	0
EASTON, Dean (GK)	28	-	-	2	0	2	0
FERGUSON, Calum	28	(5)	0	-	-	(5)	0
INGLIS, Kieran	23	27 (3)	9	7 (2)	1	34 (5)	10
KOUTSIMOUKA, Aubrel	22	5	0	1	0	6	0
LOUDON, Ewan	20	7 (20)	8	4 (6)	0	11 (26)	8
MACLEOD, Fraser	22	33 (1)	6	9 (1)	2	42 (2)	8
MCARTHUR, Michael	22	9 (6)	0	3 (1)	0	12 (7)	0
MCDONALD, Anthony	22	17 (9)	9	3 (2)	1	20 (11)	10
MCGRATH, Grady	21	31 (3)	29	10	6	41 (3)	35
MCHATTIE, Kevin	30	28 (1)	3	10	2	38 (1)	5
MCINNES, Ryan	18	(2)	0	(3)	0	(5)	0
NAGLIK, Dominic	19	(2)	1	(1)	0	(3)	1
NORTHCOTT, Jordan	21	14 (17)	4	7 (1)	2	21 (18)	6
PATRICK, Seth	23	6	1	2	0	8	1
ROSS, Cameron	25	2 (3)	1	(1)	0	2 (4)	1
SCOTT, Marc	27	34	15	10	1	44	16
SPARK, Euan	27	24	0	9	2	33	2
THOMSON, Hamish	25	12 (3)	0	2	0	14 (3)	0
WILSON, Lenny (GK)	26	34	0	8	0	42	0

Having signed from Midlands side East Craigie in the summer of 2022, Grady McGrath showed relentless form in front of goal for Brechin, netting 29 league goals in 34 appearances.
Photo: Brechin City FC

MATCH RESULTS 2022/23

Date	Opponent	Comp	Score	Scorers
Jul 23	Rothes (H)	LGE	1-0	Ross
Jul 30	Forres Mechanics (A)	LGE	1-0	McHattie
Aug 6	Formartine United (H)	LGE	3-1	Scott, McGrath
Aug 10	Hibernian B (A)	SCC R1	1-1	Northcott
Aug 13	Deveronvale (A)	LGE	3-1	Scott, Patrick, Northcott
Aug 20	Buckie Thistle (H)	LGE	1-0	McGrath
Aug 24	Stirling Albion (H)	SCC R2	1-1	Scott
Aug 27	Lossiemouth (H)	LGE	3-0	McGrath, McDonald, Macleod
Sep 3	Strathspey Thistle (A)	LGE	5-0	McHattie, Inglis (2), Loudon, McGrath
Sep 17	Jeanfield Swifts (A)	SC R1	5-1	McGrath (2), Spark, McDonald, Northcott
Sep 24	Inverness CT (A)	SCC R3	3-3	McHattie, McGrath, Spark
Oct 1	Inverurie Locos (A)	LGE	1-0	McGrath
Oct 5	Huntly (H)	LGE	2-2	McDonald, Northcott
Oct 8	Brora Rangers (A)	LGE	3-0	Macleod, Scott, McGrath
Oct 15	Keith (H)	LGE	5-0	McDonald, McGrath (2), Inglis, Biabi
Oct 22	Stirling Albion (H)	SC R2	2-2	McHattie, McGrath
Oct 29	Turriff United (A)	LGE	4-1	Biabi, Northcott, McGrath, Inglis
Nov 5	Clachnacuddin (H)	LGE	5-0	McDonald, McGrath (3), McHattie
Nov 12	Rothes (H)	HLC R1	4-2	McGrath, Biabi (3)
Nov 19	Forres Mechanics (H)	LGE	2-1	Scott, McGrath
Dec 3	Lossiemouth (A)	HLC QF	2-0	McGrath, Macleod
Dec 10	Deveronvale (H)	LGE	7-1	Inglis, McGrath (3), Loudon (2), Arnott
Dec 23	Banks o' Dee (H)	LGE	4-4	Biabi, Macleod, McGrath, Scott
Dec 30	Banks o' Dee (A)	LGE	4-1	Cruickshank, Biabi, Macleod, McGrath
Jan 7	Rothes (A)	LGE	1-0	Biabi
Jan 21	Lossiemouth (A)	LGE	3-0	Scott (2), Naglik
Jan 28	Strathspey Thistle (H)	LGE	6-0	Inglis, Scott (2), McDonald, McGrath, Biabi
Feb 4	Wick Academy (A)	LGE	3-0	Bain (2), Northcott
Feb 11	Nairn County (A)	LGE	0-0	
Feb 18	Inverurie Locos (H)	LGE	5-1	Loudon (2), Scott, Inglis, Bain
Feb 22	Formartine United (A)	LGE	0-2	
Feb 25	Huntly (A)	LGE	1-0	McDonald
Mar 4	Inverurie Locos (A)	HLC SF	0-2	
Mar 22	Nairn County (H)	LGE	3-0	McGrath, Scott, Biabi
Mar 25	Wick Academy (H)	LGE	10-0	Scott (2), McGrath (5), Loudon, Inglis (2)
Mar 29	Fraserburgh (A)	LGE	0-0	
Apr 1	Turriff United (H)	LGE	4-0	McGrath (2), McDonald (2)
Apr 5	Brora Rangers (H)	LGE	0-0	
Apr 12	Fraserburgh (H)	LGE	5-0	Biabi, Macleod, Scott (2), McGrath
Apr 15	Clachnacuddin (A)	LGE	2-1	Biabi, McDonald
Apr 19	Keith (A)	LGE	2-0	Macleod, Loudon
Apr 22	Buckie Thistle (A)	LGE	2-0	Loudon, McGrath
Apr 29	Spartans (A)	PO	0-1	
May 6	Spartans (H)	PO	3-2	Macleod, Inglis, Biabi

BRORA RANGERS F.C.
Dudgeon Park, Brora

	Age	LEAGUE		CUPS		ALL	
		Apps	Goals	Apps	Goals	Apps	Goals
DINGWALL, Tony	29	27 (4)	13	2 (2)	0	29 (6)	13
EWAN, Max	22	20 (11)	11	4	1	24 (11)	12
GAMBLE, Millar	21	17 (7)	2	2 (1)	0	19 (8)	2
GILLESPIE, Dale	34	31 (1)	8	4 (2)	0	35 (3)	8
GUNN, Ross	22	9 (19)	2	2 (3)	0	11 (22)	2
KELLY, Tom	23	30 (1)	1	4 (1)	1	34 (2)	2
MACDONALD, Ally	35	23	0	5	1	28	1
MACDONALD, Gregor	22	20 (13)	10	3 (3)	2	23 (16)	12
MACLEAN, Martin	32	19 (4)	2	4	0	23 (4)	2
MACLEOD, Andrew	18	(5)	0	-	-	(5)	0
MACRAE, Andrew	25	30 (4)	26	6	4	36 (4)	30
MACRAE, Jordan	25	29 (2)	24	5 (1)	7	34 (3)	31
MALIN, Joe (GK)	35	6	0	2	0	8	0
MEEKINGS, Josh	31	10	1	4 (1)	0	14 (1)	1
NICOL, Ruardhri (GK)	19	12 (1)	0	4	0	16 (1)	0
NICOLSON, Mark	35	24 (1)	6	4 (1)	0	28 (2)	6
ROSS, Logan (GK)	19	16	0	-	-	16	0
SUTHERLAND, Ali	27	25 (6)	6	5 (1)	0	30 (7)	6
WALLACE, James	23	(1)	0	-	-	(1)	0
WILLIAMSON, Colin	33	26 (1)	3	6	0	32 (1)	3

Ally MacDonald and Josh Meekings took on the role of player-manager and assistant in February 2023, along with player-coach Joe Malin.
Photo: Brora Rangers

Date	Opponent	Comp	Score	Scorers
Jul 23	Keith (A)	LGE	4-0	Gillespie, J MacRae, A Macrae (2)
Jul 30	Turriff United (H)	LGE	2-1	Dingwall, J MacRae
Aug 6	Clachnacuddin (A)	LGE	4-0	A Macrae, J MacRae (2), Meekings
Aug 9	Aberdeen B (H)	SCC R1	2-0	J MacRae, A Macrae
Aug 13	Banks o' Dee (H)	LGE	3-0	Dingwall (2), G MacDonald
Aug 17	Strathspey Thistle (H)	NoS QF	4-0	A Macrae, Ewan, J MacRae, G MacDonald
Aug 20	Rothes (A)	LGE	4-0	A Macrae (2), Dingwall, Ewan
Aug 24	Buckie Thistle (A)	SCC R2	1-1	A Macrae
Aug 27	Formartine United (A)	LGE	1-2	A Macrae
Aug 31	Lossiemouth (A)	NoS SF	4-1	Kelly, J MacRae (3)
Sep 3	Deveronvale (H)	LGE	5-0	Gillespie, J MacRae (2), A Macrae
Sep 24	Fraserburgh (A)	LGE	2-2	Ewan, A Macrae
Oct 1	Clachnacuddin (H)	NoS F	2-1	J MacRae, A Macrae
Oct 5	Strathspey Thistle (A)	LGE	11-0	G MacDonald (2), A Macrae, J MacRae (2), Gillespie, Sutherland, Kelly, Nicolson, Dingwall, Ewan
Oct 8	Brechin City (H)	LGE	0-3	
Oct 15	Nairn County (A)	LGE	4-0	A Macrae (3), Nicolson
Oct 22	Forres Mechanics (H)	LGE	4-1	Sutherland, Nicolson, Gunn, A Macrae
Oct 29	Inverurie Locos (H)	LGE	5-2	A Macrae (2), Dingwall, Ewan, Gillespie
Nov 5	Huntly (A)	LGE	3-1	A Macrae, Sutherland, G MacDonald
Nov 12	Banks o' Dee (H)	HLC R1	3-3	G MacDonald, A Macdonald, J MacRae
Nov 26	Clachnacuddin (H)	LGE	4-2	Williamson, A Macrae, J MacRae (2)
Jan 7	Keith (H)	LGE	6-1	A Macrae, Ewan, J MacRae (2), Williamson, Gillespie
Jan 14	Forres Mechanics (A)	LGE	8-0	Dingwall, A Macrae (2), Ewan, G MacDonald (2), Maclean, J MacRae
Jan 28	Deveronvale (A)	LGE	6-0	J MacRae (3), Maclean, Ewan, G MacDonald
Feb 4	Buckie Thistle (A)	LGE	2-4	A Macrae, Dingwall
Feb 11	Fraserburgh (H)	LGE	0-1	
Feb 18	Lossiemouth (A)	LGE	3-0	Gillespie, Ewan (2)
Feb 22	Wick Academy (A)	LGE	7-1	J MacRae, Ewan, Gillespie, A Macrae, Sutherland, Dingwall (2)
Feb 25	Strathspey Thistle (H)	LGE	2-0	Gamble, A Macrae
Mar 4	Turriff United (A)	LGE	4-0	Sutherland, G MacDonald (3)
Mar 15	Buckie Thistle (H)	LGE	0-2	
Mar 18	Nairn County (H)	LGE	2-1	J MacRae, Gamble
Mar 25	Banks o' Dee (A)	LGE	3-4	J MacRae (3)
Mar 29	Wick Academy (H)	LGE	6-1	Gunn, Dingwall (2), A Macrae, Sutherland, J MacRae
Apr 1	Inverurie Locos (A)	LGE	4-2	J MacRae, A Macrae (2), Dingwall
Apr 5	Brechin City (A)	LGE	0-0	
Apr 8	Formartine United (H)	LGE	2-1	Gillespie, Williamson
Apr 12	Lossiemouth (H)	LGE	1-0	Ewan
Apr 15	Huntly (H)	LGE	1-0	Nicolson
Apr 22	Rothes (H)	LGE	3-0	J MacRae, Nicolson (2)

PLAYING SQUAD & STATISTICS 2022/23

BUCKIE THISTLE F.C.
Victoria Park, Buckie

	Age	LEAGUE Apps	LEAGUE Goals	CUPS Apps	CUPS Goals	ALL Apps	ALL Goals
ADAMS, Scott	27	10 (14)	9	7 (5)	5	17 (19)	14
BARRY, Max	21	26 (1)	5	14	2	40 (1)	7
DEMUS, Balint (GK)	21	29	0	8	0	37	0
FRASER, Kevin	32	5	2	7	1	12	3
FYFFE, Ryan	22	15 (2)	1	8 (2)	0	23 (4)	1
GOODALL, Marcus	21	31 (2)	3	14 (2)	6	45 (4)	9
HERBERT, Lee (GK)	22	5 (1)	0	9	0	14 (1)	0
MACASKILL, Andy	31	32	15	15 (2)	5	47 (2)	20
MACKINNON, Lewis	38	11	0	5 (1)	0	16 (1)	0
MACLENNAN, Tom	26	9 (2)	0	6 (2)	0	15 (4)	0
MACLEOD, Kyle	28	13 (19)	9	4 (6)	1	17 (25)	10
MCCABE, Joe	26	24 (6)	5	11 (3)	2	35 (9)	7
MCLAUCHLAN, Mark	21	10 (5)	1	8 (5)	0	18 (10)	1
MILNE, Declan	26	(2)	1	(2)	0	(4)	1
MUNRO, Hamish	37	20 (5)	0	7 (3)	0	27 (8)	0
MURRAY, Jack	23	32 (1)	8	16	3	48 (1)	11
PETERS, Josh	27	30	23	11 (2)	6	41 (2)	29
PUGH, Sam	26	33	1	16 (1)	3	49 (1)	4
RAMSAY, Cohen	23	22 (3)	3	9 (3)	1	31 (6)	4
URQUHART, Sam	32	15 (17)	5	7 (6)	3	22 (23)	8
WOOD, Shaun	31	2 (4)	0	5 (3)	1	7 (7)	1

Josh Peters netted 23 league goals during the 2022-23 campaign, having joined the Jags from Elgin City during the summer of 2022.
Photo: Allan Robertson

MATCH RESULTS 2022/23

Date	Opponent	Comp	Score	Scorers
Jul 9	Ross County (H)	SLC GRP	1-1	Urquhart
Jul 12	Dunfermline Athletic (A)	SLC GRP	0-5	
Jul 16	Alloa Athletic (H)	SLC GRP	1-4	Urquhart
Jul 19	East Fife (A)	SLC GRP	2-3	Adams (2)
Jul 23	Wick Academy (H)	LGE	2-1	Macleod, Fraser
Jul 27	Formartine United (A)	AC R1	2-2	Fraser, Peters
Jul 30	Fraserburgh (H)	LGE	2-1	Fraser, MacAskill
Aug 6	Lossiemouth (A)	LGE	6-0	Peters, Urquhart, Macleod, Ramsay, Adams (2)
Aug 10	Hearts B (A)	SCC R1	3-2	Murray, Ramsay, Pugh
Aug 13	Strathspey Thistle (H)	LGE	8-0	Urquhart, Murray, Peters (4), Macleod, Milne
Aug 20	Brechin City (A)	LGE	0-1	
Aug 24	Brora Rangers (H)	SCC R2	1-1	Peters
Aug 27	Inverurie Locos (A)	LGE	4-0	Macleod, Peters, Ramsay, Urquhart
Sep 3	Huntly (H)	LGE	2-0	MacAskill (2)
Sep 17	Lossiemouth (A)	SC R1	2-1	Goodall (2)
Sep 24	Linfield (H)	SCC R3	1-2	Goodall
Oct 1	Turriff United (H)	LGE	7-1	MacAskill, McLauchlan, Goodall, Murray (3), Adams
Oct 5	Clachnacuddin (A)	LGE	4-1	Adams (3), Mccabe
Oct 8	Banks o' Dee (H)	LGE	2-2	Peters, Murray
Oct 12	Dyce (H)	AS R1	5-0	Urquhart, Goodall (2), MacAskill, Murray
Oct 15	Rothes (A)	LGE	4-2	MacAskill (2), Barry, Macleod
Oct 22	Broomhill (H)	SC R2	1-3	Goodall
Oct 29	Forres Mechanics (H)	LGE	2-0	Murray, Barry
Nov 2	Keith (A)	LGE	5-1	MacAskill, Peters (3), Ramsay
Nov 5	Formartine United (A)	LGE	2-1	MacAskill, Peters
Nov 12	Deveronvale (A)	HLC R1	3-1	Murray, MacAskill, Barry
Nov 16	Deveronvale (A)	AS QF	9-1	Barry, Wood, MacAskill, Mccabe (2), Peters (2), Adams (2)
Nov 19	Fraserburgh (A)	LGE	0-1	
Nov 26	Lossiemouth (H)	LGE	2-1	Peters, Adams
Dec 3	Formartine United (A)	HLC QF	3-1	Peters (2), Adams
Dec 23	Deveronvale (A)	LGE	2-1	MacAskill, Goodall
Jan 3	Deveronvale (H)	LGE	3-2	MacAskill, Peters (2)
Jan 7	Wick Academy (A)	LGE	1-0	Fyffe
Jan 11	Aberdeen B (H)	AS SF	3-2	MacAskill (2), Macleod
Jan 14	Nairn County (A)	LGE	3-1	Barry, Mccabe, Peters
Jan 21	Inverurie Locos (H)	LGE	2-0	Peters, MacAskill
Jan 28	Huntly (A)	LGE	1-1	Adams
Feb 4	Brora Rangers (H)	LGE	4-2	Adams, MacAskill, Peters
Feb 11	Keith (H)	LGE	3-0	Murray, Pugh, MacAskill
Feb 15	Fraserburgh (H)	AS F	1-2	Pugh
Feb 18	Turriff United (A)	LGE	1-0	Barry
Feb 25	Clachnacuddin (H)	LGE	5-0	Mccabe (2), Goodall, Peters, Macleod
Mar 4	Banks o' Dee (H)	HLC SF	1-1	Pugh
Mar 11	Banks o' Dee (A)	LGE	3-1	MacAskill (2), Peters
Mar 15	Brora Rangers (A)	LGE	2-0	Murray, Peters
Mar 18	Rothes (H)	LGE	1-1	Peters
Mar 25	Nairn County (H)	LGE	3-0	Peters, Mccabe, Macleod
Apr 1	Forres Mechanics (A)	LGE	3-2	Peters, Macleod, Barry
Apr 8	Strathspey Thistle (A)	LGE	2-0	Urquhart (2)
Apr 15	Formartine United (H)	LGE	1-0	Macleod
Apr 22	Brechin City (H)	LGE	0-2	

PLAYING SQUAD & STATISTICS 2022/23

CLACHNACUDDIN F.C.
Grant Street Park, Inverness

		LEAGUE		CUPS		ALL	
	Age	Apps	Goals	Apps	Goals	Apps	Goals
ANDERSON, James	22	32 (1)	14	5	1	37 (1)	15
BLACK, Calum	23	20	0	4	0	24	0
BRINDLE, Paul	31	14 (5)	7	3	1	17 (5)	8
BUNCE, Connor	22	24 (6)	6	2 (3)	3	26 (9)	9
CALLUM, Martin	35	21 (6)	1	2 (3)	0	23 (9)	1
CHALMERS, Kieran	22	8 (7)	0	(1)	0	8 (8)	0
COOPER, Troy	23	2 (8)	0	1	0	3 (8)	0
CORMACK, Ben	18	29	1	5	0	34	1
GALBRAITH, Owen (GK)	-	1	0	-	-	1	0
GILLIES, Ali	21	17 (3)	1	2 (3)	0	19 (6)	1
HENNEM, Harry	19	12 (1)	4	-	-	12 (1)	4
LAWRIE, Blair	37	6 (12)	0	1 (1)	0	7 (13)	0
LOGAN, Ross	21	7 (3)	0	(2)	0	7 (5)	0
MACKENZIE, Finlay	19	(1)	0	-	-	(1)	0
MACKENZIE, Lewis	21	18 (14)	4	4	2	22 (14)	6
MACKENZIE, Riley	19	4 (1)	0	2	0	6 (1)	0
MACKINNON, Martin (GK)	23	20	0	5	0	25	0
MACLEOD, Andrew	18	4 (1)	0	1 (1)	0	5 (2)	0
MACLEOD, Rorie	25	8 (1)	0	-	-	8 (1)	0
MORRISON, Donald	22	20 (8)	2	3 (1)	0	23 (9)	2
NICOLSON, Harry	22	14	0	-	-	14	0
RAE, Daniel (GK)	22	11	0	(1)	0	11 (1)	0
RIDDLE, Aly	19	10 (6)	0	1 (2)	1	11 (8)	1
SIENKOWSKI, Dawid (GK)	19	2	0	-	-	2	0
SUTHERLAND, Shaun	22	24 (7)	1	4 (1)	0	28 (8)	1
SYRJANEN, Keiran	20	(2)	0	-	-	(2)	0
THOMPSON, Robbie	19	18 (4)	0	5	2	23 (4)	2
WARREN, Gary	39	28 (1)	1	5	0	33 (1)	1

Clachnacuddin defender Ben Cormack impressed during his first campaign on loan from Elgin City, and had his deal extended for 2023-24.
Photo: Donald Cameron

MATCH RESULTS 2022/23

Date	Opponent	Comp	Score	Scorers
Jul 23	Inverurie Locos (H)	LGE	1-3	Morrison
Jul 30	Huntly (A)	LGE	1-0	Bunce
Aug 6	Brora Rangers (H)	LGE	0-4	
Aug 13	Keith (A)	LGE	1-2	L Mackenzie
Aug 17	Wick Academy (H)	NoS QF	3-0	Anderson, L Mackenzie, Bunce
Aug 20	Turriff United (H)	LGE	1-4	Cormack
Aug 24	Wick Academy (A)	LGE	0-1	
Aug 27	Banks o' Dee (A)	LGE	1-2	Bunce
Aug 31	Rothes (A)	NoS SF	4-1	Thompson (2), Bunce (2)
Sep 3	Rothes (H)	LGE	4-1	Brindle (2), Anderson (2)
Sep 17	Dunbar United (A)	SC R1	2-3	Brindle, Riddle
Sep 24	Formartine United (H)	LGE	1-3	Sutherland
Oct 1	Brora Rangers (A)	NoS F	1-2	L Mackenzie
Oct 5	Buckie Thistle (H)	LGE	1-4	Gillies
Oct 8	Fraserburgh (A)	LGE	0-5	
Oct 15	Lossiemouth (H)	LGE	2-1	Anderson, Brindle
Oct 22	Deveronvale (A)	LGE	3-3	Anderson (3)
Nov 2	Strathspey Thistle (H)	LGE	0-2	
Nov 5	Brechin City (A)	LGE	0-5	
Nov 12	Turriff United (A)	HLC R1	0-4	
Nov 19	Huntly (H)	LGE	2-0	Anderson (2)
Nov 26	Brora Rangers (A)	LGE	2-4	Brindle (2)
Jan 3	Nairn County (H)	LGE	0-2	
Jan 7	Inverurie Locos (A)	LGE	4-2	Bunce (3)
Jan 14	Wick Academy (H)	LGE	1-3	Anderson
Jan 28	Rothes (A)	LGE	2-3	L Mackenzie, Bunce
Feb 4	Forres Mechanics (H)	LGE	2-0	Hennem, Brindle
Feb 11	Formartine United (A)	LGE	0-4	
Feb 18	Deveronvale (H)	LGE	3-1	Anderson, Hennem, Morrison
Feb 22	Forres Mechanics (A)	LGE	0-0	
Feb 25	Buckie Thistle (A)	LGE	0-5	
Mar 4	Keith (H)	LGE	2-1	L Mackenzie, Warren
Mar 18	Lossiemouth (A)	LGE	2-0	Brindle
Mar 29	Banks o' Dee (H)	LGE	3-1	Anderson, Hennem, L Mackenzie
Apr 1	Strathspey Thistle (A)	LGE	2-2	Anderson, Callum
Apr 5	Fraserburgh (H)	LGE	1-1	Hennem
Apr 8	Nairn County (A)	LGE	0-1	
Apr 15	Brechin City (H)	LGE	1-2	Anderson
Apr 22	Turriff United (A)	LGE	1-4	Anderson

DEVERONVALE F.C.
Princess Royal Park, Banff

	Age	LEAGUE Apps	LEAGUE Goals	CUPS Apps	CUPS Goals	ALL Apps	ALL Goals
ALLAN, Ben	27	19 (3)	1	4	0	23 (3)	1
ALLAN, Robbie	37	8 (1)	0	3	0	11 (1)	0
ANGUS, Cameron	21	1 (5)	0	2 (1)	0	3 (6)	0
BALLARD, Dane	32	32 (1)	16	4	2	36 (1)	18
BASHUA, Sam	29	8 (1)	0	3	0	11 (1)	0
BRADFORD, Jaydan	19	31 (1)	0	4	0	35 (1)	0
DAVIDSON, Rory	26	(1)	0	-	-	(1)	0
DLUGOSZ, Alexsander	19	1 (4)	2	-	-	1 (4)	2
GOLDIE, Jay	19	26 (1)	0	2	0	28 (1)	0
HAMILTON, Aaron	27	8	0	1	0	9	0
HAY, Charlie	20	12 (3)	0	2 (1)	0	14 (4)	0
IMBERT-THOMAS, Caiden	25	7 (1)	0	2	0	9 (1)	0
JAM, Antonio	19	5 (8)	1	(3)	1	5 (11)	2
JAMIESON, Matt	20	14 (1)	5	3 (1)	1	17 (2)	6
LAIRD, Zane	19	9	2	-	-	9	2
MACKILLOP-HALL, Kyle	21	8 (11)	2	1 (1)	0	9 (12)	2
MCINTOSH, Sean (GK)	29	32	0	4	0	36	0
MCKAY, Innes	23	30 (1)	2	5	1	35 (1)	3
NOBLE, Grant	36	4 (6)	0	1	0	5 (6)	0
NOBLE, Harry	28	31	2	5	0	36	2
ORMSBY, Horace	28	32	10	3 (1)	0	35 (1)	10
READ, Rogan	22	8 (2)	0	1	1	9 (2)	1
SHINGLER, Jamie (GK)	19	-	-	1	0	1	0
STEWART, Max	20	18 (4)	1	2 (1)	0	20 (5)	1
STILL, Gavin (GK)	26	(1)	0	-	-	(1)	0
TINNOCK, Jamie	20	6 (4)	1	1	0	7 (4)	1
WATSON, Michael	23	22 (3)	1	1 (3)	0	23 (6)	1
WILLIAMSON, Jamie (GK)	20	2	0	-	-	2	0

Midfielder Horace Ormsby, known as 'H', netted 10 goals across all competitions for Vale after signing during the summer of 2022 from Stansted FC in Essex.
Photo: Deveronvale FC

MATCH RESULTS 2022/23

Date	Opponent	Comp	Score	Scorers
Jul 23	Fraserburgh (A)	LGE	0-3	
Jul 27	Hermes (A)	AC R1	1-1	Jam
Jul 30	Lossiemouth (H)	LGE	2-0	Ballard, MacKillop-Hall
Aug 6	Strathspey Thistle (A)	LGE	2-2	Ballard, H Noble
Aug 13	Brechin City (H)	LGE	1-3	Ballard
Aug 17	Formartine United (A)	AC QF	1-2	Jamieson
Aug 20	Nairn County (A)	LGE	2-2	Ballard, Tinnock
Aug 24	Inverurie Locos (H)	LGE	0-3	
Aug 27	Huntly (A)	LGE	0-1	
Sep 3	Brora Rangers (A)	LGE	0-5	
Sep 17	East Kilbride (H)	SC R1	2-4	McKay, Ballard
Sep 24	Turriff United (A)	LGE	1-5	Ormsby
Oct 1	Keith (H)	LGE	4-3	B Allan, Ballard, Ormsby, Jamieson
Oct 5	Banks o' Dee (A)	LGE	0-2	
Oct 8	Rothes (H)	LGE	0-1	
Oct 15	Forres Mechanics (A)	LGE	1-4	McKay
Oct 22	Clachnacuddin (H)	LGE	3-3	Ballard (2), Stewart
Nov 2	Formartine United (H)	LGE	0-3	
Nov 5	Wick Academy (A)	LGE	1-2	H Noble
Nov 12	Buckie Thistle (H)	HLC R1	1-3	Ballard
Nov 16	Buckie Thistle (H)	AS QF	1-9	Read
Nov 19	Lossiemouth (A)	LGE	3-2	Ormsby, Watson
Nov 26	Strathspey Thistle (H)	LGE	7-0	Jamieson (3), Ormsby (2), Ballard, Jam
Dec 10	Brechin City (A)	LGE	1-7	Ormsby
Dec 23	Buckie Thistle (H)	LGE	1-2	
Jan 3	Buckie Thistle (A)	LGE	2-3	Jamieson, Ballard
Jan 7	Fraserburgh (H)	LGE	2-3	MacKillop-Hall, Dlugosz
Jan 14	Inverurie Locos (A)	LGE	0-4	
Jan 21	Huntly (H)	LGE	1-3	Ballard
Jan 28	Brora Rangers (H)	LGE	0-6	
Feb 4	Keith (A)	LGE	1-1	Dlugosz
Feb 11	Turriff United (H)	LGE	2-0	Ballard, Laird
Feb 18	Clachnacuddin (A)	LGE	1-3	Ballard
Feb 25	Banks o' Dee (H)	LGE	1-4	Ormsby
Mar 18	Forres Mechanics (H)	LGE	2-1	McKay, Ormsby
Apr 1	Formartine United (A)	LGE	1-2	Ballard
Apr 8	Rothes (A)	LGE	1-1	Laird
Apr 15	Wick Academy (H)	LGE	3-3	Ormsby (2), Ballard
Apr 22	Nairn County (H)	LGE	2-3	Ballard (2)

FORMARTINE UNITED F.C.
North Lodge Park, Pitmedden

	Age	LEAGUE Apps	LEAGUE Goals	CUPS Apps	CUPS Goals	ALL Apps	ALL Goals
ADAMS, Kieran	32	22 (4)	3	10	1	32 (4)	4
ADDISON, Murray	21	(6)	0	(2)	0	(8)	0
ALBERTS, Brody	-	(1)	0	(2)	0	(3)	0
ANDERSON, Cole	21	2 (12)	2	2 (6)	1	4 (18)	3
CAMPBELL, Paul	30	13 (2)	11	-	-	13 (2)	11
COMBE, Aidan	26	9 (5)	5	2 (1)	2	11 (6)	7
CRAWFORD, Jonathan	33	24 (1)	4	12	3	36 (1)	7
DIMOV, Danail	23	2 (3)	1	(2)	0	2 (5)	1
GALLAGHER, Mark	22	34	6	12	2	46	8
HANRATTY, Kevin	20	2 (6)	0	-	-	2 (6)	0
LAWRENCE, Kieran	27	7 (1)	0	4 (1)	0	11 (2)	0
LISLE, Scott	25	20 (8)	5	4 (3)	2	24 (11)	7
LYNCH, Jordan	20	(2)	0	-	-	(2)	0
MACDONALD, Ewen (GK)	27	34	0	12	0	46	0
MACIVER, Jack	20	11 (6)	1	7 (2)	1	18 (8)	2
MCLEAN, Matthew	24	30 (1)	3	12	0	42 (1)	3
MYKYTA, Tyler	21	12 (5)	2	4	0	16 (5)	2
NORRIS, Aaron	25	28 (4)	1	9 (2)	1	37 (6)	2
PARK, Daniel	33	14 (10)	0	5 (2)	0	19 (12)	0
RODGER, Graeme	32	23 (1)	5	4 (2)	1	27 (3)	6
SMITH, Jonny	35	10 (3)	9	7 (2)	1	17 (5)	10
SMITH, Stuart	34	21 (3)	1	6 (3)	0	27 (6)	1
SPINK, Ryan	26	16 (5)	0	8	0	24 (5)	0
THOMAS, Rhys	21	8 (4)	0	-	-	8 (4)	0
WADE, Julian	33	32	21	12	6	44	27

MATCH RESULTS 2022/23

Date	Opponent	Comp	Score	Scorers
Jul 23	Lossiemouth (A)	LGE	3-1	Gallagher, Lisle, Wade
Jul 27	Buckie Thistle (H)	AC R1	2-2	Wade (2)
Jul 30	Strathspey Thistle (H)	LGE	6-1	Gallagher, J Smith (3), Wade (2)
Aug 6	Brechin City (A)	LGE	1-3	Wade
Aug 13	Nairn County (H)	LGE	3-1	Mykyta, J Smith, Rodger
Aug 17	Deveronvale (H)	AC QF	2-1	Gallagher, Lisle
Aug 20	Inverurie Locos (A)	LGE	1-1	Wade
Aug 24	Huntly (A)	LGE	2-1	J Smith, Gallagher
Aug 27	Brora Rangers (H)	LGE	2-1	McLean, Lisle
Sep 3	Keith (A)	LGE	0-1	
Sep 7	Huntly (H)	AC SF	1-0	Wade
Sep 17	East Stirling (H)	SC R1	3-1	Adams, Norris
Sep 24	Clachnacuddin (A)	LGE	3-1	Wade, Dimov, Lisle
Sep 30	Fraserburgh (H)	AC F	1-1	Lisle
Oct 5	Rothes (A)	LGE	2-2	Wade, Crawford
Oct 8	Forres Mechanics (H)	LGE	2-0	C Anderson, Crawford
Oct 11	Hermes (A)	AS R1	2-0	C Anderson, Crawford
Oct 15	Wick Academy (A)	LGE	3-0	J Smith (2), Crawford
Oct 22	Carnoustie Panmure (A)	SC R2	2-1	Maciver, Wade
Oct 29	Wick Academy (A)	HLC PR.	2-0	J Smith, Gallagher
Nov 2	Deveronvale (A)	LGE	3-0	Crawford, J Smith (2)
Nov 5	Buckie Thistle (H)	LGE	1-2	Maciver
Nov 12	Huntly (A)	HLC R1	3-2	Crawford (2), Combe
Nov 19	Strathspey Thistle (A)	LGE	2-0	Wade, Rodger
Nov 26	Stenhousemuir (H)	SC R3	1-3	Wade
Dec 3	Buckie Thistle (H)	HLC QF	1-3	Rodger
Dec 6	Aberdeen B (H)	AS QF	2-2	Wade, Combe
Dec 10	Nairn County (A)	LGE	1-1	Rodger
Dec 23	Fraserburgh (H)	LGE	0-1	
Dec 30	Fraserburgh (A)	LGE	2-2	Combe (2)
Jan 7	Lossiemouth (H)	LGE	5-0	Wade (2), Rodger, Combe, Norris
Jan 14	Huntly (H)	LGE	2-0	Adams, Combe
Jan 28	Keith (H)	LGE	6-0	Gallagher, McLean, Campbell, Combe, Lisle, C Anderson
Feb 4	Turriff United (A)	LGE	4-2	S Smith, Wade, Campbell (2)
Feb 11	Clachnacuddin (H)	LGE	4-0	Campbell (3), Adams
Feb 18	Banks o' Dee (A)	LGE	3-2	Campbell (2), Rodger
Feb 22	Brechin City (H)	LGE	2-0	Campbell, Wade
Feb 25	Rothes (H)	LGE	2-1	Wade
Mar 11	Forres Mechanics (A)	LGE	1-1	Wade
Mar 15	Turriff United (H)	LGE	2-1	Adams, Campbell
Mar 18	Wick Academy (H)	LGE	6-0	Mykyta, Lisle, Wade (3), McLean
Mar 22	Banks o' Dee (H)	LGE	2-0	Wade, Gallagher
Apr 1	Deveronvale (H)	LGE	2-1	Wade, Gallagher
Apr 8	Brora Rangers (A)	LGE	1-2	Wade
Apr 15	Buckie Thistle (A)	LGE	0-1	
Apr 22	Inverurie Locos (H)	LGE	2-1	Campbell, Wade

FORRES MECHANICS F.C.
Mosset Park, Forres

	Age	LEAGUE		CUPS		ALL	
		Apps	Goals	Apps	Goals	Apps	Goals
BARRON, Ben	18	26 (5)	15	4	1	30 (5)	16
BRADY, Thomas	21	15 (7)	0	1 (2)	0	16 (9)	0
CAIRNS, Ethan	18	20 (3)	3	4	0	24 (3)	3
CAMERON, Shaun	20	(1)	0	-	-	(1)	0
DAVIDSON, Lucas	22	4 (6)	0	-	-	4 (6)	0
DAVIES, Kane	20	9 (8)	3	1 (2)	0	10 (10)	3
DONALDSON, Robert (GK)	30	5 (1)	0	2	0	7 (1)	0
EWAN, Connall	18	33	4	4	0	37	4
FRASER, Graham	30	5 (1)	0	1	1	6 (1)	1
FRASER, Lee	30	18 (9)	5	3 (1)	0	21 (10)	5
FRASER, Ruari	22	23 (1)	0	2	0	25 (1)	0
GRANT, Jack	22	19 (5)	2	3	0	22 (5)	2
GROAT, Martin	28	24 (2)	2	2 (1)	0	26 (3)	2
HENDERSON, Harvey	19	(8)	0	(2)	0	(10)	0
JOHNSTON, Callum	24	22 (1)	1	2 (1)	1	24 (2)	2
KNIGHT, Stuart (GK)	36	24 (1)	0	2	0	26 (1)	0
MACDONALD, Aidan (GK)	25	1	0	-	-	1	0
MACKENZIE, Craig	20	28	2	3	0	31	2
MACLEMAN, Ryan	19	31	3	3 (1)	2	34 (1)	5
MCCULLIE, Luca	-	(1)	0	-	-	(1)	0
MCKAY, Conor	-	(1)	0	-	-	(1)	0
MORRISON, Shaun	19	14 (18)	10	1 (3)	0	15 (21)	10
MURRAY, Callum	27	2 (1)	3	1 (1)	0	3 (2)	3
PATERSON, Corey (GK)	-	4	0	-	-	4	0
PATERSON, Owen	25	(2)	0	-	-	(2)	0
SKINNER, Andrew	29	16 (1)	0	1	0	17 (1)	0
THAIN, Taylor	21	1 (4)	0	-	-	1 (4)	0
WOOD, Dale	26	30 (1)	2	4	0	34 (1)	2

Date	Opponent	Comp	Score	Scorers
Jul 23	Strathspey Thistle (A)	LGE	4-0	Murray (3), Barron
Jul 30	Brechin City (H)	LGE	0-1	
Aug 6	Nairn County (A)	LGE	5-0	Morrison (3), Groat, Ewan
Aug 13	Inverurie Locos (A)	LGE	1-0	
Aug 17	Lossiemouth (H)	NoS QF	0-2	
Aug 20	Huntly (H)	LGE	3-0	Groat, Barron, Cairns
Aug 27	Keith (H)	LGE	1-2	Barron
Sep 3	Turriff United (A)	LGE	0-2	
Sep 17	Glasgow University (H)	SC R1	2-3	G Fraser, MacLeman
Sep 24	Banks o' Dee (A)	LGE	0-2	
Oct 1	Rothes (H)	LGE	4-3	Barron, Mackenzie, Ewan, Cairns
Oct 5	Wick Academy (H)	LGE	4-2	Barron, MacLeman, Davies (2)
Oct 8	Formartine United (A)	LGE	0-2	
Oct 15	Deveronvale (H)	LGE	4-1	Barron (3), Morrison
Oct 22	Brora Rangers (A)	LGE	1-4	Mackenzie
Oct 29	Buckie Thistle (A)	LGE	0-2	
Nov 5	Fraserburgh (H)	LGE	1-1	Barron
Nov 12	Keith (A)	HLC R1	2-0	Barron
Nov 19	Brechin City (A)	LGE	1-2	Grant
Nov 26	Nairn County (H)	LGE	3-4	Grant, Barron, Davies
Dec 3	Banks o' Dee (A)	HLC QF	2-3	MacLeman, Johnston
Dec 10	Inverurie Locos (H)	LGE	1-1	Cairns
Dec 23	Lossiemouth (H)	LGE	1-0	L Fraser
Dec 30	Lossiemouth (A)	LGE	0-0	
Jan 7	Strathspey Thistle (H)	LGE	8-1	Barron (2), Wood, Morrison (2), L Fraser (2)
Jan 14	Brora Rangers (H)	LGE	0-8	
Jan 28	Turriff United (H)	LGE	1-2	Johnston
Feb 4	Clachnacuddin (A)	LGE	0-2	
Feb 11	Banks o' Dee (H)	LGE	1-2	Morrison
Feb 18	Rothes (A)	LGE	1-2	Ewan
Feb 22	Clachnacuddin (H)	LGE	0-0	
Feb 25	Wick Academy (A)	LGE	1-1	MacLeman
Mar 4	Huntly (A)	LGE	1-2	Ewan
Mar 11	Formartine United (H)	LGE	1-1	Wood
Mar 18	Deveronvale (A)	LGE	1-2	MacLeman
Mar 25	Keith (A)	LGE	6-2	Morrison (2), L Fraser (2), Barron (2)
Apr 1	Buckie Thistle (H)	LGE	2-3	Morrison, Barron
Apr 15	Fraserburgh (A)	LGE	0-3	

FRASERBURGH F.C.
Bellslea Park, Fraserburgh

	Age	LEAGUE		CUPS		ALL	
		Apps	Goals	Apps	Goals	Apps	Goals
AITKEN, Ross	26	27 (1)	3	15	0	42 (1)	3
BARBOUR, Joe (GK)	30	30	0	11	0	41	0
BARBOUR, Scott	31	31 (3)	22	10 (5)	5	41 (8)	27
BEAGRIE, Jamie	32	15 (4)	2	6	0	21 (4)	2
BOLTON, Josh	24	6 (10)	5	(1)	0	6 (11)	5
BUCHAN, Greg	25	26 (2)	1	8	1	34 (2)	2
BUTCHER, Sean	29	18 (10)	11	10 (5)	7	28 (15)	18
CAMPBELL, Paul	30	7 (7)	7	5 (4)	1	12 (11)	8
COMBE, Aidan	26	2 (4)	1	5 (1)	0	7 (5)	1
COWIE, Ryan	32	12 (2)	0	1	0	13 (2)	0
DAVIDSON, Lewis	31	8	0	2 (1)	0	10 (1)	0
DUNCAN, Lewis	21	-	-	4	0	4	0
GRANT, Connor	19	3 (2)	0	1 (3)	0	4 (5)	0
GUILD, Jordan	30	(4)	0	5 (2)	0	5 (6)	0
HAWKINS, Joshua	-	1	0	-	-	1	0
HAY, Bryan	34	26 (1)	4	14	0	40 (1)	4
INGLIS, Sam (GK)	-	4 (1)	0	1	0	5 (1)	0
KELLY, Callum	18	1 (2)	0	1 (1)	0	2 (3)	0
LAIRD, Zane	19	2 (10)	1	3 (4)	0	5 (14)	1
LAWRENCE, Marc	25	4 (6)	2	2	0	6 (6)	2
LEASK, Paul (GK)	34	-	-	4	0	4	0
MACLELLAN, Jamie	19	(1)	0	1 (4)	0	1 (5)	0
MURISON, Scott	21	-	-	1	0	1	0
SARGENT, Ryan	22	25 (8)	10	13 (2)	5	38 (10)	15
SIMPSON, Kieran	22	27	1	15	1	42	2
SUTHERLAND, Ethan	-	(1)	0	(1)	0	(2)	0
TAYLOR, Ross	18	-	-	(2)	0	(2)	0
WATT, Logan	20	21 (9)	7	7 (6)	1	28 (15)	8
WEST, Willie	35	28 (2)	5	11 (2)	0	39 (4)	5
WOOD, Connor	23	19 (6)	3	5 (4)	4	24 (10)	7
WOOD, Kyle	-	(2)	0	2	0	2 (2)	0
YOUNG, Paul	31	31	3	13 (2)	0	44 (2)	3

MATCH RESULTS 2022/23

Date	Opponent	Comp	Score	Scorers
Jul 9	Kilmarnock (H)	SLC GRP	1-3	Butcher
Jul 12	Montrose (H)	SLC GRP	2-4	Butcher (2)
Jul 16	Stenhousemuir (A)	SLC GRP	0-3	
Jul 19	Partick Thistle (A)	SLC GRP	0-2	
Jul 23	Deveronvale (H)	LGE	3-0	Butcher, Sargent, S Barbour
Jul 27	Banks o' Dee (H)	AC R1	1-0	Sargent
Jul 30	Buckie Thistle (A)	LGE	1-2	Campbell
Aug 6	Wick Academy (H)	LGE	3-0	Sargent, West, S Barbour
Aug 9	St Johnstone B (H)	SCC R1	0-2	
Aug 13	Lossiemouth (A)	LGE	7-0	S Barbour (3), Butcher (2), Combe
Aug 17	Inverurie Locos (H)	AC QF	1-1	S Barbour
Aug 20	Strathspey Thistle (A)	LGE	9-0	C Wood, S Barbour (3), Butcher, Campbell, Laird, West, Sargent
Aug 27	Nairn County (A)	LGE	4-0	S Barbour, Simpson, Watt, Campbell
Sep 3	Inverurie Locos (H)	LGE	1-2	S Barbour
Sep 17	Civil Service Strollers (A)	SC R1	2-1	C Wood, Butcher
Sep 24	Brora Rangers (H)	LGE	2-2	Aitken, S Barbour
Sep 30	Formartine United (A)	AC F	1-1	A Norris o.g.
Oct 5	Turriff United (A)	LGE	4-1	Watt (2), S Barbour, Hay
Oct 8	Clachnacuddin (H)	LGE	5-0	Aitken (2), Watt, Butcher, Campbell
Oct 11	Banks o' Dee (H)	AS R1	3-3	Butcher, Campbell, S Barbour
Oct 14	Banks o' Dee (A)	LGE	1-1	Hay
Oct 22	Stranraer (H)	SC R2	2-1	Buchan, C Wood
Oct 29	Rothes (H)	LGE	2-0	Campbell (2)
Nov 2	Huntly (A)	LGE	4-1	S Barbour, Campbell, West, Young
Nov 5	Forres Mechanics (A)	LGE	1-1	M Groat o.g.
Nov 12	Inverurie Locos (H)	HLC R1	1-2	Butcher
Nov 16	Aberdeen Uni. (H)	AS QF	4-0	Sargent, Watt, S Barbour (2)
Nov 19	Buckie Thistle (H)	LGE	1-0	S Barbour
Nov 26	Arbroath (H)	SC R3	0-2	
Dec 3	Keith (A)	LGE	2-2	Young, S Barbour
Dec 23	Formartine United (A)	LGE	1-0	Beagrie
Dec 30	Formartine United (H)	LGE	2-2	Bolton, West
Jan 7	Deveronvale (A)	LGE	3-2	S Barbour, Bolton (2)
Jan 21	Nairn County (H)	LGE	2-2	Sargent, West
Jan 25	Huntly (A)	AS SF	6-0	Sargent (3), C Wood (2), Simpson
Jan 28	Inverurie Locos (A)	LGE	4-0	Hay, C Wood, Sargent, S Barbour
Feb 4	Huntly (H)	LGE	3-0	Sargent (2), Lawrence
Feb 11	Brora Rangers (A)	LGE	1-0	Sargent
Feb 15	Buckie Thistle (A)	AS F	2-1	S Barbour, Butcher
Feb 18	Keith (H)	LGE	4-0	Butcher, S Barbour, Sargent, Bolton
Feb 25	Turriff United (H)	LGE	2-3	Young, Buchan
Mar 4	Wick Academy (A)	LGE	6-0	Beagrie, S Barbour (2), Butcher, Lawrence, Watt
Mar 18	Banks o' Dee (H)	LGE	0-3	
Mar 24	Lossiemouth (H)	LGE	3-0	Watt, Butcher, Sargent
Mar 29	Brechin City (H)	LGE	0-0	
Apr 1	Rothes (A)	LGE	3-0	Butcher, S Barbour
Apr 5	Clachnacuddin (A)	LGE	1-1	Butcher
Apr 12	Brechin City (A)	LGE	0-5	
Apr 15	Forres Mechanics (H)	LGE	3-0	C Wood, S Barbour, Watt
Apr 22	Strathspey Thistle (H)	LGE	3-1	Butcher, Bolton, Hay

HUNTLY F.C.
Christie Park, Huntly

	Age	LEAGUE Apps	Goals	CUPS Apps	Goals	ALL Apps	Goals
ALLEN, Brodie	26	14 (16)	3	(6)	1	14 (22)	4
BERTON, Max	28	(2)	0	-	-	(2)	0
BLACKLOCK, Cammy	19	18 (7)	2	3 (1)	0	21 (8)	2
BOOTH, Lyall	20	29	1	4	0	33	1
BUCHAN, Greg	25	5	0	1	1	6	1
CHARLESWORTH, Colin	32	(3)	0	-	-	(3)	0
CLARK, Michael	29	24 (1)	3	4	0	28 (1)	3
CONNELLY, James	22	32	2	4 (1)	0	36 (1)	2
DALLING, Kyle	21	29	2	5	0	34	2
DANGANA, Michael	20	12 (3)	3	(1)	0	12 (4)	3
ELPHINSTONE, Gavin	30	18 (3)	2	3 (1)	3	21 (4)	5
FOSTER, Robbie	22	14 (10)	6	4	3	18 (10)	9
GAULD, Joe	21	1 (4)	0	-	-	1 (4)	0
GRANT, Angus	25	7 (15)	1	1 (4)	0	8 (19)	1
HAY, Chris	26	(2)	0	-	-	(2)	0
HESLOP, Cameron	22	10	0	1	0	11	0
HOBDAY, Fraser (GK)	28	25	0	4	0	29	0
HUNTER, Andy	30	26 (4)	11	6	4	32 (4)	15
JACK, Alexander	32	(1)	0	-	-	(1)	0
LAMB, Callum	19	5	0	1	0	6	0
MATTHEW, Cai	22	1 (1)	0	(1)	0	1 (2)	0
MCCORMICK, Jack	20	5 (2)	0	1 (1)	0	6 (3)	0
MCKEOWN, Reece	23	1 (2)	0	1	0	2 (2)	0
MORRIS, Adam	20	22 (4)	0	5	1	27 (4)	1
MORRIS, Owen	19	(1)	0	-	-	(1)	0
MURRAY, Callum	27	18 (4)	2	4	0	22 (4)	2
SEWELL, Ryan	25	20 (7)	0	4 (2)	0	24 (9)	0
STILL, Ross	28	25	2	5	0	30	2
STORRIER, Euan (GK)	24	9 (2)	0	2	0	11 (2)	0
THOIRS, Alexander	35	4 (3)	0	3	0	7 (3)	0

Date	Opponent	Comp	Score	Scorers
Jul 23	Turriff United (A)	LGE	1-2	
Jul 27	Keith (A)	AC R1	4-0	Elphinstone, Hunter (2), Buchan
Jul 30	Clachnacuddin (H)	LGE	0-1	
Aug 6	Banks o' Dee (A)	LGE	2-5	Allen (2)
Aug 13	Rothes (H)	LGE	1-1	Foster
Aug 20	Forres Mechanics (A)	LGE	0-3	
Aug 24	Formartine United (H)	LGE	1-2	Elphinstone
Aug 27	Deveronvale (H)	LGE	1-0	Elphinstone
Sep 3	Buckie Thistle (A)	LGE	0-2	
Sep 7	Formartine United (A)	AC SF	0-1	
Sep 24	Lossiemouth (A)	LGE	4-1	Booth, Blacklock, Hunter
Oct 1	Strathspey Thistle (H)	LGE	2-0	Connelly
Oct 5	Brechin City (A)	LGE	2-2	Hunter (2)
Oct 8	Nairn County (H)	LGE	3-1	Still, Hunter, Connelly
Oct 12	Turriff United (H)	AS R1	5-3	Hunter (2), Elphinstone (2), A Morris
Oct 15	Inverurie Locos (A)	LGE	0-0	
Nov 2	Fraserburgh (H)	LGE	1-4	Murray
Nov 5	Brora Rangers (H)	LGE	1-3	Clark
Nov 12	Formartine United (H)	HLC R1	2-3	Foster (2)
Nov 16	Inverurie Locos (A)	AS QF	2-1	Foster, Allen
Nov 19	Clachnacuddin (A)	LGE	0-2	
Nov 26	Banks o' Dee (H)	LGE	0-2	
Dec 3	Wick Academy (H)	LGE	5-2	Hunter (2), Still, Grant, Blacklock
Jan 7	Turriff United (H)	LGE	2-0	Dalling, Clark
Jan 14	Formartine United (A)	LGE	0-2	
Jan 21	Deveronvale (A)	LGE	3-1	Murray, Foster (2)
Jan 25	Fraserburgh (H)	AS SF	0-6	
Jan 28	Buckie Thistle (H)	LGE	1-1	Hunter
Feb 4	Fraserburgh (A)	LGE	0-3	
Feb 11	Lossiemouth (H)	LGE	2-1	Foster, Dalling
Feb 22	Keith (H)	LGE	1-0	Dangana
Feb 25	Brechin City (H)	LGE	0-1	
Mar 4	Forres Mechanics (H)	LGE	2-1	Hunter (2)
Mar 11	Nairn County (A)	LGE	0-2	
Mar 18	Inverurie Locos (H)	LGE	1-1	Hunter
Mar 29	Strathspey Thistle (A)	LGE	4-1	Dangana (2), Allen, Foster
Apr 1	Wick Academy (A)	LGE	1-0	Clark
Apr 8	Keith (A)	LGE	1-1	
Apr 15	Brora Rangers (A)	LGE	0-1	
Apr 19	Rothes (A)	LGE	2-0	Hunter, Foster

PLAYING SQUAD & STATISTICS 2022/23

INVERURIE LOCO WORKS F.C.
Harlaw Park, Inverurie

	Age	LEAGUE		CUPS		ALL	
		Apps	Goals	Apps	Goals	Apps	Goals
ALBERTS, Fergus	21	11 (8)	2	2 (5)	0	13 (13)	2
ANDERSON, Cole	21	4 (2)	0	-	-	4 (2)	0
BUCHAN, Josh	18	3 (1)	0	-	-	3 (1)	0
BURNETT, Sam	26	8 (4)	0	5	2	13 (4)	2
DINGWALL, Calum	30	31 (1)	3	7 (1)	0	38 (2)	3
DUNCAN, Callum	18	(1)	0	-	-	(1)	0
GILL, Craig	24	6 (11)	0	1 (3)	0	7 (14)	0
HALLIDAY, Jay	21	12 (8)	3	3 (2)	1	15 (10)	4
JOHNSTONE, Logan	23	27	1	7	0	34	1
MASON, Taylor	18	1 (1)	0	-	-	1 (1)	0
MERES, Nathan	22	20 (4)	2	6 (2)	1	26 (6)	3
MICHIE, Jamie	32	15 (9)	4	3 (5)	0	18 (14)	4
MITCHELL, Greg	28	30	4	9	0	39	4
PETERMANN, Matthew	19	5 (8)	1	2 (1)	0	7 (9)	1
REID, Andy (GK)	38	34	0	9	0	43	0
REID, Thomas	24	31 (2)	0	8	0	39 (2)	0
ROBERTSON, Lloyd	22	21 (6)	7	4 (2)	0	25 (8)	7
ROBERTSON, Sam	26	10 (1)	4	2	1	12 (1)	5
SMITH, Blair	-	2 (5)	0	1	1	3 (5)	1
SMITH, Jonny	35	9 (1)	6	-	-	9 (1)	6
SOUTER, Mark	29	31	1	9	1	40	2
THAIN, Taylor	21	2 (12)	0	3 (2)	0	5 (14)	0
WARD, Robert	22	28 (2)	11	9	3	37 (2)	14
WILSON, David	23	9	0	2	0	11	0
WOOD, Garry	35	24 (1)	11	7	2	31 (1)	13

MATCH RESULTS 2022/23

Date	Opponent	Comp	Score	Scorers
Jul 23	Clachnacuddin (A)	LGE	3-1	Dingwall, L Robertson, Ward
Jul 27	Dyce (A)	AC R1	2-1	Burnett, Ward
Jul 30	Banks o' Dee (H)	LGE	1-1	Alberts
Aug 6	Rothes (A)	LGE	5-0	Wood, Ward, Petermann, Dingwall, Johnstone
Aug 13	Forres Mechanics (H)	LGE	0-1	
Aug 17	Fraserburgh (A)	AC QF	1-1	Ward
Aug 20	Formartine United (H)	LGE	1-1	
Aug 24	Deveronvale (A)	LGE	3-0	L Robertson, Wood
Aug 27	Buckie Thistle (H)	LGE	0-4	
Sep 3	Fraserburgh (A)	LGE	2-1	Souter, Halliday
Sep 17	Hill of Beath (A)	SC R1	1-3	Souter
Sep 24	Strathspey Thistle (A)	LGE	2-2	Alberts, Ward
Oct 1	Brechin City (H)	LGE	0-1	
Oct 5	Nairn County (A)	LGE	2-2	Dingwall, Michie
Oct 8	Wick Academy (A)	LGE	2-1	Wood, Halliday
Oct 12	Keith (A)	AS R1	2-0	Halliday, Wood
Oct 15	Huntly (H)	LGE	0-0	
Oct 22	Lossiemouth (H)	LGE	3-2	Michie, Mitchell, Ward
Oct 29	Brora Rangers (A)	LGE	2-5	Wood (2)
Nov 5	Keith (H)	LGE	2-0	Mitchell, Ward
Nov 12	Fraserburgh (A)	HLC R1	2-1	Meres, Wood
Nov 16	Huntly (H)	AS QF	1-2	Ward
Nov 19	Banks o' Dee (A)	LGE	4-3	Wood (2), Michie, Ward
Nov 26	Rothes (H)	LGE	1-1	Mitchell
Dec 3	Turriff United (A)	HLC QF	1-0	B Smith
Dec 10	Forres Mechanics (A)	LGE	1-1	L Robertson
Dec 30	Turriff United (A)	LGE	2-3	Wood, Mitchell
Jan 7	Clachnacuddin (H)	LGE	2-4	Ward (2)
Jan 14	Deveronvale (H)	LGE	4-0	L Robertson, Wood (3)
Jan 21	Buckie Thistle (A)	LGE	0-2	
Jan 28	Fraserburgh (H)	LGE	0-4	
Feb 4	Lossiemouth (A)	LGE	0-1	
Feb 11	Strathspey Thistle (H)	LGE	4-0	S Robertson, J Smith (2), Meres
Feb 18	Brechin City (A)	LGE	1-5	L Robertson
Feb 25	Nairn County (H)	LGE	2-1	J Smith, Ward
Mar 4	Brechin City (H)	HLC SF	2-0	S Robertson, Burnett
Mar 18	Huntly (A)	LGE	1-1	Ward
Mar 25	Turriff United (H)	LGE	3-1	J Smith, S Robertson, Meres
Apr 1	Brora Rangers (H)	LGE	2-4	S Robertson, Ward
Apr 8	Banks o' Dee (H)	HLC F	0-1	
Apr 12	Wick Academy (H)	LGE	4-0	L Robertson (2), J Smith, Halliday
Apr 15	Keith (A)	LGE	3-2	S Robertson, J Smith
Apr 22	Formartine United (A)	LGE	1-2	Michie

KEITH F.C.
Kynoch Park, Keith

		LEAGUE		CUPS		ALL	
	Age	Apps	Goals	Apps	Goals	Apps	Goals
ABDULKARIM, Nizam	20	13 (1)	0	2	0	15 (1)	0
ADDISON, Murray	21	13 (1)	0	-	-	13 (1)	0
ANDREWS, Tom	24	10 (1)	1	3	0	13 (1)	1
BROWNIE, James	32	27 (1)	5	4	0	31 (1)	5
COLLIN, Aiden	19	(1)	0	-	-	(1)	0
COULL, Lewis	19	19 (5)	2	3	0	22 (5)	2
CUMMING, Dylan	20	(6)	0	-	-	(6)	0
DUNCAN, Liam	23	19 (1)	5	1 (1)	0	20 (2)	5
ELPHINSTONE, Gavin	30	8 (1)	3	-	-	8 (1)	3
EMMETT, Luke	22	7	0	2	0	9	0
GRANT, Connor	19	14	0	2	0	16	0
GRAY, Scott	23	(1)	0	-	-	(1)	0
HUTCHEON, Stewart	30	18 (10)	3	(2)	0	18 (12)	3
IRONSIDE, Michael	24	12 (10)	0	(4)	0	12 (14)	0
IRVINE, Kyle (GK)	20	5	0	1	0	6	0
JARVIE, Cameron (GK)	24	1	0	-	-	1	0
KILLOH, Connor	21	28 (2)	0	3	0	31 (2)	0
MCKEOWN, Nathan	21	3 (15)	0	1 (2)	0	4 (17)	0
MOONEY, Kieran	23	17 (3)	7	2	0	19 (3)	7
MURRAY, Ewan	19	8	0	-	-	8	0
NAWROCKI, Przemyslaw	26	4 (6)	4	2	0	6 (6)	4
REID, Craig (GK)	28	28	0	3	0	31	0
ROBERTSON, Ryan	32	19	1	3	0	22	1
SMITH, Ethan	22	5 (1)	0	-	-	5 (1)	0
THOMAS, Rhys	21	11	0	2	0	13	0
TOUGH, Matthew	22	17 (15)	4	3 (1)	1	20 (16)	5
WILSON, Joey	21	8 (16)	0	(3)	0	8 (19)	0
YEATS, Kieran	23	27 (1)	0	3	0	30 (1)	0
YUNUS, Demi	21	33	3	4	0	37	3

MATCH RESULTS 2022/23

Date	Opponent	Comp	Score	Scorers
Jul 23	Brora Rangers (H)	LGE	0-4	
Jul 27	Huntly (H)	AC R1	0-4	
Jul 30	Wick Academy (A)	LGE	0-1	
Aug 6	Turriff United (A)	LGE	1-1	Nawrocki
Aug 13	Clachnacuddin (H)	LGE	2-1	Yunus (2)
Aug 20	Banks o' Dee (A)	LGE	0-8	
Aug 24	Rothes (H)	LGE	2-3	Mooney, Nawrocki
Aug 27	Forres Mechanics (A)	LGE	2-1	Nawrocki (2)
Sep 3	Formartine United (H)	LGE	1-0	Mooney
Sep 17	Cumnock (H)	SC R1	1-2	Tough
Oct 1	Deveronvale (A)	LGE	3-4	Mooney, Andrews, Brownie
Oct 5	Lossiemouth (A)	LGE	0-2	
Oct 8	Strathspey Thistle (H)	LGE	6-1	Mooney (3), Robertson, Tough, Hutcheon
Oct 12	Inverurie Locos (H)	AS R1	0-2	
Oct 15	Brechin City (A)	LGE	0-5	
Oct 22	Rothes (A)	LGE	0-3	
Oct 29	Nairn County (H)	LGE	1-1	Hutcheon
Nov 2	Buckie Thistle (H)	LGE	1-5	Duncan
Nov 5	Inverurie Locos (A)	LGE	0-2	
Nov 12	Forres Mechanics (H)	HLC R1	0-2	
Nov 26	Turriff United (H)	LGE	2-1	Brownie, Duncan
Dec 3	Fraserburgh (H)	LGE	2-2	Mooney, Yunus
Jan 7	Brora Rangers (A)	LGE	1-6	Hutcheon
Jan 28	Formartine United (A)	LGE	0-6	
Feb 4	Deveronvale (H)	LGE	1-1	Duncan
Feb 11	Buckie Thistle (A)	LGE	0-3	
Feb 18	Fraserburgh (A)	LGE	0-4	
Feb 22	Huntly (A)	LGE	0-1	
Feb 25	Lossiemouth (H)	LGE	0-2	
Mar 4	Clachnacuddin (A)	LGE	1-2	Elphinstone
Mar 25	Forres Mechanics (H)	LGE	2-6	Elphinstone, Coull
Apr 1	Nairn County (A)	LGE	2-2	Duncan, Brownie
Apr 5	Wick Academy (H)	LGE	2-0	Brownie, Tough
Apr 8	Huntly (H)	LGE	1-1	Coull
Apr 12	Strathspey Thistle (A)	LGE	1-0	Tough
Apr 15	Inverurie Locos (H)	LGE	2-3	Tough, Elphinstone
Apr 19	Brechin City (H)	LGE	0-2	
Apr 22	Banks o' Dee (H)	LGE	2-3	Brownie, Duncan

LOSSIEMOUTH F.C.
Grant Park, Lossiemouth

	Age	LEAGUE Apps	LEAGUE Goals	CUPS Apps	CUPS Goals	ALL Apps	ALL Goals
ALLEN, Harry	22	(3)	0	(1)	0	(4)	0
ARCHIBALD, Liam	32	30	7	6	2	36	9
ARCHIBALD, Ross	32	12 (7)	2	5	3	17 (7)	5
BREW, Darren	25	(4)	0	-	-	(4)	0
CAMPBELL, Baylee	23	12 (10)	4	3 (2)	0	15 (12)	4
CHARLESWORTH, Martin	35	4	1	-	-	4	1
EDWARDS, Fergus	23	1	0	-	-	1	0
ELLIOTT, Ross	25	16 (7)	4	2 (3)	0	18 (10)	4
FARQUHAR, Cameron (GK)	27	16	0	-	-	16	0
FARQUHAR, Ryan	29	23 (3)	0	6	1	29 (3)	1
FORBES, Fraser	30	16 (12)	3	2 (3)	0	18 (15)	3
KENNEDY, Jared	25	21 (1)	0	3	0	24 (1)	0
KENNEDY, Niall	24	28 (1)	5	5	0	33 (1)	5
LESLIE, James	22	27 (3)	0	5	0	32 (3)	0
MACARTHUR, Jack	24	1 (8)	0	1	0	2 (8)	0
MACLEOD, Adam	30	9 (12)	3	1 (1)	0	10 (13)	3
MCANDREW, Lewis	22	26 (1)	0	4	0	30 (1)	0
MILLER, Scott	30	1 (2)	0	-	-	1 (2)	0
MORRISON, Ross	27	31 (1)	2	5 (1)	0	36 (2)	2
O'HALLORAN, Ryan	23	12 (2)	0	4 (1)	0	16 (3)	0
PATERSON, Ross	27	9	0	-	-	9	0
ROSS, Logan (GK)	19	18	0	6	0	24	0
STEWART, Dean	26	15 (3)	4	3	0	18 (3)	4
STUART, Ryan	28	19 (10)	2	4	1	23 (10)	3
THOMSON, Scott	27	9 (5)	0	(2)	0	9 (7)	0
WEIR, Michael	25	18 (1)	0	1	0	19 (1)	0

Liam Archibald finished as the Coasters' top scorer at the end of the 2022-23 campaign with 9 goals to his name.
Photo: Lossiemouth FC

Date	Opponent	Comp	Score	Scorers
Jul 23	Formartine United (H)	LGE	1-3	Charlesworth
Jul 30	Deveronvale (A)	LGE	0-2	
Aug 6	Buckie Thistle (H)	LGE	0-6	
Aug 13	Fraserburgh (H)	LGE	0-7	
Aug 17	Forres Mechanics (A)	NoS QF	2-0	R Farquhar, R Archibald
Aug 20	Wick Academy (H)	LGE	2-1	L Archibald, Macleod
Aug 24	Strathspey Thistle (H)	LGE	4-2	L Archibald, Elliott, R Archibald, Campbell
Aug 27	Brechin City (A)	LGE	0-3	
Aug 31	Brora Rangers (H)	NoS SF	1-4	L Archibald
Sep 3	Nairn County (H)	LGE	5-1	Elliott, Stewart (2), Campbell, L Archibald
Sep 17	Buckie Thistle (H)	SC R1	1-2	R Archibald
Sep 24	Huntly (H)	LGE	1-4	Stewart
Oct 5	Keith (H)	LGE	2-0	L Archibald, Forbes
Oct 8	Turriff United (A)	LGE	2-1	L Archibald, Macleod
Oct 15	Clachnacuddin (A)	LGE	1-2	R Morrison
Oct 22	Inverurie Locos (A)	LGE	2-3	Stuart, Campbell
Oct 29	Strathspey Thistle (A)	HLC PR.	3-2	Stuart, R Archibald, L Archibald
Nov 5	Rothes (A)	LGE	1-3	Stewart
Nov 12	Nairn County (H)	HLC R1	0-3	
Nov 19	Deveronvale (H)	LGE	2-3	Elliott
Nov 26	Buckie Thistle (A)	LGE	1-2	Stuart
Dec 3	Brechin City (H)	HLC QF	0-2	
Dec 23	Forres Mechanics (A)	LGE	0-1	
Dec 30	Forres Mechanics (H)	LGE	0-0	
Jan 7	Formartine United (A)	LGE	0-5	
Jan 14	Strathspey Thistle (A)	LGE	3-1	L Archibald, Forbes, R Archibald
Jan 21	Brechin City (H)	LGE	0-3	
Jan 28	Nairn County (A)	LGE	0-2	
Feb 4	Inverurie Locos (H)	LGE	1-0	N Kennedy
Feb 11	Huntly (A)	LGE	1-2	Elliott
Feb 18	Brora Rangers (H)	LGE	0-3	
Feb 22	Banks o' Dee (H)	LGE	1-2	R Morrison
Feb 25	Keith (A)	LGE	2-0	Macleod, Forbes
Mar 11	Turriff United (H)	LGE	2-2	L Archibald, N Kennedy
Mar 18	Clachnacuddin (H)	LGE	0-2	
Mar 24	Fraserburgh (A)	LGE	0-3	
Apr 1	Banks o' Dee (A)	LGE	0-7	
Apr 12	Brora Rangers (A)	LGE	0-1	
Apr 15	Rothes (H)	LGE	2-4	N Kennedy, Campbell
Apr 22	Wick Academy (A)	LGE	2-2	N Kennedy (2)

PLAYING SQUAD & STATISTICS 2022/23

NAIRN COUNTY F.C.
Station Park, Nairn

	Age	LEAGUE		CUPS		ALL	
		Apps	Goals	Apps	Goals	Apps	Goals
COUNSELL, Will (GK)	24	3	0	-	-	3	0
CRUICKSHANK, Aidan	18	1 (7)	0	-	-	1 (7)	0
DAVIDSON, Scott	29	22 (3)	6	1 (1)	0	23 (4)	6
DEY, Angus	29	27 (4)	3	2	0	29 (4)	3
DINGWALL, Fraser	25	28	4	2	0	30	4
EADIE, Tyler	22	2	0	-	-	2	0
GETHINS, Conor	40	25 (3)	14	2	0	27 (3)	14
GILLIES, Ali	21	5 (1)	0	-	-	5 (1)	0
GORDON, Sam	24	8 (19)	1	2 (1)	0	10 (20)	1
GRANT, John	21	3 (1)	0	1	0	4 (1)	0
GRANT, Nathan	21	2 (1)	0	-	-	2 (1)	0
GREIG, Andrew	30	24	4	3	1	27	5
HOGG, Grant	20	2	0	1	0	3	0
HOWARTH, Calum	27	14 (4)	0	1	0	15 (4)	0
LISLE, Cameron	25	19 (5)	0	2	0	21 (5)	0
MACDONALD, Owen	18	(1)	0	-	-	(1)	0
MACINNES, Kenneth	19	10 (3)	0	-	-	10 (3)	0
MACKAY, Steven	42	3 (4)	3	-	-	3 (4)	3
MACKINTOSH, Wayne	36	20	0	1	0	21	0
MACLEAN, Callum	32	19 (1)	1	1	0	20 (1)	1
MACLEAN, Dylan (GK)	27	26	0	2	0	28	0
MACLEOD, Paul	34	4	0	1	0	5	0
MAIN, Glenn	38	6 (1)	0	2	0	8 (1)	0
MCCONAGHY, Seamus	23	1 (3)	0	(2)	0	1 (5)	0
MCKENZIE, Kenny	31	21 (3)	1	1	0	22 (3)	1
MCNAB, Gordon	35	4 (2)	0	1	0	5 (2)	0
MITCHELL, Lewis	22	(1)	0	-	-	(1)	0
MUNRO, Lewis (GK)	18	5	0	1	0	6	0
PORRITT, Adam	29	11 (1)	0	1 (1)	0	12 (2)	0
RENNIE, Stephen	26	11 (3)	0	1 (1)	0	12 (4)	0
SHEWAN, Liam	28	11 (5)	2	(3)	1	11 (8)	3
STRACHAN, Matthew	18	7 (1)	1	-	-	7 (1)	1
TOKELY, Ross	44	19	3	1	0	20	3
WILLIAMSON, Rory	19	(2)	0	1 (1)	1	1 (3)	1
YOUNG, Ciaran	22	11 (14)	6	2	2	13 (14)	8

Former Inverness Caledonian Thistle defender Ross Tokely made the move from North Caledonian League side St Duthus to join Nairn County in November 2022, and featured 20 times over the season for the Wee County.
Photo: Nairn County FC

MATCH RESULTS 2022/23

Date	Opponent	Comp	Score	Scorers
Jul 23	Banks o' Dee (A)	LGE	1-1	Shewan
Jul 26	Elgin City (H)	NoS R1	1-2	Williamson
Jul 30	Rothes (H)	LGE	2-2	Greig (2)
Aug 6	Forres Mechanics (H)	LGE	0-5	
Aug 13	Formartine United (A)	LGE	1-3	Dey
Aug 20	Deveronvale (H)	LGE	2-2	Davidson, Young
Aug 27	Fraserburgh (H)	LGE	0-4	
Sep 3	Lossiemouth (A)	LGE	1-5	Shewan
Sep 17	Drumchapel United (H)	SC R1	1-3	Greig
Oct 5	Inverurie Locos (H)	LGE	2-2	Gethins, Davidson
Oct 8	Huntly (A)	LGE	1-3	Gethins
Oct 15	Brora Rangers (H)	LGE	0-4	
Oct 22	Strathspey Thistle (H)	LGE	4-2	C Maclean, Gethins (2), Davidson
Oct 29	Keith (A)	LGE	1-1	
Nov 2	Wick Academy (H)	LGE	3-0	Young, Gethins
Nov 5	Turriff United (H)	LGE	2-1	Young, Dingwall
Nov 12	Lossiemouth (A)	HLC R1	3-0	Young (2), Shewan
Nov 26	Forres Mechanics (A)	LGE	4-3	Gordon, Gethins (3)
Dec 10	Formartine United (H)	LGE	1-1	Dey
Jan 3	Clachnacuddin (A)	LGE	2-0	Greig, Young
Jan 7	Banks o' Dee (H)	LGE	3-0	McKenzie, Tokely, Greig
Jan 14	Buckie Thistle (H)	LGE	1-3	Tokely
Jan 21	Fraserburgh (A)	LGE	2-2	Tokely, Davidson
Jan 28	Lossiemouth (H)	LGE	2-0	Gethins, Young
Feb 4	Strathspey Thistle (A)	LGE	1-1	Dingwall
Feb 11	Brechin City (H)	LGE	0-0	
Feb 18	Wick Academy (A)	LGE	2-1	Dey, Mackay
Feb 25	Inverurie Locos (A)	LGE	1-2	Young
Mar 4	Rothes (A)	LGE	0-2	
Mar 11	Huntly (H)	LGE	2-0	Gethins, Strachan
Mar 18	Brora Rangers (A)	LGE	1-2	Dingwall
Mar 22	Brechin City (A)	LGE	0-3	
Mar 25	Buckie Thistle (A)	LGE	0-3	
Apr 1	Keith (H)	LGE	2-2	Davidson, Gethins
Apr 8	Clachnacuddin (H)	LGE	1-0	Gethins
Apr 15	Turriff United (A)	LGE	3-1	Gethins, Dingwall, Davidson
Apr 22	Deveronvale (A)	LGE	3-2	Gethins, Mackay (2)

41

PLAYING SQUAD & STATISTICS 2022/23

ROTHES F.C.
MacKessack Park, Rothes

	Age	LEAGUE		CUPS		ALL	
		Apps	Goals	Apps	Goals	Apps	Goals
FINNIS, Michael	33	34	1	3	1	37	2
HARKNESS, Shane	20	2 (9)	1	(2)	0	2 (11)	1
JOHNSTONE, Ben	22	29	1	4	0	33	1
KERR, Gary	32	7 (7)	4	1	0	8 (7)	4
MACCALLUM, Michael (GK)	34	1	0	-	-	1	0
MACHADO, Matheus	22	14 (2)	5	2	0	16 (2)	5
MACKAY, Steven	42	8	3	3	1	11	4
MACKENZIE, Allen	33	25 (1)	1	1 (1)	0	26 (2)	1
MACKENZIE, Iain (GK)	27	11 (1)	0	-	-	11 (1)	0
MAIN, Gregg	37	2 (1)	0	-	-	2 (1)	0
MALEY, Jack	27	14	1	1 (1)	0	15 (1)	1
MCCARTHY, Sean (GK)	30	22	0	4	0	26	0
MCLAUCHLAN, Ewan	24	1	0	-	-	1	0
MCRITCHIE, Ryan	24	17 (1)	3	4	0	21 (1)	3
MILNE, Bruce	35	28 (3)	2	4	0	32 (3)	2
MORRISON, Greg	25	29	7	4	2	33	9
NEIL, Ewan	22	8 (11)	1	2	0	10 (11)	1
POLLOCK, Alan	33	26 (3)	5	3	0	29 (3)	5
ROBERTSON, Fraser	28	27 (1)	6	2 (1)	0	29 (2)	6
SHEPHERD, Kenzie	18	(2)	0	-	-	(2)	0
SHEWAN, Liam	28	10 (2)	3	-	-	10 (2)	3
SOPEL, Aidan	24	12 (1)	1	-	-	12 (1)	1
THOMSON, Jake	22	10 (21)	1	2 (2)	1	12 (23)	2
WHYTE, Kyle	29	3 (5)	1	-	-	3 (5)	1
WILLIAMSON, Ben	20	8 (5)	0	-	-	8 (5)	0
WILSON, Aidan	23	26 (4)	16	4	2	30 (4)	18

Date	Opponent	Comp	Score	Scorers
Jul 23	Brechin City (A)	LGE	0-1	
Jul 30	Nairn County (A)	LGE	2-2	Finnis, Mackay
Aug 6	Inverurie Locos (H)	LGE	0-5	
Aug 13	Huntly (A)	LGE	1-1	Whyte
Aug 17	Elgin City (H)	NoS QF	3-2	Wilson, J Thomson, Morrison
Aug 20	Brora Rangers (H)	LGE	0-4	
Aug 24	Keith (A)	LGE	3-2	Machado, Morrison (2)
Aug 27	Turriff United (H)	LGE	6-1	McRitchie, Machado, Mackay (2), Morrison, Harkness
Aug 31	Clachnacuddin (H)	NoS SF	1-4	Finnis
Sep 3	Clachnacuddin (A)	LGE	1-4	Pollock
Sep 17	Carnoustie Panmure (A)	SC R1	1-3	Mackay
Sep 24	Wick Academy (A)	LGE	1-1	McRitchie
Oct 1	Forres Mechanics (A)	LGE	3-4	Machado, Robertson, Maley
Oct 5	Formartine United (H)	LGE	2-2	Robertson, Kerr
Oct 8	Deveronvale (A)	LGE	1-0	Wilson
Oct 15	Buckie Thistle (H)	LGE	2-4	Machado (2)
Oct 22	Keith (H)	LGE	3-0	Wilson (2), Pollock
Oct 29	Fraserburgh (A)	LGE	0-2	
Nov 2	Banks o' Dee (H)	LGE	2-0	Wilson, Robertson
Nov 5	Lossiemouth (H)	LGE	3-1	Morrison (2), Milne
Nov 12	Brechin City (A)	HLC R1	2-4	Wilson, Morrison
Nov 26	Inverurie Locos (A)	LGE	1-1	McRitchie
Dec 3	Strathspey Thistle (A)	LGE	7-0	Robertson, Milne, Wilson (3), Kerr (2)
Jan 7	Brechin City (H)	LGE	0-1	
Jan 28	Clachnacuddin (H)	LGE	3-2	Robertson (2), Shewan
Feb 4	Banks o' Dee (A)	LGE	0-2	
Feb 11	Wick Academy (H)	LGE	2-2	Pollock, Wilson
Feb 18	Forres Mechanics (H)	LGE	2-1	Sopel, A Mackenzie
Feb 22	Strathspey Thistle (H)	LGE	9-0	Wilson (5), Shewan (2), Neil, Pollock
Feb 25	Formartine United (A)	LGE	1-2	Pollock
Mar 4	Nairn County (H)	LGE	2-0	Morrison
Mar 18	Buckie Thistle (A)	LGE	1-1	Wilson
Mar 22	Turriff United (A)	LGE	1-3	Wilson
Apr 1	Fraserburgh (H)	LGE	0-3	
Apr 8	Deveronvale (H)	LGE	1-1	Kerr
Apr 15	Lossiemouth (A)	LGE	4-2	Morrison, Wilson, Johnstone, J Thomson
Apr 19	Huntly (H)	LGE	0-2	
Apr 22	Brora Rangers (A)	LGE	0-3	

PLAYING SQUAD & STATISTICS 2022/23

STRATHSPEY THISTLE F.C.
Seafield Park, Grantown-on-Spey

	Age	LEAGUE Apps	LEAGUE Goals	CUPS Apps	CUPS Goals	ALL Apps	ALL Goals
AUSTIN, Connor	21	21	1	2	0	23	1
BREW, Darren	25	10 (3)	0	1 (1)	0	11 (4)	0
CRUICKSHANK, Aidan	18	7 (4)	3	1 (1)	1	8 (5)	4
CULLEN, Ben	32	4 (2)	1	(1)	1	4 (3)	2
CUTHBERT, Joe	23	21 (10)	0	1 (2)	0	22 (12)	0
DAVISON, Jack	21	32 (1)	2	3	0	35 (1)	2
FRASER, James	23	5	0	-	-	5	0
GILES, Cairn	22	2 (2)	0	-	-	2 (2)	0
GILLILAND, Jack	22	27 (2)	0	3	0	30 (2)	0
GRANT, Liam	22	13	1	3	0	16	1
GRIMES, Michael	29	7	0	-	-	7	0
KELLY, Oliver (GK)	22	20	0	2	0	22	0
KELLY, Stephen	20	5	1	-	-	5	1
KENDALL, James (GK)	32	5	0	-	-	5	0
KERR, Alan	31	21 (5)	1	3	0	24 (5)	1
LOCKETT, Jake	27	1 (4)	1	-	-	1 (4)	1
LOGAN, Ross	21	12 (3)	1	-	-	12 (3)	1
LOVELAND, Owen	21	22 (6)	2	2	0	24 (6)	2
MACCALLUM, Michael (GK)	34	8	0	1	0	9	0
MACKENZIE, Craig	20	3	0	-	-	3	0
MACLEOD, Connor	27	1 (2)	0	(1)	0	1 (3)	0
MCCONAGHY, Seamus	23	(7)	0	-	-	(7)	0
MCDADE, Liam	22	32	0	3	0	35	0
MCINNES, Thomas	22	4 (6)	0	2	0	6 (6)	0
MCKENZIE, Michael	28	8	3	-	-	8	3
MCSHANE, James	29	25	0	2	0	27	0
PATERSON, Owen	25	24 (1)	0	2	0	26 (1)	0
RITCHIE, Stefan	22	(1)	0	-	-	(1)	0
ROSS, David	41	5 (2)	0	-	-	5 (2)	0
RUSSELL, Fraser	21	(1)	0	-	-	(1)	0
SHAW, Jordan	21	(4)	0	(1)	0	(5)	0
TAYLOR, Liam	27	13 (2)	4	1 (1)	0	14 (3)	4
VALENTE, Nathanial (GK)	30	1	0	-	-	1	0
WARDROP, Jack	24	(6)	0	-	-	(6)	0
WHITEHORN, Daniel	28	15 (4)	2	1	0	16 (4)	2
WILLIAMSON, Rory	19	(3)	0	-	-	(3)	0

MATCH RESULTS 2022/23

Date	Opponent	Comp	Score	Scorers
Jul 23	Forres Mechanics (H)	LGE	0-4	
Jul 30	Formartine United (A)	LGE	1-6	Cullen
Aug 6	Deveronvale (H)	LGE	2-2	S Kelly, Taylor
Aug 13	Buckie Thistle (A)	LGE	0-8	
Aug 17	Brora Rangers (A)	NoS QF	0-4	
Aug 20	Fraserburgh (H)	LGE	0-9	
Aug 24	Lossiemouth (A)	LGE	2-4	Loveland, Taylor
Aug 27	Wick Academy (H)	LGE	1-2	Taylor
Sep 3	Brechin City (H)	LGE	0-5	
Sep 17	Camelon (H)	SC R1	0-5	
Sep 24	Inverurie Locos (H)	LGE	2-2	Davison, Taylor
Oct 1	Huntly (A)	LGE	0-2	
Oct 5	Brora Rangers (H)	LGE	0-11	
Oct 8	Keith (A)	LGE	1-6	Cruickshank
Oct 15	Turriff United (H)	LGE	1-6	Loveland
Oct 22	Nairn County (A)	LGE	2-4	Cruickshank (2)
Oct 29	Lossiemouth (H)	HLC PR.	2-3	Cruickshank, Cullen
Nov 2	Clachnacuddin (A)	LGE	2-0	Austin, Grant
Nov 5	Banks o' Dee (H)	LGE	0-7	
Nov 19	Formartine United (H)	LGE	0-2	
Nov 26	Deveronvale (A)	LGE	0-7	
Dec 3	Rothes (H)	LGE	0-7	
Jan 7	Forres Mechanics (A)	LGE	1-8	
Jan 14	Lossiemouth (H)	LGE	1-3	Kerr
Jan 28	Brechin City (A)	LGE	0-6	
Feb 4	Nairn County (H)	LGE	1-1	Whitehorn
Feb 11	Inverurie Locos (A)	LGE	0-4	
Feb 22	Rothes (A)	LGE	0-9	
Feb 25	Brora Rangers (A)	LGE	0-2	
Mar 18	Turriff United (A)	LGE	0-5	
Mar 22	Wick Academy (A)	LGE	2-1	Whitehorn, McKenzie
Mar 29	Huntly (H)	LGE	1-4	Lockett
Apr 1	Clachnacuddin (H)	LGE	2-2	Davison, Logan
Apr 8	Buckie Thistle (H)	LGE	0-2	
Apr 12	Keith (H)	LGE	0-1	
Apr 15	Banks o' Dee (A)	LGE	1-9	McKenzie
Apr 22	Fraserburgh (A)	LGE	1-3	McKenzie

TURRIFF UNITED F.C.
The Haughs, Turriff

	Age	LEAGUE		CUPS		ALL	
		Apps	Goals	Apps	Goals	Apps	Goals
ALBERTS, Fergus	21	6 (4)	4	-	-	6 (4)	4
BROWN, Rory	22	3 (10)	2	1 (2)	0	4 (12)	2
CHALMERS, James	29	24 (2)	0	5 (1)	0	29 (3)	0
CHEYNE, Liam	26	21 (3)	1	4 (1)	0	25 (4)	1
CLARK, Ewan	30	26 (3)	7	6	10	32 (3)	17
CLARK, Rhys	20	15 (5)	1	2 (1)	0	17 (6)	1
COOPER, Jordan	24	17 (6)	1	5 (1)	0	22 (7)	1
CORMACK, Murray	19	12 (5)	1	1 (1)	0	13 (6)	1
DEY, David (GK)	26	31	0	5	0	36	0
ESSON, Murray	22	(2)	0	-	-	(2)	0
FINDLAY, Tim (GK)	20	3	0	1	0	4	0
FOSTER, Max	24	17 (1)	4	3	0	20 (1)	4
GORDON, Kyle	26	11 (7)	4	1 (3)	3	12 (10)	7
GRAY, Callan	21	24 (6)	6	4	1	28 (6)	7
HUTCHEON, Stewart	30	1	0	-	-	1	0
KINSELLA, Luke	20	3 (2)	0	-	-	3 (2)	0
KINSELLA, Owen	24	27 (1)	1	3 (1)	0	30 (2)	1
LENNOX, Jamie	35	(1)	0	-	-	(1)	0
LIVINGSTONE, Stevie	-	(1)	0	(1)	0	(2)	0
MCKENZIE, Jack	20	23 (5)	3	3 (2)	0	26 (7)	3
MCKEOWN, Reece	23	17 (10)	6	3 (2)	0	20 (12)	6
NICOL, Callum	19	(3)	0	(1)	0	(4)	0
REID, Aaron	19	14	11	3 (1)	4	17 (1)	15
SMITH, Ethan	22	6 (3)	0	2 (1)	0	8 (4)	0
SMITH, Keir	24	23 (5)	2	6	0	29 (5)	2
STRACHAN, Liam	25	23	0	3 (1)	0	26 (1)	0
STUART, Dylan	21	25 (1)	0	5	1	30 (1)	1
THOMPSON, Murray	19	1 (8)	0	(1)	0	1 (9)	0
WATT, Andrew	23	1	0	-	-	1	0

Date	Opponent	Comp	Score	Scorers
Jul 23	Huntly (H)	LGE	2-1	Reid (2)
Jul 30	Brora Rangers (A)	LGE	1-2	Reid
Aug 6	Keith (H)	LGE	1-1	Reid
Aug 13	Wick Academy (A)	LGE	0-2	
Aug 17	Aberdeen Uni. (A)	AC QF	10-0	E Clark (5), Gray, Gordon (3), Reid
Aug 20	Clachnacuddin (A)	LGE	4-1	E Clark, Reid (2), Cheyne
Aug 24	Banks o' Dee (H)	LGE	1-1	Brown
Aug 27	Rothes (A)	LGE	1-6	E Clark
Sep 3	Forres Mechanics (H)	LGE	2-0	McKeown, Brown
Sep 17	Banks o' Dee (A)	SC R1	0-4	
Sep 24	Deveronvale (H)	LGE	5-1	McKeown, Reid (3), E Clark
Oct 1	Buckie Thistle (A)	LGE	1-7	E Clark
Oct 5	Fraserburgh (H)	LGE	1-4	Cormack
Oct 8	Lossiemouth (H)	LGE	1-2	McKenzie
Oct 12	Huntly (A)	AS R1	3-5	E Clark, Reid, Stuart
Oct 15	Strathspey Thistle (A)	LGE	6-1	E Clark (2), Reid, Foster (2)
Oct 22	Dunipace (A)	SC R2	2-5	Reid (2)
Oct 29	Brechin City (H)	LGE	1-4	Gray
Nov 5	Nairn County (A)	LGE	1-2	
Nov 12	Clachnacuddin (H)	HLC R1	4-0	E Clark (4)
Nov 26	Keith (A)	LGE	1-2	McKeown
Dec 3	Inverurie Locos (H)	HLC QF	0-1	
Dec 30	Inverurie Locos (H)	LGE	3-2	O Kinsella, Gray, Reid
Jan 7	Huntly (A)	LGE	0-2	
Jan 14	Banks o' Dee (A)	LGE	0-2	
Jan 28	Forres Mechanics (A)	LGE	2-1	Gray, K Smith
Feb 4	Formartine United (H)	LGE	2-4	Gray (2)
Feb 11	Deveronvale (A)	LGE	0-2	
Feb 18	Buckie Thistle (H)	LGE	0-1	
Feb 25	Fraserburgh (A)	LGE	3-2	McKeown (2), Gordon
Mar 4	Brora Rangers (H)	LGE	0-4	
Mar 11	Lossiemouth (A)	LGE	2-2	Gordon, Alberts
Mar 15	Formartine United (A)	LGE	1-2	K Smith
Mar 18	Strathspey Thistle (H)	LGE	5-0	Cooper, Gordon (2), McKenzie, E Clark
Mar 22	Rothes (H)	LGE	3-1	R Clark, Alberts, Gray
Mar 25	Inverurie Locos (A)	LGE	1-3	McKeown
Apr 1	Brechin City (A)	LGE	0-4	
Apr 8	Wick Academy (H)	LGE	0-3	
Apr 15	Nairn County (H)	LGE	1-3	Alberts
Apr 22	Clachnacuddin (H)	LGE	4-1	Alberts, Foster (2), McKenzie

PLAYING SQUAD & STATISTICS 2022/23 *

WICK ACADEMY F.C.
Harmsworth Park, Wick

	Age	LEAGUE		CUPS		ALL	
		Apps	Goals	Apps	Goals	Apps	Goals
AITKENHEAD, Matthew	-	(4)	0	(1)	0	(5)	0
ALLAN, Ross	30	30 (1)	0	4 (1)	0	34 (2)	0
ANDERSON, Joe	19	17 (3)	0	4	0	21 (3)	0
ANDERSON, Steven	31	1	0	-	-	1	0
ANGUS, Chris	33	1	0	-	-	1	0
BAIN, Liam	19	(2)	0	-	-	(2)	0
CAMPBELL, Grant	33	1 (1)	0	-	-	1 (1)	0
CAMPBELL, Ryan	24	31	2	4 (1)	0	35 (1)	2
CAMPBELL, Sean	26	12 (1)	1	4	2	16 (1)	3
FARQUHAR, Alan	35	8 (1)	0	1	0	9 (1)	0
FARQUHAR, Conor	19	8 (7)	1	(3)	0	8 (10)	1
FLETT, Jamie	24	6	2	(1)	0	6 (1)	2
HALLIDAY, Jack	29	14 (5)	0	5	1	19 (5)	1
HENNEM, Harry	19	11 (2)	1	4 (1)	0	15 (3)	1
HENRY, Jack	32	19 (1)	5	2 (1)	0	21 (2)	5
HUGHES, Alan	28	31	0	5	0	36	0
INNES, Roddy	21	1 (2)	0	-	-	1 (2)	0
MACADIE, Mark	20	27 (3)	6	5	1	32 (3)	7
MACADIE, Richard	36	27 (2)	2	5	0	32 (2)	2
MACGREGOR, Marc	28	10	3	-	-	10	3
MACKINTOSH, James	24	13 (8)	2	1 (2)	0	14 (10)	2
MACLEOD, Toby	24	4 (2)	0	(1)	0	4 (3)	0
MACNAB, Gordon	29	27 (1)	7	3 (2)	2	30 (3)	9
MANSON, Gary	39	10 (5)	1	-	-	10 (5)	1
MCLEAN, Robert	26	4	0	-	-	4	0
MILLER, Billy (GK)	23	1	0	-	-	1	0
MONTGOMERY, Cameron	21	7 (9)	0	(1)	0	7 (10)	0
MORE, James (GK)	35	5	0	-	-	5	0
MUNRO, Mark	18	6 (9)	0	1 (2)	1	7 (11)	1
MUNRO, Sean	31	9 (2)	1	2	0	11 (2)	1
PATERSON, Corey (GK)	-	1	0	-	-	1	0
RENDALL, Owen	25	3	0	-	-	3	0
WEIR, Gary	36	2	0	-	-	2	0
WILLIAMSON, Graeme (GK)	33	27	0	5	0	32	0

* Players with less than 1 full appearance not displayed due to size of squad.

48

Date	Opponent	Comp	Score	Scorers
Jul 23	Buckie Thistle (A)	LGE	1-2	R Campbell
Jul 30	Keith (H)	LGE	1-0	MacNab
Aug 6	Fraserburgh (A)	LGE	0-3	
Aug 13	Turriff United (H)	LGE	2-0	Henry, M MacAdie
Aug 17	Clachnacuddin (A)	NoS QF	0-3	
Aug 20	Lossiemouth (A)	LGE	1-2	MacNab
Aug 24	Clachnacuddin (H)	LGE	1-0	Hennem
Aug 27	Strathspey Thistle (A)	LGE	2-1	MacNab, M MacAdie
Sep 3	Banks o' Dee (H)	LGE	0-8	
Sep 17	Lochee United (H)	SC R1	5-1	Halliday, S Campbell, M MacAdie, MacNab, M Munro
Sep 24	Rothes (H)	LGE	1-1	R Campbell
Oct 5	Forres Mechanics (A)	LGE	2-4	S Campbell, M MacAdie
Oct 8	Inverurie Locos (H)	LGE	1-2	R MacAdie
Oct 15	Formartine United (H)	LGE	0-3	
Oct 22	Benburb (H)	SC R2	2-0	S Campbell, MacNab
Oct 29	Formartine United (H)	HLC PR.	0-2	
Nov 2	Nairn County (A)	LGE	0-3	
Nov 5	Deveronvale (H)	LGE	2-1	S Munro, MacNab
Nov 26	Falkirk (H)	SC R3	0-6	
Dec 3	Huntly (A)	LGE	2-5	M MacAdie, Henry
Jan 7	Buckie Thistle (H)	LGE	0-1	
Jan 14	Clachnacuddin (A)	LGE	3-1	Henry (2), Flett
Jan 28	Banks o' Dee (A)	LGE	0-6	
Feb 4	Brechin City (H)	LGE	0-3	
Feb 11	Rothes (A)	LGE	2-2	C Farquhar, Mackintosh
Feb 18	Nairn County (H)	LGE	1-2	Macgregor
Feb 22	Brora Rangers (H)	LGE	1-7	Macgregor
Feb 25	Forres Mechanics (H)	LGE	1-1	Henry
Mar 4	Fraserburgh (H)	LGE	0-6	
Mar 18	Formartine United (A)	LGE	0-6	
Mar 22	Strathspey Thistle (H)	LGE	1-2	Macgregor
Mar 25	Brechin City (A)	LGE	0-10	
Mar 29	Brora Rangers (A)	LGE	1-6	Mackintosh
Apr 1	Huntly (H)	LGE	0-1	
Apr 5	Keith (A)	LGE	0-2	
Apr 8	Turriff United (A)	LGE	3-0	R MacAdie, M MacAdie, MacNab
Apr 12	Inverurie Locos (A)	LGE	0-4	
Apr 15	Deveronvale (A)	LGE	3-3	Flett, Manson, M MacAdie
Apr 22	Lossiemouth (H)	LGE	2-2	MacNab (2)

FIRST HIGHLAND LEAGUE HONOUR FOR NEW BOYS

Banks o' Dee are the newest holders of the Scottish Highland League Cup, claiming their first silverware since making the step up from the ranks of the north juniors.

Defeating Abereenshire rivals Inverurie Locos at Bellslea Park on Saturday April 8., the Spain Park men etched their name in the Highland League history books for the first time thanks to a solitary goal in the second half of the game.

There were chances for Kane Winton and Robert Ward in the early going of a grim first half, with both sides watching opportunities go astray, and neither side really testing the goalkeepers.

Dee were forced to make a change in the 33rd minute, when a back injury meant Lachie Macleod went off to be replaced by former Aberdeen forward Chris Antoniazzi.

The action heated up in the second period, thirteen minutes in, when a Locos mistake allowed Magnus Watson to fire the ball high into the net past Reid to make it 1-0, after being sent clear by a through pass from Antoniazzi.

Shearer at the other end was called into action to deal with a chance for Logan Johnstone, who delivered an inviting low cross into the box.

An Inverurie free-kick also brought about the need for a block, struck well by Dingwal before Shearer blocked it.

Meres, with the rebound, could do no better.

Watson had a good chance to double his contribution and make sure of the win midway through the second half, but could not capitalise.

Locos believed they should have had a penalty award towards the end of the match when substitute Jay Halliday appeared to be fouled, but referee Duncan Nicolson waved play on.

Shearer was the Dee hero again in the 66th minute, when he made a brilliant diving save to prevent a 22-yard drive from Dingwall finding the net.

Alas, time ran out on Locos' hopes for an equaliser, and the 'Dee' went on to lift the cup - their first as a senior football club.

Banks o' Dee co-manager Paul Lawson dedicated the historic victory to the club's backroom staff and loyal band of supporters.

Paul, who masterminded the triumph along with Josh Winton, said: "It's times like these when you have to think of all the people who had dedicated many years of hard work to ensure we were in the position to be able to win this trophy.

"I'm speaking about the army of volunteers we see on match days, many of whom have been there for decades, giving up their time for the sheer love of the club.

"I know the players appreciate what

The Highland League Cup win was Banks o' Dee's first honour since moving up to join the senior ranks of the Highland League. Photo: Craig Duff Photography

they do for them and that they were eager to win the cup for them.

"It was also great to give the Dee fans something back for sticking with us during what we all know has been a strange and at times very challenging first season for the club at Highland League level.

"The club winning this trophy at the first time of asking is a huge achievement."

Paul confirmed efforts to ensure we can build on the cup triumph are already underway.

He added: "We have shown we can compete with the teams at the top level, the aim now is to make sure we are able to do that on a consistent basis.

"We already have a number of top players at Spain Park, the task now is to add to that to maybe take us to the next level, which is backing up our great cup record with a serious title challenge.

BANKS O' DEE.........................1 (0)
Watson 58
INVERURIE LOCO WORKS......0 (0)
Dee: Shearer, Stark, Lewecki, Kelly (Armstrong), Anderson, Winton, Watson (Henderson), Gilmour, Gauld, L Macleod (Antoniazzi), Philipson. *Not used: Alexander, Davidson, Wallace, Salmon.*

Locos: A Reid, Mitchell, Dingwall, Souter, Johnstone (L Robertson), Ward, S Robertson, Burnett (Halliday), Wilson, Michie, Meres. *Not used: Buchan, T Reid, B Smith, Gill, Shingler.*

Referee: D Nicolson

CALENDAR YEAR TROPHY DOUBLE FOR CATTACHS

The North of Scotland Cup victory proved to be Craig Campbell's last trophy win as manager with Brora Rangers.   Photo: Donald Cameron

Craig Campbell's impressive Brora Rangers completed a cup double for the calendar year with a 2–1 win over hosts Clachnacuddin on Saturday, October 1st.

With the scores level at the interval, it took a goal from Andrew Macrae midway through the second period to decide upon the destination of the trophy, as the Cattachs lifted their sixth North of Scotland Challenge Cup in the last ten years.

The final itself was originally set to be played at Lossiemouth's Grant Park, but was moved to Grant Street Park in a bid to attract more spectators to the game. The move, which was agreed following a consultation with the both clubs, handed finalists Clachnacuddin an unlikely home advantage.

But it was visitors Brora who took the initiative after just seven minutes – the opening goal coming after good work between Dale Gillespie and Jordan MacRae, the latter sending the ball beyond the keeper and over the line with the Clach defence in close quarters.

The home side remained undeterred though, and they could have had an

The cup final between Clach and Brora was locked at 1-1 until deep into the second half.
Photo: Donald Cameron

equaliser moments later when Brora keeper Ruardhri Nicol was called into action to prevent a net bound header from Lilywhites defender Gary Warren.

Shaun Sutherland also came close for Clach with a shot that rattled the crossbar and it was only to be a matter of time before the equaliser arrived on 28 minutes.

A ball from Robbie Thompson through the middle of the Brora defence found Lewis Mackenzie and the midfielder made no mistake with a low driven shot past Nicol to make it 1–1.

With both sides in pursuit of a second half winner, it was the Cattachs who eventually found the net with a goal from Andrew Macrae.

The in-form striker fired his side in front on 66 minutes when he connected with a Martin Maclean ball across goal, making no mistake from six yards out.

Despite a valiant effort from Clach, Brora held on to their slender lead to secure victory.

The Sutherland club now hold possession of two of the north's most senior cups at the same time, having won the Highland League Cup back in April with a win over Buckie Thistle.

CLACHNACUDDIN.........................1 (1)
L Mackenzie 28
BRORA RANGERS.........................2 (1)
J MacRae 7, A Macrae 66
Clach: Mackinnon, Morrison, Black, Cormack, Warren, Sutherland, Callum (Logan), Anderson, Thompson, Brindle (Bunce), L Mackenzie (Gillies). Not used: Riddle, Macleod, Chalmers, Rae.
Brora: Nicol, Kelly (Sutherland), A Macdonald, Williamson, Nicolson, Gillespie, Maclean, Meekigns, J MacRae (Gamble), A Macrae, Ewan (G Macdonald). Not used: Gunn.
Referee: G Seago

SHIRE CUP DELIGHT FOR BROCH AFTER PENALTIES

Scott Barbour's 50th minute chance was turned into the net by Formartine player Aaron Norris to level the scores.

Photo: Barry Walker

Fraserburgh secured the first of two Aberdeenshire honours in 2022-23 with a penalty shoot-out victory over Formartine United on September 30th.

Formartine fell short in front of a Friday night crowd at the Haughs in Turriff, despite taking the lead through Scott Lisle just before half-time.

Their efforts were undone shortly after the break, however, when Fraserburgh equalised courtesy of a Scott Barbour corner which came off Aaron Norris on its way into the goal.

With the match 1-1 at full-time, it went straight to spot-kicks which The Broch won 3-2.

Fraserburgh had an early chance through Ross Aitken whose shot was just wide and smacked off an advertising board.

Formartine's Julian Wade proved to be a constant threat in the first half. An opportunity from a corner was just too low and bounced beyond him.

Fraserburgh goalkeeper Joe Barbour struggled with a long throw-in from Matthew McLean but none of the

United's players could capitalise on the loose ball. It eventually came to Kieran Adams who missed it completely with his shot.

Jonny Smith then got a good shot away which was just over the crossbar.

At the other end Paul Young hit an effort first time on the volley that flew wide of the target.

Wade sent in an inviting cross to Norris who was just unable to get a header onto it and the ball went out.

United were continuing to pressure and a pass was played to Jonny Smith in a close position to the goal, however, his effort was weak and saved by Joe Barbour.

Paul Campbell had an opportunity for Fraserburgh but he screwed his effort wide of the goal.

Just before the break United opened the scoring. Wade managed some positive play and saw his shot blocked, which was latched onto by Lisle who ran in and shot low past Joe Barbour.

Fraserburgh came back into the game after the break and it meant that Formartine struggled to get out of their own half.

The Broch set the tone for the half when Scott Barbour received the ball in a good position, ran towards goal and fired in an effort which was blocked by Ewen Macdonald.

The equaliser then came when Scott Barbour's corner was guided home off Norris.

Fraserburgh pushed for a second goal with Connor Wood having a chance which deflected off a couple United players and out for a corner that was saved by Macdonald.

The goalkeeper had to be lively again when Jamie Beagrie struck a shot, which the custodian managed to save.

At the other end Lisle, Wade and Jonny Smith had opportunities but Formartine were struggling to create the forward play they enjoyed in the first half.

They were then reduced to 10 men when McLean received a straight red card from referee Duncan Nicolson for a late challenge on Beagrie.

It was all square at the full-time whistle and the match went straight to penalties to decide who would lift the cup.

In the shootout Kieran Simpson, Sean Butcher and Campbell all scored for Fraserburgh, while Scott Barbour's spot-kick was saved.

For Formartine Jonathan Crawford scored, Wade hit the post, Mark Gallagher's penalty was saved, Daniel Park scored and Joe Barbour saved Cole Anderson's effort to secure the cup victory.

Report by Kyle Ritchie
Highland News & Media

FORMARTINE UNITED...............1 (0)
Lisle 43
FRASERBURGH........................1 (1)
Norris o.g. 50
Broch win 3-2 on pens
Formartine: MacDonald, Spink, Adams, Crawford, McLean, Lawrence (Park 77), Lisle (S Smith 90), Gallagher, J Smith, Wade, Norris (C Anderson 81). Not used: Watson, Addison, Dimov, Maciver

Broch: J Barbour, Simpson, West, Aitken, Hay, Young, Beagrie, C Wood (Butcher 73), Sargent, S Barbour, Campbell. Not used: Inglis, Davidson, Laird, Watt, Combe
Referee: D Nicolson

BUTCHER GOAL NETS DOUBLE FOR BROCH

Sean Butcher's 88th minute winner secured the shield for Fraserburgh at Kynoch Park.
Photo: Barry Walker

Defending Highland League champions Fraserburgh were crowned Aberdeenshire Shield winners for 2022-23 with a 2–1 win over Buckie Thistle under the lights at Kynoch Park.

Mark Cowie's side saw a change in goal with sixteen year old Sam Inglis stepping in for the injured Joe Barbour.

Both sides flirted with goal in the early going, with Andy MacAskill cutting across and shooting over the bar for Buckie, and Scott Barbour firing a low cross across goal.

Broch were the side to take the lead ithough, finding the net in 24 minutes with a goal from top scorer Barbour. The striker fired a deflected shot past Lee Herbert from seven yards after the keeper had beaten away an earlier effort from Ryan Sargent.

Cohen Ramsay, Josh Peters and Max Barry each threatened to equalise for Thistle as time wore on, coming agonisingly close to equalising before Connor Wood at the other forced a save from Herbert.

A Scott Adams shot cannoned off the upright on the hour mark, but it was only to be another three minutes before his side drew level.

An Andy MacAskill free kick provided the danger as Sam Pugh pounced to fire the ball home from close range.

The sides could not be separated until the 88th minute when a right footed cross from Ross Aitken found the head of Sean Butcher who found the bottom right corner of the net.

There was still time for Buckie to pull themselves back level, and they nearly did that when substitute Kyle Macleod headed the ball down to Urquhart who fired just wide.

The win brings the ninth piece of silverware to Bellslea Park during the tenure of Fraserburgh manager Mark Cowie. It is the third time that Cowie's Broch have won the trophy.

For Buckie, the loss continued a six year weight for silverware, having last tasted success with the winning of the Highland League in 2016-17.

BUCKIE THISTLE.......................1 (0)
Pugh 63
FRASERBURGH.........................2 (1)
S Barbour 25, Butcher 88

Buckie: Herbert, McCabe, Munro, Murray, Ramsay (Macleod 89), Pugh, Goodall, MacAskill, Barry, Adams (Urquhart 61), Peters. Not used: MacKinnon, Fyffe, McLauchlan, Morrison, Macleod

Broch: Inglis, Hay, Cowie, Simpson, Beagrie, Lawrence (Butcher 82), S Barbour (West 89), C Wood (Watt 61), Buchan, Sargent, Aitken. Not used: Davidson, West, Bolton, Grant, Flinn

Referee: H Bruce

Fraserburgh lifted the Aberdeenshire & District Shield for a record ninth time.
Photo: Barry Walker

PLAYING SQUAD & STATISTICS 2022/23 *

ALNESS UNITED F.C.
Dalmore Park, Alness

	Age	LEAGUE Apps	Goals	CUPS Apps	Goals	ALL Apps	Goals
ALLISON, Logan	18	1 (6)	0	1	0	2 (6)	0
CARSON, Keir	21	(2)	0	-	-	(2)	0
COLI, Callum	21	5 (11)	6	1	0	6 (11)	6
DRYBURGH, Ryan	20	18	1	1	0	19	1
DUNCAN, James (GK)	26	3	0	-	-	3	0
FRASER, Jude	22	10 (3)	6	1	0	11 (3)	6
GRAHAM, Chris	34	10 (3)	0	1	0	11 (3)	0
GRIMES, Michael	29	13	5	2	0	15	5
HENDERSON, Euan	21	15 (3)	4	(1)	0	15 (4)	4
HUDSON, Jack	31	16	1	2	0	18	1
HUTCHINSON, Liam	29	(2)	0	-	-	(2)	0
KEITH, Stan	22	1 (1)	1	1	0	2 (1)	1
LYON, Roy	-	1 (1)	0	(1)	0	1 (2)	0
MACDONALD, Finlay	-	1	0	-	-	1	0
MACDONALD, Paul	26	2 (3)	1	-	-	2 (3)	1
MACGRUER, Dave	33	7 (1)	0	-	-	7 (1)	0
MACKAY, Alexander	21	11 (3)	11	(1)	0	11 (4)	11
MACKAY, Gregor	24	8 (3)	1	1	0	9 (3)	1
MACLEOD, Fraser	26	1 (1)	0	-	-	1 (1)	0
MCFEE, Ryan	21	22	20	1	0	23	20
MCKENZIE, Michael	28	13 (1)	3	1	1	14 (1)	4
MICHAEL, Stuart	28	18 (2)	1	2	0	20 (2)	1
MITCHELL, Jack	28	2 (1)	0	-	-	2 (1)	0
MITCHELL, Jordan	34	7	0	-	-	7	0
MORRISON, Robbie	21	1	0	-	-	1	0
MUNRO, Craig	37	1 (2)	0	-	-	1 (2)	0
RAE, Michael	28	13	1	1	0	14	1
ROSS, Iain	26	1	0	1	0	2	0
ROSS, Ryan	21	3 (8)	1	1	0	4 (8)	1
SHAW, Jordan	21	2 (2)	0	-	-	2 (2)	0
SINCLAIR, Fraser	31	2	0	-	-	2	0
SKINNER, Aaron	17	3	1	-	-	3	1
SMITH, Brandon (GK)	21	10 (5)	0	1 (1)	0	11 (6)	0
STEWART, Ryan	30	17	2	2	0	19	2
TAYLOR, Kyle	26	4 (7)	0	-	-	4 (7)	0
THAIN, Arran	18	1 (2)	0	-	-	1 (2)	0
VALENTE, Nathanial (GK)	30	9	0	1	0	10	0
WARDROP, Louie	-	1 (4)	0	-	-	1 (4)	0
WILSON, Reece	-	(7)	0	(1)	0	(8)	0

* Players with less than 1 full appearance not displayed due to size of squad.

Date	Opponent	Comp	Score	Scorers
Aug 20	Invergordon (H)	LGE	2-1	Mcfee (2)
Aug 27	St Duthus (H)	FTC R1	0-5	
Sep 3	Halkirk United (H)	LGE	0-1	
Sep 14	Inverness Athletic (H)	LGE	1-3	Henderson
Sep 24	Orkney (A)	LGE	0-0	
Sep 28	Loch Ness (H)	LGE	0-2	
Oct 1	Bonar Bridge (H)	LGE	10-1	Fraser (2), Hudson, Mcfee (2), Coli (3), A Mackay, Rae
Oct 8	Thurso (A)	LGE	5-0	Coli, Fraser, A Mackay (2), McKenzie
Oct 15	Clachnacuddin A (A)	LGE	4-0	Michael, Stewart, A Mackay, Mcfee
Oct 22	St Duthus (H)	LGE	7-0	Mcfee (2), Grimes (2), Henderson (2), A Mackay
Nov 5	Nairn County A (A)	LGE	2-3	A Mackay (2)
Nov 12	Golspie Sutherland (H)	LGE	6-2	A Mackay (2), Grimes, McKenzie, Mcfee, Fraser
Nov 19	Fort William (H)	LGE	2-4	A Mackay, Grimes
Nov 26	Halkirk United (A)	LGE	2-3	McKenzie, B Reid o.g.
Dec 3	Nairn County A (H)	LGE	4-3	Mcfee (2), R Ross, Keith
Dec 10	St Duthus (A)	LCE	1-9	Mcfee
Jan 7	Fort William (A)	LGE	2-4	Grimes, Skinner
Feb 4	Nairn County A (A)	NCC QF	1-2	McKenzie
Feb 11	Golspie Sutherland (A)	LGE	3-3	A Mackay, Mcfee, Fraser
Feb 18	Clachnacuddin A (II)	LCE	2-1	Fraser, P Macdonald
Feb 25	Orkney (H)	LGE	2-5	G Mackay, Mcfee
Mar 11	Bonar Bridge (A)	LGE	4-3	Coli (2), Stewart, Mcfee
Mar 25	Thurso (H)	LGE	9-2	Mcfee (6), Dryburgh, A Porteous o.g., Winter
Mar 29	Invergordon (A)	LGE	1-3	Henderson
Apr 1	Inverness Athletic (A)	LGE	0-2	
Apr 15	Loch Ness (A)	LGE	0-8	

BONAR BRIDGE F.C.
Midgale Playing Fields, Bonar Bridge

		LEAGUE		CUPS		ALL	
	Age	Apps	Goals	Apps	Goals	Apps	Goals
ALI, Shadi	20	10 (9)	0	-	-	10 (9)	0
BROWN, Jack	20	(1)	0	(1)	0	(2)	0
CAMERON, Archie	19	4 (4)	0	-	-	4 (4)	0
COGILL, Dean	26	3 (1)	0	-	-	3 (1)	0
CORBETT, Jack	26	11	4	1	0	12	4
CREIGHTON, Liam	27	2	0	1	0	3	0
DRYBURGH, Craig	23	10	0	-	-	10	0
DUNCAN, Jamie	20	4 (6)	0	-	-	4 (6)	0
FLETT, Liam	21	3	0	-	-	3	0
HAMILTON, Ryan	24	15 (5)	0	2	0	17 (5)	0
HEATH, Fraser	32	8 (2)	0	-	-	8 (2)	0
HOUSTON, Cammy	29	3	0	-	-	3	0
HUTCHISON, Daniel	32	14 (1)	1	1	0	15 (1)	1
MACCULLOCH, Dylan	27	7 (2)	0	1	0	8 (2)	0
MACDONALD, Scott	23	5	2	1	0	6	2
MACKAY, Adam	25	19	5	2	0	21	5
MACKENZIE, Ross	19	4 (4)	0	(2)	0	4 (6)	0
MACLENNAN, Stuart	22	2 (7)	0	(1)	0	2 (8)	0
MATHESON, Ayden	23	2	0	1	0	3	0
MCCLENAGHAN, Michael	22	10	0	-	-	10	0
MCKAY, Jamie	23	5 (1)	0	-	-	5 (1)	0
MONAGHAN, Euan	18	9 (12)	0	(2)	0	9 (14)	0
MORRISON, Callum	22	7 (2)	0	1	0	8 (2)	0
MORRISON, Robbie	21	1 (3)	0	1	0	2 (3)	0
MUNRO, Ian	27	2 (1)	0	-	-	2 (1)	0
MUNRO, Jack	24	2	0	-	-	2	0
PIETRZIC, Stefan (GK)	26	10 (3)	0	1	0	11 (3)	0
ROSS, Connor	27	3	0	1	1	4	1
ROSS, Liam	23	3	0	-	-	3	0
RYDER, Archie	20	1 (1)	0	2	0	3 (1)	0
SANGWIN, Paul	33	7	0	1	0	8	0
SHAND, Gary	31	5	0	-	-	5	0
SMITH, Paul	22	2 (2)	0	-	-	2 (2)	0
STAINKE, Aiden	21	19	1	2	0	21	1
SUTHERLAND, Drew	23	3	2	-	-	3	2
TRAYNOR, Jack	24	9	0	1	0	10	0
URQUHART, Bruce	23	24	4	2	0	26	4
WILSON, Stuart (GK)	25	6 (3)	0	-	-	6 (3)	0

* Players with less than 2 appearances not displayed due to size of squad.

MATCH RESULTS 2022/23

Date	Opponent	Comp	Score	Scorers
Aug 27	Nairn County A (A)	LGE	0-1	
Sep 3	Orkney (A)	LGE	1-3	Corbett
Sep 14	Golspie Sutherland (A)	LGE	2-5	S Macdonald, Corbett
Sep 17	Invergordon (A)	FTC QF	0-3	
Sep 24	Thurso (H)	LGE	1-5	Stainke
Oct 1	Alness United (A)	LGE	1-10	Mackay
Oct 8	Halkirk United (H)	LGE	1-8	Urquhart
Oct 15	Inverness Athletic (H)	LGE	1-3	Mackay
Oct 22	Nairn County A (H)	LGE	4-2	Mackay, Corbett (2), Urquhart
Oct 29	Halkirk United (A)	LGE	1-5	Mackay
Nov 5	Invergordon (H)	LGE	1-5	Hutchison
Nov 19	St Duthus (A)	LGE	2-3	W Ross o.g., S Macdonald
Nov 26	Loch Ness (A)	LGE	0-10	
Dec 3	Clachnacuddin A (A)	LGE	0-6	
Jan 14	Golspie Sutherland (H)	NCC R1	1-6	C Ross
Jan 28	Inverness Athletic (A)	LGE	0-8	
Feb 11	Thurso (A)	LGE	0-10	
Feb 18	Invergordon (A)	LGE	0-9	
Feb 25	St Duthus (H)	LGE	0-5	
Mar 4	Loch Ness (H)	LGE	1-12	Urquhart
Mar 11	Alness United (H)	LGE	3-4	Sutherland (2), Mackay
Mar 18	Fort William (A)	LGE	0-8	
Mar 25	Golspie Sutherland (H)	LGE	0-7	
Apr 1	Fort William (H)	LGE	0-4	
Apr 7	Clachnacuddin A (H)	LGE	1-6	Urquhart
Apr 15	Orkney (H)	LGE	0-4	

CLACHNACUDDIN F.C. 'A'
Inverness Royal Academy, Inverness

	Age	LEAGUE		CUPS		ALL	
		Apps	Goals	Apps	Goals	Apps	Goals
BRAY, Declan	21	(8)	0	-	-	(8)	0
CALDER, Jamie	19	5	0	1	0	6	0
CHALMERS, Ollie	19	1 (2)	0	-	-	1 (2)	0
COLI, Struan	19	1 (11)	1	(1)	1	1 (12)	2
COOPER, Troy	23	8	4	1	0	9	4
DAVIDSON, Aiden	20	2 (3)	0	-	-	2 (3)	0
DUNCAN, Michael	19	11 (3)	0	3	0	14 (3)	0
EAGLESHAM, Caillean	20	8 (2)	0	-	-	8 (2)	0
EAGLESHAM, Charlie	18	5	0	-	-	5	0
FARQUHARSON, Scott	19	4 (8)	0	(3)	0	4 (11)	0
GORDON, Ross	19	(2)	0	-	-	(2)	0
GRANT, Aaron	19	(1)	0	(1)	0	(2)	0
GREGORY, Jamie	22	3 (3)	0	(1)	0	3 (4)	0
HAMILTON, Evan	19	3 (15)	0	3	0	6 (15)	0
KINNEAR, Dylan	19	(3)	0	-	-	(3)	0
LAWRENCE, Ross	19	(2)	0	(1)	0	(3)	0
LEWIS, Thomas	20	19 (1)	5	2	0	21 (1)	5
LOGAN, Ross	21	3	0	-	-	3	0
MACIVER, Scott	20	1 (6)	0	-	-	1 (6)	0
MACKENZIE, Donald	-	(4)	1	-	-	(4)	1
MACKENZIE, Finlay	19	9	2	2	1	11	3
MACKINNON, Aidan	20	3 (4)	2	(1)	0	3 (5)	2
MACLEAN, Cameron	23	11 (1)	0	1	0	12 (1)	0
MACLEOD, Kian	18	2 (4)	1	(1)	0	2 (5)	1
MACMORRAN, Thomas (GK)	20	2	0	-	-	2	0
MCBRIDE, Ronan	22	2	0	-	-	2	0
MCGORAN, Ethan	18	2 (4)	1	1	0	3 (4)	1
MUNRO, Jamie	19	(2)	0	(1)	0	(3)	0
NEVILLE, Cameron	18	19 (3)	5	3	0	22 (3)	5
PATIENCE, Lewis	18	(2)	0	-	-	(2)	0
QUATE, Lachlan	18	16 (4)	1	3	0	19 (4)	1
REID, Kai	21	9 (2)	2	1	0	10 (2)	2
REID-NICOL, Sean	19	18 (4)	2	2 (1)	0	20 (5)	2
RODGERS, Jack	20	1 (2)	0	-	-	1 (2)	0
SHAW, Reece	22	12	0	1 (1)	0	13 (1)	0
SIENKOWSKI, Dawid (GK)	19	16	0	2	0	18	0
SYRJANEN, Keiran	20	19 (2)	14	2	2	21 (2)	16
URQUHART, Robert	18	14	0	(1)	0	14 (1)	0
WALKER, Ryan	21	19	3	1	0	20	3
WHITE, Cal	20	9 (1)	0	2	0	11 (1)	0
YOUNG, Jamie	17	2 (1)	0	1	0	3 (1)	0

* Players with less than 1 full appearance not displayed due to size of squad.

Date	Opponent	Comp	Score	Scorers
Aug 20	Inverness Athletic (A)	LGE	1-2	Lewis
Aug 27	Loch Ness (H)	LGE	1-7	Lewis
Sep 17	Golspie Sutherland (A)	FTC QF	3-0	A Sutherland o.g., Syrjanen, Coli
Oct 1	Halkirk United (A)	LGE	5-2	F Mackenzie, Syrjanen, Neville (2), C Cormack o.g.
Oct 8	St Duthus (A)	FTC SF	2-2	F Mackenzie, Syrjanen
Oct 15	Alness United (H)	LGE	0-4	
Oct 19	St Duthus (H)	LGE	0-3	
Oct 22	Invergordon (A)	LGE	0-4	
Oct 29	Golspie Sutherland (A)	LGE	1-4	A Bremner o.g.
Nov 4	Fort William (A)	LGE	3-4	Lewis (2), Syrjanen
Nov 12	Nairn County A (H)	LGE	1-0	Reid
Nov 19	Thurso (A)	LGE	4-3	Neville, Syrjanen (3)
Nov 26	Orkney (A)	LGE	2-3	Walker (2)
Dec 3	Bonar Bridge (H)	LGE	6-0	Reid, Reid-Nicol, Neville (2), Syrjanen (2)
Jan 14	Nairn County A (H)	NCC R1	0-5	
Jan 28	Halkirk United (H)	LGE	1-3	Syrjanen
Feb 4	Orkney (H)	LGE	0-7	
Feb 11	St Duthus (A)	LGE	2-1	L Flett o.g., Brindle
Feb 18	Alness United (A)	LGE	1-2	Macleod
Feb 25	Loch Ness (A)	LGE	1-3	Syrjanen
Mar 4	Fort William (H)	LGE	2-8	McGoran, Syrjanen
Mar 11	Inverness Athletic (H)	LGE	0-1	
Mar 18	Thurso (H)	LGE	7-0	Syrjanen (4), Cooper (3)
Mar 22	Invergordon (H)	LGE	1-2	Walker
Mar 25	Nairn County A (A)	LGE	3-0	Lewis, Cooper, Mackinnon
Apr 7	Bonar Bridge (A)	LGE	6-1	Mackinnon, Reid-Nicol, D Macculloch o.g., Coli, D Mackenzie, Quate
Apr 15	Golspie Sutherland (H)	LGE	2-0	F Mackenzie, A Sutherland o.g.

GOLSPIE SUTHERLAND F.C.
King George V Park, Golspie

	Age	LEAGUE		CUPS		ALL	
		Apps	Goals	Apps	Goals	Apps	Goals
BREMNER, Andrew	40	11	2	-	-	11	2
CAIRNS, Billy	28	17	11	5	1	22	12
CAIRNS, Kevin	23	4 (2)	3	-	-	4 (2)	3
CAMERON, Korbyn	24	5 (1)	1	1	0	6 (1)	1
CANNOP, Christopher (GK)	39	2	0	-	-	2	0
DOOGAN, Danny	27	2 (6)	0	(1)	0	2 (7)	0
GORDON, Paul	34	5 (7)	1	2 (1)	1	7 (8)	2
HARROLD, Owen	27	9	1	4	1	13	2
INNES, Grant	21	(3)	0	1	0	1 (3)	0
KEITH, Austin	18	1 (1)	0	-	-	1 (1)	0
MACBEATH, Luke	23	4	0	1	0	5	0
MACKAY, Alfie	18	1 (5)	0	1 (2)	0	2 (7)	0
MACKAY, Joe	20	2	0	-	-	2	0
MACKAY, Miller	27	12 (3)	3	1 (1)	0	13 (4)	3
MACKAY, Sam	34	5 (1)	2	3	3	8 (1)	5
MACKENZIE, Gary	28	3	0	-	-	3	0
MACKENZIE, Mark	23	5 (6)	2	1 (1)	0	6 (7)	2
MACLEOD, Ally	41	16	0	5	0	21	0
MACPHERSON, Louis	20	16 (6)	3	5 (2)	1	21 (8)	4
MURRAY, Robbie	21	15	6	6	2	21	8
PULLEN, Gary	19	17 (4)	3	6	2	23 (4)	5
RENWICK, Ryan (GK)	26	17	0	6	0	23	0
ROSS, Craig	29	1	0	1 (1)	0	2 (1)	0
ROSS, Donnie	-	8 (5)	1	(2)	0	8 (7)	1
ROSS, James	27	7	2	2	0	9	2
SUTHERLAND, Adam	35	14 (4)	3	6 (1)	0	20 (5)	3
SUTHERLAND, Cameron	24	18	4	5 (1)	0	23 (1)	4
SUTHERLAND, Joe	30	19	0	4 (2)	0	23 (2)	0
SUTHERLAND, Robbie	22	(7)	0	(2)	1	(9)	1
SUTHERLAND, Steven	24	6 (1)	1	2 (1)	1	8 (2)	2
URQUHART, Shaun	24	17	5	6	0	23	5
YUILL, Cameron (GK)	22	1	0	1	0	2	0

* Players with less than 2 appearances not displayed due to size of squad.

MATCH RESULTS 2022/23

Date	Opponent	Comp	Score	Scorers
Aug 20	Fort William (A)	LGE	2-0	Matheson, Murray
Aug 27	Glasgow University (A)	SC PR.	0-2	
Sep 3	Inverness Athletic (H)	FTC R1	2-2	Murray, B Cairns
Sep 14	Bonar Bridge (H)	LGE	5-2	M Mackay (2), Murray (2), A Sutherland
Sep 17	Clachnacuddin A (H)	FTC QF	0-3	
Sep 24	Nairn County A (H)	LGE	2-1	Bremner, Gordon
Sep 28	Halkirk United (H)	LGE	2-1	Murray, Urquhart
Oct 1	Thurso (A)	LGE	2-1	C Sutherland, K Cairns
Oct 8	Orkney (H)	LGE	1-6	B Cairns
Oct 15	Loch Ness (H)	LGE	3-4	B Cairns (3)
Oct 22	Inverness Athletic (A)	LGE	3-2	C Sutherland (3)
Oct 29	Clachnacuddin A (H)	LGE	4-1	S Mackay, K Cairns (2), B Cairns
Nov 12	Alness United (A)	LGE	2-6	Bremner, M Mackay
Nov 26	Invergordon (H)	LGE	0-1	
Dec 3	St Duthus (A)	LGE	0-1	
Jan 7	Thurso (H)	LGE	2-1	Cameron, B Cairns
Jan 14	Bonar Bridge (A)	NCC R1	6-1	Pullen, S Sutherland, Macpherson, Gordon, R Sutherland, S Mackay
Feb 1	Inverness Athletic (H)	LGE	0-1	
Feb 4	Halkirk United (H)	NCC QF	3-2	Harrold, Murray, Bryan Reid o.g.
Feb 11	Alness United (H)	LGE	3-3	Urquhart, Murray, David Macgruer o.g.
Feb 18	Fort William (H)	LGE	3-2	Macpherson, Pullen, S Mackay
Feb 25	Nairn County A (A)	LGE	2-0	A Sutherland, Urquhart
Mar 4	St Duthus (H)	LGE	4-2	Harrold, B Cairns, A Sutherland, Macpherson
Mar 11	Loch Ness (A)	LGE	3-1	Urquhart, Pullen, D Ross
Mar 18	Loch Ness (A)	NCC SF	2-1	S Mackay (2)
Mar 25	Bonar Bridge (A)	LGE	7-0	J Ross (2), B Cairns (3), Macpherson, Pullen
Mar 29	Halkirk United (A)	LGE	2-2	B Cairns, S Sutherland
Apr 1	Orkney (A)	LGE	2-2	M Mackenzie, Murray
Apr 12	Invergordon (A)	LGE	2-6	Urquhart, M Mackenzie
Apr 15	Clachnacuddin A (A)	LGE	0-2	
Apr 29	Invergordon (A)	NCC F	1-2	Pullen

FORT WILLIAM F.C.
Claggan Park, Fort William

	Age	LEAGUE		CUPS		ALL	
		Apps	Goals	Apps	Goals	Apps	Goals
AHMED, Asad	24	15	8	1	0	16	8
BARKER, Logan	29	8	4	-	-	8	4
BENYOUCEF, Amin	23	9 (1)	6	1	0	10 (1)	6
CAMPBELL, Lewis	29	3	0	-	-	3	0
CAMPBELL, Steven	23	9	0	-	-	9	0
DIGNAM, Kyle	21	3	0	-	-	3	0
DUXBURY, Cameron	20	4 (2)	0	1	0	5 (2)	0
FEJZO, Elgi (GK)	24	11	0	1	0	12	0
FERGUSON, John	31	4	0	-	-	4	0
FLETCHER, Kit (GK)	24	7	0	-	-	7	0
FORBES, David	33	11 (5)	1	(1)	0	11 (6)	1
GILLESPIE, Michael	37	6 (1)	0	-	-	6 (1)	0
HAY, Lerlah	24	17 (5)	4	1	0	18 (5)	4
HYLTON, Carsel	26	2 (5)	0	1	0	3 (5)	0
KEBE, Mohamed	20	1 (2)	0	-	-	1 (2)	0
KELLY, Taylor	21	5	0	1	0	6	0
KULBACKI, Mateusz (GK)	29	5 (1)	0	-	-	5 (1)	0
LAZARO, Diego	22	4	1	-	-	4	1
LELLOUCH, Niels	20	10 (1)	0	1	0	11 (1)	0
LOPEZ, Kieran	28	4	0	-	-	4	0
MACDONALD, Ryan	22	3 (1)	0	-	-	3 (1)	0
MACKINTOSH, Danny	37	2 (1)	0	-	-	2 (1)	0
MACLELLAN, Iain	30	2 (4)	4	-	-	2 (4)	4
MARTHA, Kuerten	21	2 (1)	0	(1)	0	2 (2)	0
MARTIN, Andrew	37	7 (5)	1	-	-	7 (5)	1
MCCONNELL, Jamie	19	5	2	1	0	6	2
MCDONALD, Finlay	22	3 (1)	1	-	-	3 (1)	1
MCLEAN, Andrew	27	16	8	-	-	16	8
MOORE, Lamar	20	5 (4)	0	-	-	5 (4)	0
MUNRO, Martin	28	17 (1)	19	-	-	17 (1)	19
NOBLE, Sean	28	2 (4)	0	-	-	2 (4)	0
PALUGA, Damian	20	2 (1)	0	-	-	2 (1)	0
QUIGG, Darren	35	5	2	-	-	5	2
REID, Andrew	26	6 (1)	0	-	-	6 (1)	0
RODGERS, Michael	29	21 (1)	4	(1)	0	21 (2)	4
RYDINGS, Robbie	19	1 (3)	1	-	-	1 (3)	1
SNEDDON, Andrew	20	3 (3)	3	-	-	3 (3)	3
TREASURER, John	26	3 (1)	0	-	-	3 (1)	0
WYNTER-COLES, Shaquille	23	6 (3)	4	-	-	6 (3)	4

* Players with less than 3 appearances not displayed due to size of squad.

MATCH RESULTS 2022/23

Date	Opponent	Comp	Score	Scorers
Aug 20	Golspie Sutherland (H)	LGE	0-2	
Aug 27	Benburb (H)	SC PR.	0-4	
Sep 3	Thurso (A)	LGE	2-1	Ahmed, Benyoucef
Sep 17	Orkney (H)	LGE	5-1	Benyoucef (2), Munro (2), MacLellan
Sep 24	Halkirk United (A)	LGE	6-1	Barker, Munro, Rodgers, Ahmed, H Bremner o.g., Benyoucef
Oct 1	Loch Ness (H)	LGE	1-2	Munro
Oct 15	Nairn County A (H)	LGE	4-0	Munro (3), Benyoucef
Oct 29	Inverness Athletic (H)	LGE	1-2	Benyoucef
Nov 4	Clachnacuddin A (H)	LGE	4-3	Rodgers, Wynter-Coles (2), Ahmed
Nov 19	Alness United (A)	LGE	4-2	Wynter-Coles (2), Hay, Munro
Nov 26	St Duthus (A)	LGE	0-3	
Dec 3	Thurso (H)	LGE	6-0	S Ellis (2), A McLean (2), Lazaro, Sneddon
Jan 7	Alness United (H)	LGE	4-2	A McLean, A Martin, Munro, Ahmed
Jan 21	Nairn County A (A)	LGE	6-1	A McLean (2), Ahmed, MacLellan (3)
Jan 28	Invergordon (H)	LGE	1-2	Hay
Feb 11	Inverness Athletic (A)	LGE	5-3	Rodgers, Munro (2), Sneddon (2)
Feb 18	Golspie Sutherland (A)	LGE	2-3	Ahmed, Rodgers
Feb 25	Halkirk United (H)	LGE	3-1	A McLean, Ahmed, Hay
Mar 4	Clachnacuddin A (A)	LGE	8-2	Munro (3), Forbes, Barker (2), Ahmed, Rydings
Mar 18	Bonar Bridge (H)	LGE	8-0	Munro (3), Quigg (2), A McLean, Barker, J Duncan o.g.
Mar 25	Orkney (A)	LGE	0-4	
Apr 1	Bonar Bridge (A)	LGE	4-0	Birrell, Hay, McDonald, McConnell
Apr 8	Loch Ness (A)	LGE	0-5	
Apr 15	Invergordon (A)	LGE	1-6	A Martin
Apr 22	St Duthus (H)	LGE	4-0	A McLean, McConnell, Munro (2)

HALKIRK UNITED F.C.
Morrison Park, Halkirk

	Age	LEAGUE		CUPS		ALL	
		Apps	Goals	Apps	Goals	Apps	Goals
ANDERSON, Steven	31	11	8	1	0	12	8
BAIN, Liam	19	13 (8)	0	1 (1)	0	14 (9)	0
BARCLAY, Sam	20	14 (7)	3	1	0	15 (7)	3
BREMNER, Hasheem	32	8 (5)	1	1	0	9 (5)	1
CAMPBELL, Stuart	20	17 (1)	1	1	0	18 (1)	1
CANNOP, William	19	7 (9)	0	(2)	1	7 (11)	1
CLARK, Gordon (GK)	28	1	0	1	0	2	0
COGHILL, Marc	28	15 (2)	0	2	0	17 (2)	0
CORMACK, Conor	24	4 (2)	0	(1)	0	4 (3)	0
GOW, Andrew (GK)	26	2	0	-	-	2	0
GRANT, Euan (GK)	25	4	0	-	-	4	0
HENDERSON, Kyle	24	12 (2)	9	1	1	13 (2)	10
HENSTRIDGE, Colin	23	7 (2)	3	-	-	7 (2)	3
HOWDEN, Jordan	28	1	0	(1)	0	1 (1)	0
KOZIOL, Kuba	28	20 (1)	9	2	0	22 (1)	9
LOCKHART, Owen	20	(3)	0	-	-	(3)	0
MACDONALD, Shaun	20	(2)	0	-	-	(2)	0
MACKAY, Andrew	25	9 (1)	3	1	0	10 (1)	3
MACKAY, Murray	27	1 (1)	0	-	-	1 (1)	0
MACKINTOSH, Alasdair	20	1 (10)	0	-	-	1 (10)	0
MACKINTOSH, Innes	24	12 (2)	0	1	0	13 (2)	0
MACNAB, Grant	32	3	0	-	-	3	0
MARTENS, Jonah	29	2	0	1	2	3	2
MATHIESON, Alan	19	10 (4)	5	1	0	11 (4)	5
MCKECHNIE, Lewis	22	(2)	0	-	-	(2)	0
MCLEAN, John	38	1 (1)	0	-	-	1 (1)	0
MCLEOD, Kieron (GK)	27	12	0	1	0	13	0
MCNICOL, Aaron	25	18 (1)	2	2	0	20 (1)	2
MILLER, Billy (GK)	23	2	0	-	-	2	0
PEARSON, Tomas	19	3 (2)	0	-	-	3 (2)	0
REID, Aidan	24	7	1	1	0	8	1
REID, Bryan	32	10 (3)	1	1	0	11 (3)	1
ROSS, Ian	25	2 (2)	0	-	-	2 (2)	0
SINCLAIR, Ben	21	4	5	-	-	4	5
SINCLAIR, Stuart	35	3	0	-	-	3	0
SUTHERLAND, Ryan	24	3 (1)	0	-	-	3 (1)	0
SWANSON, Don	20	1 (2)	0	-	-	1 (2)	0
TRUEMAN, Conor	27	17	1	2	0	19	1
WEBSTER, Mark	26	1 (2)	0	-	-	1 (2)	0

* Players with less than 2 appearances not displayed due to size of squad.

MATCH RESULTS 2022/23

Date	Opponent	Comp	Score	Scorers
Aug 20	St Duthus (A)	LGE	2-4	Barclay, B Reid
Aug 27	Thurso (H)	FTC R1	2-2	Martens (2)
Sep 3	Alness United (A)	LGE	1-0	Mathieson
Sep 14	Thurso (H)	LGE	3-0	A Mackay, A Reid, Mathieson
Sep 24	Fort William (H)	LGE	1-6	Anderson
Sep 28	Golspie Sutherland (A)	LGE	1-2	Koziol
Oct 1	Clachnacuddin A (H)	LGE	2-5	Henstridge, Barclay
Oct 8	Bonar Bridge (A)	LGE	8-1	Anderson (2), B Sinclair (2), Henstridge, Koziol (2), Bremner
Oct 15	Invergordon (H)	LGE	1-2	Koziol
Oct 22	Loch Ness (A)	LGE	4-7	Anderson (2), A Mackay, Henderson
Oct 29	Bonar Bridge (H)	LGE	5-1	Henderson (2), Koziol (3)
Nov 5	Inverness Athletic (A)	LGE	3-2	B Sinclair, Henderson, Anderson
Nov 12	Orkney (H)	LGE	3-1	Henderson (2), A Mackay
Nov 19	Nairn County A (A)	LGE	3-4	Koziol, B Sinclair (2)
Nov 26	Alness United (H)	LGE	3-2	Henderson, McNicol, Mathieson
Dec 10	Loch Ness (H)	LGE	1-4	Mathieson
Jan 7	Nairn County A (H)	LGE	1-0	McNicol
Jan 28	Clachnacuddin A (A)	LGE	3-1	Henderson (2), J Calder o.g.
Feb 4	Golspie Sutherland (A)	NCC QF	2-3	Henderson, Cannop
Feb 18	Inverness Athletic (H)	LGE	2-0	Anderson, Koziol
Feb 25	Fort William (A)	LGE	1-3	Trueman
Mar 4	Invergordon (A)	LGE	1-3	Anderson
Mar 18	Orkney (A)	LGE	0-3	
Mar 29	Golspie Sutherland (H)	LGE	2-2	Campbell, Barclay
Apr 7	Thurso (A)	LGE	0-0	
Apr 15	St Duthus (H)	LGE	2-3	Mathieson, Henstridge

INVERGORDON F.C.
Recreation Grounds, Invergordon

		LEAGUE		CUPS		ALL	
	Age	Apps	Goals	Apps	Goals	Apps	Goals
ADAMSON, Robert (GK)	-	1	0	-	-	1	0
CAMPBELL, Oscar	21	(1)	0	-	-	(1)	0
CRUICKSHANK, Kai	30	(1)	0	-	-	(1)	0
DOCHERTY, Niall	27	16 (2)	3	7	1	23 (2)	4
DUFF, Alan	30	2	0	2	0	4	0
GOLLER, Darran	34	(1)	0	(1)	0	(2)	0
GOW, Callum	28	3 (6)	0	1 (2)	0	4 (8)	0
HOUSTON, Scott	36	1	0	-	-	1	0
KELLY, Ben	25	20 (1)	22	7	9	27 (1)	31
KERR, Shaun	37	(4)	0	(1)	0	(5)	0
KNIGHT, Jordan	31	13 (8)	8	4	1	17 (8)	9
LAIDLAW, Jordan	26	17 (1)	0	4	0	21 (1)	0
LESLIE, Stuart	33	7 (1)	6	3	2	10 (1)	8
LOCKETT, Jake	27	1	0	2	2	3	2
MACCALLUM, Michael (GK)	34	2	0	-	-	2	0
MACDONALD, Charlie	28	19	1	8	1	27	2
MACDONALD, Kyle	29	(2)	1	(1)	0	(3)	1
MACDONALD, Neil	36	(1)	0	-	-	(1)	0
MACKAY, Jack	26	22	5	8	1	30	6
MACLEAN, Kyle	35	12 (2)	3	5 (1)	0	17 (3)	3
MASON, Colin	37	15 (2)	3	3	0	18 (2)	3
MILLER, Andrew	36	14 (5)	7	2 (5)	3	16 (10)	10
MORRISON, Blair	25	15	2	4 (1)	0	19 (1)	2
MORRISON, Kenneth	27	19 (2)	6	7 (1)	1	26 (3)	7
MUNRO, Ross	25	(1)	0	-	-	(1)	0
MURRAY, Callum	19	4 (18)	5	(5)	1	4 (23)	6
PATIENCE, Ruaraidh	23	12 (4)	2	5 (1)	1	17 (5)	3
PENWRIGHT, Ian	34	1 (2)	0	-	-	1 (2)	0
ROBERTSON, Christopher	44	(1)	0	-	-	(1)	0
SLANEY, Ryan (GK)	28	21	0	6	0	27	0
SMITH, Paul	33	16 (4)	0	2 (4)	0	18 (8)	0
SUTHERLAND, Taylor	26	11 (7)	1	6 (1)	0	17 (8)	1
WARDROP, Jack	24	(1)	0	-	-	(1)	0

MATCH RESULTS 2022/23

Date	Opponent	Comp	Score	Scorers
Aug 20	Alness United (A)	LGE	1-2	K Macdonald
Aug 27	Newtongrange Star (H)	SC PR.	1-5	Lockett
Sep 3	Loch Ness (A)	LGE	1-3	Maclean
Sep 17	Bonar Bridge (H)	FTC QF	3-0	Kelly (2), Lockett
Sep 24	Inverness Athletic (A)	LGE	5-0	B Morrison, Knight (3), Miller
Sep 28	Nairn County A (A)	LGE	2-1	Mackay, Kelly
Oct 8	Loch Ness (H)	FTC SF	3-1	Kelly, Patience, Knight
Oct 15	Halkirk United (A)	LGE	2-1	Knight, Kelly
Oct 22	Clachnacuddin A (H)	LGE	4-0	Kelly (2), Docherty, Mason
Oct 29	Thurso (H)	LGE	5-0	Knight, Kelly (2), Mason, K Morrison
Nov 5	Bonar Bridge (A)	LGE	5-1	Mackay (2), Kelly, K Morrison, Murray
Nov 12	St Duthus (H)	FTC F	3-1	K Morrison, Miller (2)
Nov 26	Golspie Sutherland (A)	LGE	1-0	Mason
Dec 3	Loch Ness (H)	LGE	1-3	B Morrison
Jan 7	St Duthus (H)	LGE	3-1	Kelly, Mackay, Murray
Jan 14	Thurso (A)	NCC R1	7-0	Kelly (3), Mackay, Murray, Miller, Leslie
Jan 28	Fort William (A)	LGE	2-1	Kelly, K Morrison
Feb 4	Inverness Athletic (H)	NCC QF	3-2	Kelly, Leslie, Docherty
Feb 11	Nairn County A (H)	LGE	4-0	K Morrison (2), C Macdonald, Sutherland
Feb 18	Bonar Bridge (H)	LGE	9-0	Murray, Maclean, Kelly (4), Mackay, Miller, Knight
Feb 25	Thurso (A)	LGE	5-1	Leslie (3), K Morrison, Docherty
Mar 4	Halkirk United (H)	LGE	3-1	Leslie (2), Kelly
Mar 18	Nairn County A (A)	NCC SF	2-0	Kelly, R Peterkin o.g.
Mar 22	Clachnacuddin A (A)	LGE	2-1	Kelly, Miller
Mar 25	Inverness Athletic (H)	LGE	2-1	Miller, Kelly
Mar 29	Alness United (H)	LGE	3-1	Maclean, Miller (2)
Apr 1	St Duthus (A)	LGE	0-1	
Apr 8	Orkney (H)	LGE	1-1	Patience
Apr 12	Golspie Sutherland (H)	LGE	6-2	Miller, Leslie, Kelly (3), Murray
Apr 15	Fort William (H)	LGE	6-1	Murray, Knight, Docherty, Kelly (3)
Apr 22	Orkney (A)	LGE	2-1	Knight, Patience
Apr 29	Golspie Sutherland (H)	NCC F	2-1	Kelly, C Macdonald

INVERNESS ATHLETIC F.C.
Ferry Brae, North Kessock

		LEAGUE		CUPS		ALL	
	Age	Apps	Goals	Apps	Goals	Apps	Goals
ALLISON, Dean	28	4 (3)	2	-	-	4 (3)	2
BAIN, Martin	42	14	0	2	0	16	0
BRUCE, Danni	22	18 (2)	5	2	0	20 (2)	5
CAMERON, Paul	37	(1)	0	(1)	0	(2)	0
CHISHOLM, Scott	30	(5)	0	-	-	(5)	0
GODDARD, Kieran	-	(7)	0	-	-	(7)	0
GRESHAM, Connel	35	8 (5)	6	1	0	9 (5)	6
HERSEE, Aidan	27	11 (2)	2	2	0	13 (2)	2
IRVING, Sam	18	1 (6)	0	(1)	0	1 (7)	0
MACAULAY, Dominic	24	1 (3)	3	2	0	3 (3)	3
MACGREGOR, Darren	31	2	0	-	-	2	0
MACKAY, Luke	23	14 (2)	7	(1)	0	14 (3)	7
MACKAY, Luke	28	9 (4)	1	1	0	10 (4)	1
MACKENZIE, Matthew	29	(2)	0	-	-	(2)	0
MACKINNON, Ross	20	1 (5)	0	(1)	0	1 (6)	0
MACKINNON, Willie	22	1	0	(1)	0	1 (1)	0
MACLEOD, Ryan	28	17 (2)	11	2	3	19 (2)	14
MACLEOD, Ryan (GK)	26	18	0	2	0	20	0
MACRAE, Ally	23	1 (3)	0	(1)	0	1 (4)	0
MARTIN, Liam	27	3 (2)	0	-	-	3 (2)	0
MCBEATH, Craig	21	5 (3)	0	-	-	5 (3)	0
MCCHEYNE, Cameron	22	20 (3)	0	2	0	22 (3)	0
MCLEOD, John	35	7 (1)	6	-	-	7 (1)	6
MCROBERT, Michael	31	(2)	0	-	-	(2)	0
MCWILLIAM, Fergus	21	14 (6)	1	1 (1)	0	15 (7)	1
MCWILLIAM, Sandy	18	(3)	0	-	-	(3)	0
MORRISON, Craig	28	10	0	1	0	11	0
MORRISON, Max	18	(4)	0	-	-	(4)	0
PATERSON, Corey (GK)	-	6	0	-	-	6	0
SHEWAN, Harry	23	19 (2)	3	1	0	20 (2)	3
SMITH, Liam	22	20 (1)	0	1	0	21 (1)	0
THOMSON, Arran	22	1 (1)	0	-	-	1 (1)	0
WATSON, Brodie	20	11 (2)	0	-	-	11 (2)	0
WHITE, Cal	20	5 (2)	0	-	-	5 (2)	0
WHITE, Sandy	39	20 (1)	2	2	0	22 (1)	2

* Players with less than 2 appearances not displayed due to size of squad.

MATCH RESULTS 2022/23

Date	Opponent	Comp	Score	Scorers
Aug 20	Clachnacuddin A (H)	LGE	2-1	Broomfield, Shewan
Aug 27	Orkney (A)	LGE	3-2	Bruce, Shewan, L Mackay
Sep 3	Golspie Sutherland (A)	FTC R1	2-2	R Macleod, Mark Mackenzie o.g.
Sep 14	Alness United (A)	LGE	3-1	R Macleod, Gresham (2)
Sep 24	Invergordon (H)	LGE	0-5	
Oct 1	St Duthus (A)	LGE	0-4	
Oct 8	Nairn County A (A)	LGE	3-3	Hersee, Allison, L Mackay
Oct 15	Bonar Bridge (A)	LGE	3-1	Allison, L Mackay, R Macleod
Oct 22	Golspie Sutherland (H)	LGE	2-3	S White, Hersee
Oct 29	Fort William (A)	LGE	2-1	Gresham (2)
Nov 5	Halkirk United (H)	LGE	2-3	Bruce (2)
Nov 12	Thurso (H)	LGE	2-1	R Macleod (2)
Nov 19	Loch Ness (A)	LGE	2-3	R Macleod (2)
Nov 26	Nairn County A (H)	LGE	3-1	R Macleod, Bruce, L Mackay
Dec 3	Orkney (H)	LGE	1-2	R Macleod
Jan 7	Loch Ness (H)	LGE	2-1	Bruce, Gresham
Jan 28	Bonar Bridge (H)	LGE	8-0	Mcleod (3), Macaulay, Gresham, F McWilliam, L Mackay (2)
Feb 1	Golspie Sutherland (A)	LGE	1-0	Macaulay
Feb 4	Invergordon (A)	NCC QF	2-3	R Macleod (2)
Feb 11	Fort William (H)	LGE	3-5	Mcleod, L Mackay, R Macleod
Feb 18	Halkirk United (A)	LGE	0-2	
Mar 4	Thurso (A)	LGE	2-1	R Macleod (2)
Mar 11	Clachnacuddin A (A)	LGE	1-0	Shewan
Mar 18	St Duthus (H)	LGE	2-3	S White, Mcleod
Mar 25	Invergordon (A)	LGE	1-2	Mcleod
Apr 1	Alness United (H)	LGE	2-0	L Mackay, Macaulay

PLAYING SQUAD & STATISTICS 2022/23

LOCH NESS F.C.
King George V Park, Fortrose

	Age	LEAGUE Apps	Goals	CUPS Apps	Goals	ALL Apps	Goals
BOYCE, Dean	19	14 (8)	1	1 (1)	0	15 (9)	1
DONOGHUE, Glenn	30	(10)	1	(1)	1	(11)	2
FRASER, James Lee	33	22 (1)	0	4	0	26 (1)	0
HARKNESS, Shane	20	4 (4)	3	1 (1)	0	5 (5)	3
HOSIE, Ben	32	(11)	0	-	-	(11)	0
INGRAM, Ryan	34	5	1	-	-	5	1
INNES, Chris	35	3 (1)	0	2	0	5 (1)	0
KENNEDY, Mark	40	8 (9)	5	-	-	8 (9)	5
KERR, Jacob	20	23	0	4	0	27	0
LEE, Ricky	33	12 (4)	0	2 (1)	0	14 (5)	0
MACDONALD, Phil	37	15 (2)	16	2	2	17 (2)	18
MACDONALD, Steven	33	5 (1)	1	1	0	6 (1)	1
MACGREGOR, Darren	31	(1)	0	-	-	(1)	0
MACLEAN, Scott	27	10 (1)	0	2	0	12 (1)	0
MACPHEE, Allan	26	22	29	4	2	26	31
MACPHEE, Conor	25	20 (1)	6	4	0	24 (1)	6
MAINLAND, Craig (GK)	32	6	0	-	-	6	0
MAINLAND, Martin	32	8 (6)	0	1 (1)	0	9 (7)	0
MASON, Keith	37	13 (1)	1	3	2	16 (1)	3
MIELE, Michael (GK)	30	10 (2)	0	3 (1)	0	13 (3)	0
MORRISON, Sam	25	(1)	0	-	-	(1)	0
MORRISON, Scott	36	11 (1)	5	2	0	13 (1)	5
MUNRO, Lewis (GK)	18	8	0	1	0	9	0
NEIL, Calum	27	12 (7)	4	3 (1)	1	15 (8)	5
RACE, Josh	25	18	8	1	0	19	8
SEAGO, Luke	19	7 (5)	0	1 (1)	1	8 (6)	1
TAYLOR, Liam	27	8 (1)	16	2	1	10 (1)	17
VENTERS, Ross	33	(2)	0	-	-	(2)	0

MATCH RESULTS 2022/23

Date	Opponent	Comp	Score	Scorers
Aug 20	Orkney (H)	LGE	0-0	
Aug 27	Clachnacuddin A (A)	LGE	7-1	Kennedy (2), P Macdonald (2), A MacPhee, S Morrison, Boyce
Sep 3	Invergordon (H)	LGE	3-1	P Macdonald (2), A MacPhee
Sep 17	Nairn County A (H)	FTC QF	6-0	Mason, A MacPhee (2), Seago, Neil, Donoghue
Sep 24	St Duthus (H)	LGE	2-1	A MacPhee, Neil
Sep 28	Alness United (A)	LGE	2-0	C MacPhee, P Macdonald
Oct 1	Fort William (A)	LGE	2-1	A MacPhee, P Macdonald
Oct 8	Invergordon (A)	FTC SF	1-3	P Macdonald
Oct 15	Golspie Sutherland (A)	LGE	4-3	A MacPhee, Adam Sutherland o.g., S Morrison, Cameron Sutherland o.g.
Oct 22	Halkirk United (H)	LGE	7-4	Kennedy, A MacPhee, P Macdonald (2), Race (3)
Oct 29	Nairn County A (H)	LGE	7-1	A MacPhee (3), P Macdonald, Neil (2), Grant Hogg o.g.
Nov 5	Thurso (A)	LGE	0-0	
Nov 19	Inverness Athletic (H)	LGE	3-2	A MacPhee (2), Ingram
Nov 26	Bonar Bridge (H)	LGE	10-0	S Morrison, Race, P Macdonald (3), A MacPhee (3), Euan Monaghan o.g., Donoghue
Dec 3	Invergordon (A)	LCE	3-1	S Macdonald, Race, A MacPhee
Dec 10	Halkirk United (A)	LGE	4-1	A MacPhee (2), C MacPhee, Race
Jan 7	Inverness Athletic (A)	LGE	1-2	A MacPhee
Jan 28	Nairn County A (A)	LGE	5-3	A MacPhee (3), Taylor (2)
Feb 4	St Duthus (A)	NCC QF	2-1	Taylor, P Macdonald
Feb 11	Orkney (A)	LGE	5-1	Taylor (4), P Macdonald
Feb 18	Thurso (H)	LGE	2-0	P Macdonald (2)
Feb 25	Clachnacuddin A (H)	LGE	3-1	Race, Mason, A MacPhee
Mar 4	Bonar Bridge (A)	LGE	12-1	Taylor (6), C MacPhee, A MacPhee (2), Harkness, Kennedy (2)
Mar 11	Golspie Sutherland (H)	LGE	1-3	Taylor
Mar 18	Golspie Sutherland (H)	NCC SF	1-2	Mason
Mar 25	St Duthus (A)	LGE	5-1	C MacPhee (2), Taylor, S Morrison, A MacPhee
Apr 8	Fort William (H)	LGE	5-0	S Morrison, Race, Taylor, A MacPhee, Harkness
Apr 15	Alness United (H)	LGE	8-0	C MacPhee, Harkness, A MacPhee (3), Neil, P Macdonald, Taylor

NAIRN COUNTY F.C. 'A'
Nairn Academy

	Age	LEAGUE		CUPS		ALL	
		Apps	Goals	Apps	Goals	Apps	Goals
BALFOUR, Liam	20	13 (2)	1	4	0	17 (2)	1
DAWSON, Ewan	18	(2)	0	(1)	0	(3)	0
DUFFTY, Kieran	22	18 (3)	6	4	4	22 (3)	10
EADIE, Tyler	22	20	3	4	0	24	3
GORDON, Sam	24	5	4	-	-	5	4
GRANT, Nathan	21	8 (1)	1	2	0	10 (1)	1
HALLAM, Logan	21	(2)	0	-	-	(2)	0
HOGG, Grant	20	8 (1)	1	1	0	9 (1)	1
HOWARTH, Calum	27	2	1	-	-	2	1
JACK, Will	18	2 (2)	0	(1)	0	2 (3)	0
LEAN, Robbie	19	19 (3)	1	4	1	23 (3)	2
LOGAN, Euan	21	7 (1)	0	2	0	9 (1)	0
MACCORMACK, Jack	-	(3)	0	(1)	0	(4)	0
MACDONALD, Campbell	-	1 (5)	0	-	-	1 (5)	0
MACDONALD, Kyle	19	6 (4)	2	2 (1)	0	8 (5)	2
MACDONALD, Owen	18	3 (3)	1	(2)	0	3 (5)	1
MACKINTOSH, Wayne	36	1 (1)	0	-	-	1 (1)	0
MACLEAN, Dylan (GK)	27	2	0	-	-	2	0
MALLINSON, Kyle (GK)	25	2	0	(1)	0	2 (1)	0
MCCONAGHY, Seamus	23	8	0	-	-	8	0
MCKENZIE, Kenny	31	2	0	-	-	2	0
MITCHELL, Lewis	22	9	0	-	-	9	0
MOODIE, Ryan	21	5 (2)	0	1	1	6 (2)	1
MUNRO, Kieran	19	10 (2)	0	3	0	13 (2)	0
MUTCH, Scott	22	21	0	3 (1)	1	24 (1)	1
PETERKIN, Reid (GK)	19	13	0	3 (1)	0	16 (1)	0
PETERS, Ross	20	5 (3)	1	(1)	0	5 (4)	1
PORRITT, Adam	29	3	0	-	-	3	0
RAE, Charlie	-	1 (2)	0	-	-	1 (2)	0
RENNIE, Stephen	26	2	0	-	-	2	0
ROBERTSON, Duncan	22	4 (5)	0	(1)	0	4 (6)	0
SCOTT, Max	18	(2)	0	-	-	(2)	0
STEPHENSON, Joshua	-	2 (2)	0	-	-	2 (2)	0
STEWART, Scott	18	3 (9)	0	1 (2)	0	4 (11)	0
THOMPSON, Kieran	20	1 (6)	1	-	-	1 (6)	1
TORRIE, Kyle	24	13 (2)	0	1 (1)	0	14 (3)	0
WILLIAMSON, Rory	19	12 (1)	2	2	0	14 (1)	2
WILSON, Gus (GK)	21	5	0	2	0	7	0
WILSON, Murray	31	14	2	3	0	17	2
YOUNG, Ciaran	22	3 (1)	3	2	0	5 (1)	3
YOUNG, Jamie	18	3	0	-	-	3	0

* Players with less than 2 appearances not displayed due to size of squad.

Date	Opponent	Comp	Score	Scorers
Aug 20	Thurso (H)	LGE	2-4	K Macdonald, Duffty
Aug 27	Bonar Bridge (H)	LGE	1-0	Balfour
Sep 3	St Duthus (A)	LGE	1-4	Williamson
Sep 17	Loch Ness (A)	FTC QF	0-6	
Sep 24	Golspie Sutherland (A)	LGE	1-2	Duffty
Sep 28	Invergordon (H)	LGE	1-2	C Young
Oct 1	Orkney (H)	LGE	0-5	
Oct 8	Inverness Athletic (H)	LGE	3-3	C Young (2), Peters
Oct 15	Fort William (A)	LGE	0-4	
Oct 22	Bonar Bridge (A)	LGE	2-4	Lean, Thompson
Oct 29	Loch Ness (A)	LGE	1-7	Gordon
Nov 5	Alness United (H)	LGE	3-2	M Wilson, Hogg, Eadie
Nov 12	Clachnacuddin A (A)	LGE	0-1	
Nov 19	Halkirk United (H)	LGE	4-3	Gordon (2), H Bremner o.g., Howarth
Nov 26	Inverness Athletic (A)	LGE	1-3	Eadie
Dec 3	Alness United (A)	LGE	3-4	Williamson, C Maclean, M Wilson
Jan 7	Halkirk United (A)	LGE	0-1	
Jan 14	Clachnacuddin A (A)	NCC R1	5-0	Duffty (3), Moodie, Lean
Jan 21	Fort William (H)	LGE	1-6	K Macdonald
Jan 28	Loch Ness (H)	LCE	3-5	Duffty (3)
Feb 4	Alness United (H)	NCC QF	2-1	Mutch, Duffty
Feb 11	Invergordon (A)	LGE	0-4	
Feb 25	Golspie Sutherland (H)	LGE	0-2	
Mar 4	Orkney (A)	LGE	0-1	
Mar 18	Invergordon (H)	NCC SF	0-2	
Mar 25	Clachnacuddin A (H)	LGE	0-3	
Apr 11	St Duthus (H)	LGE	4-2	Eadie, Macinnes, Gordon, O Macdonald
Apr 15	Thurso (A)	LGE	2-1	Grant, Duffty

ORKNEY F.C.
KGS Sports Centre, Orkney

		LEAGUE		CUPS		ALL	
	Age	Apps	Goals	Apps	Goals	Apps	Goals
ADAM, Jamie (GK)	19	1	0	-	-	1	0
ARCHIBALD, Connor	25	1	0	-	-	1	0
COOPER, Aiden	-	3 (9)	4	-	-	3 (9)	4
COOPER, Findley (GK)	20	5 (2)	0	-	-	5 (2)	0
CRAIGIE, Jimmy	28	1	0	-	-	1	0
DELDAY, Liam	25	12	8	-	-	12	8
DOWELL, Gregor	21	6 (2)	1	-	-	6 (2)	1
DREVER, Aiden	28	5 (3)	1	-	-	5 (3)	1
DREVER, Kyle	27	1 (2)	0	-	-	1 (2)	0
DUNCAN, Kern (GK)	28	2 (1)	0	-	-	2 (1)	0
FLETT, Jamie	24	3	3	-	-	3	3
FOUBISTER, Jay	21	1	0	-	-	1	0
GILLON, Craig	35	(2)	0	-	-	(2)	0
HARRISON, Craig	20	4 (3)	0	-	-	4 (3)	0
HELLEWELL, Chris	33	3 (4)	1	-	-	3 (4)	1
HELLEWELL, Steven	28	5	0	-	-	5	0
HOURSTON, Daniel	24	9 (1)	0	-	-	9 (1)	0
JESSIMAN, Callan	22	17 (1)	1	-	-	17 (1)	1
KIRKNESS, Wayne	30	13	0	-	-	13	0
MACKAY, Niall	23	16	0	-	-	16	0
MACLEOD, Toby	24	6	3	-	-	6	3
MOFFAT, DJ	30	11 (1)	0	-	-	11 (1)	0
PATERSON, Jack	26	1 (2)	0	-	-	1 (2)	0
PICKLES, James	33	12	3	-	-	12	3
PICKLES, John	29	15	0	-	-	15	0
RENDALL, Lee	26	10 (4)	1	-	-	10 (4)	1
RENDALL, Owen	25	19	15	-	-	19	15
RISBRIDGER, Colin	47	1 (3)	0	-	-	1 (3)	0
SCOTT, Christopher	19	1	0	-	-	1	0
SCOTT, Glen	22	8 (4)	0	-	-	8 (4)	0
SCOTT, Greg	24	1	0	-	-	1	0
SCOTT, Jason	18	8 (5)	1	-	-	8 (5)	1
SCOTT, Robbie	24	1	0	-	-	1	0
SIMPSON, Chris	35	17	6	-	-	17	6
STOUT, Thorfinn	30	2	0	-	-	2	0
TULLOCH, Jamie	18	3 (4)	2	-	-	3 (4)	2
VALENTINE, Liam (GK)	32	15	0	-	-	15	0
WILSON, Joe	25	7 (1)	3	-	-	7 (1)	3
YOUNG, Owen	20	7 (3)	1	-	-	7 (3)	1

* Players with less than 1 full appearance not displayed due to size of squad.

MATCH RESULTS 2022/23

Date	Opponent	Comp	Score	Scorers
Aug 20	Loch Ness (A)	LGE	0-0	
Aug 27	Inverness Athletic (H)	LGE	2-3	J Scott, O Rendall
Sep 3	Bonar Bridge (H)	LGE	3-1	J Pickles, Simpson, L Delday
Sep 17	Fort William (A)	LGE	1-5	Wilson
Sep 24	Alness United (H)	LGE	0-0	
Oct 1	Nairn County A (A)	LGE	5-0	Wilson, Flett (2), O Rendall, L Rendall
Oct 8	Golspie Sutherland (A)	LGE	6-1	O Rendall, Macleod (2), Dowell, J Pickles, Wilson
Oct 22	Thurso (A)	LGE	1-1	Flett
Oct 29	St Duthus (A)	LGE	2-2	O Rendall, J Pickles
Nov 12	Halkirk United (A)	LGE	1-3	C Hellewell
Nov 26	Clachnacuddin A (H)	LGE	3-2	Reece Shaw o.g., O Rendall (2)
Dec 3	Inverness Athletic (A)	LGE	2-1	O Rendall, Simpson
Dec 10	Thurso (H)	LGE	0-2	
Feb 4	Clachnacuddin A (A)	LGE	7-0	Jessiman, L Delday, O Rendall (3), Simpson, A Cooper
Feb 11	Loch Ness (H)	LGE	1-5	L Delday
Feb 18	St Duthus (H)	LGE	2-2	A Cooper, L Delday
Feb 25	Alness United (A)	LGE	5-2	Simpson, A Cooper, O Rendall (2), Ryan Dryburgh o.g.
Mar 4	Nairn County A (H)	LGE	1-0	O Rendall
Mar 18	Halkirk United (H)	LGE	3-0	Simpson, O Rendall, Young
Mar 25	Fort William (H)	LGE	4-0	Tulloch (2), A Cooper, L Delday
Apr 1	Golspie Sutherland (H)	LGE	2-2	L Delday (2)
Apr 8	Invergordon (A)	LGE	1-1	Ryan Slaney o.g.
Apr 15	Bonar Bridge (A)	LGE	4-0	L Delday, A Drever, O Rendall, Simpson
Apr 22	Invergordon (H)	LGE	1-2	Macleod

PLAYING SQUAD & STATISTICS 2022/23

ST DUTHUS F.C.
Grant Park, Tain

	Age	LEAGUE		CUPS		ALL	
		Apps	Goals	Apps	Goals	Apps	Goals
ALLAN, Adam	22	15 (1)	0	2 (1)	0	17 (2)	0
ALLAN, John (GK)	27	11	0	2	0	13	0
AS-CHAINEY, Finn	23	22	7	5	3	27	10
BEATTIE, Johnie	18	(3)	0	-	-	(3)	0
BRUCE, Ben	28	3 (1)	2	1 (1)	2	4 (2)	4
CAMPBELL, Christopher	35	-	-	(1)	0	(1)	0
CHRISTIE, Arron	37	4	0	-	-	4	0
CHRISTIE, Daniel	32	2 (1)	0	-	-	2 (1)	0
DAVIDSON, Duncan	32	1 (3)	0	2	0	3 (3)	0
FLETT, Liam	21	4	0	-	-	4	0
GAIR, Paul	35	20 (1)	1	4	0	24 (1)	1
GODDING, William (GK)	26	12	0	3	0	15	0
GRAY, Michael (GK)	47	1	0	-	-	1	0
HULME, Bradi	23	18 (5)	10	4 (1)	2	22 (6)	12
IRVINE, Kaden	18	(1)	0	-	-	(1)	0
LOCKETT, Jake	27	12 (1)	14	1	0	13 (1)	14
MACKAY, James	29	18 (1)	5	5	0	23 (1)	5
MACKENZIE, Connor	18	(7)	0	(1)	0	(8)	0
MACKENZIE, Harris	18	(1)	0	-	-	(1)	0
MACKENZIE, Kyle	25	6 (11)	1	2 (3)	1	8 (14)	2
MACLELLAN, John	30	3 (10)	0	(1)	0	3 (11)	0
MACRITCHIE, Stefan	27	17 (1)	2	4	0	21 (1)	2
MARSHALL, Shaun	19	5 (14)	2	(3)	1	5 (17)	3
PATERSON, Reece	27	1 (1)	0	1	0	2 (1)	0
ROSS, Sam	26	12	3	3	0	15	3
ROSS, Will	25	19	2	5	1	24	3
SEARS, Louis	19	1 (4)	1	-	-	1 (4)	1
SKINNER, Jamie	24	19 (3)	1	4	0	23 (3)	1
SKINNER, John	50	16	0	5	0	21	0
SMITH, Lewis	26	4 (2)	0	(1)	0	4 (3)	0
SPENCE, Harry	19	1	0	-	-	1	0
TOKELY, Ross	44	3	2	1	1	4	3
VOIGT, Adrian	20	14 (9)	7	1 (3)	0	15 (12)	7

Date	Opponent	Comp	Score	Scorers
Aug 20	Halkirk United (H)	LGE	4-2	Bruce, As-Chainey, Lockett (2)
Aug 27	Alness United (A)	FTC R1	5-0	K Mackenzie, As-Chainey (2), Bruce, Marshall
Sep 3	Nairn County A (H)	LGE	4-1	Murray Wilson o.g., As-Chainey, Bruce, Voigt
Sep 17	Thurso (A)	FTC QF	3-1	W Ross, Allan Munro o.g., Hulme
Sep 24	Loch Ness (A)	LGE	1-2	Tokely
Oct 1	Inverness Athletic (H)	LGE	4-0	As-Chainey, Hulme, MacRitchie, Voigt
Oct 8	Clachnacuddin A (H)	FTC SF	2-2	Tokely, Bruce
Oct 15	Thurso (H)	LGE	3-1	Lockett, MacRitchie, Marshall
Oct 19	Clachnacuddin A (A)	LGE	3-0	Mackay, Tokely, As-Chainey
Oct 22	Alness United (A)	LGE	0-7	
Oct 29	Orkney (H)	LGE	2-2	Lockett (2)
Nov 12	Invergordon (A)	FTC Final	1-3	Hulme
Nov 19	Bonar Bridge (H)	LGE	3-2	S Ross, Hulme (2)
Nov 26	Fort William (H)	LGE	3-0	Gair, Hulme, Voigt
Dec 3	Golspie Sutherland (H)	LGE	1-0	S Ross
Dec 10	Alness United (H)	LGE	9-1	Lockett (4), Voigt (2), As-Chainey, J Skinner, Hulme
Jan 7	Invergordon (A)	LGE	1-3	Voigt
Jan 28	Thurso (A)	LGE	5-3	Hulme, Lockett (3), As-Chainey
Feb 4	Loch Ness (H)	NCC QF	1-2	As-Chainey
Feb 11	Clachnacuddin A (H)	LGE	1-2	Lockett
Feb 18	Orkney (A)	LGE	2-2	W Ross, Lockett
Feb 25	Bonar Bridge (A)	LGE	5-0	S Ross, Marshall, Hulme, As-Chainey, Sears
Mar 4	Golspie Sutherland (A)	LGE	2-4	Christopher Cannop o.g., K Mackenzie
Mar 18	Inverness Athletic (A)	LGE	3-2	Mackay, Hulme, S White o.g.
Mar 25	Loch Ness (H)	LGE	1-5	Hulme
Apr 1	Invergordon (H)	LGE	1-0	Mackay
Apr 11	Nairn County A (A)	LGE	2-4	Hulme, Mackay
Apr 15	Halkirk United (A)	LGE	3-2	W Ross, Voigt, Mackay
Apr 22	Fort William (A)	LGE	0-4	

THURSO F.C.
Sir George's Park, Thurso

	Age	LEAGUE		CUPS		ALL	
		Apps	Goals	Apps	Goals	Apps	Goals
AITKENHEAD, Grant	21	12 (1)	2	2	0	14 (1)	2
ALEXANDER, Dylan	19	18 (1)	1	1 (1)	0	19 (2)	1
BAIN, Ryan (GK)	32	12	0	2	0	14	0
BANKS, Martin	31	2 (1)	0	-	-	2 (1)	0
BREMNER, Michael	40	3 (8)	0	-	-	3 (8)	0
BREMNER, Saleem	29	4	0	-	-	4	0
CAIRNS, Kevin	23	5 (1)	0	-	-	5 (1)	0
CAMPBELL, Taylor	27	11 (2)	0	1 (1)	0	12 (3)	0
CANNOP, Owen	19	(1)	0	(1)	0	(2)	0
COGHILL, Daniel	26	2	1	-	-	2	1
DAVIDSON, Scott	32	1 (4)	0	-	-	1 (4)	0
DUNNETT, Jake	19	2 (1)	0	-	-	2 (1)	0
FINLAYSON, Kyle	19	3	0	-	-	3	0
GREEN, Christopher	28	11 (1)	2	2	0	13 (1)	2
GUNN, Adam	23	7 (1)	3	(1)	0	7 (2)	3
GUNN, Bobby	32	11 (2)	4	-	-	11 (2)	4
HALE, David	31	15 (2)	1	(1)	0	15 (3)	1
HARDWICK, Andrew	31	7 (1)	1	1	0	8 (1)	1
HARROLD, Owen	27	6	0	1	0	7	0
INNES, Kyle	32	3	1	(1)	0	3 (1)	1
KENNEDY, Craig	23	10 (6)	1	(1)	0	10 (7)	1
MACGREGOR, Marc	28	1	0	2	1	3	1
MACKAY, Alfie	18	5 (3)	0	-	-	5 (3)	0
MACLEOD, Conor	25	3 (4)	0	(1)	0	3 (5)	0
MACRAE, Colin	25	2 (1)	0	1	0	3 (1)	0
MANSON, Luke	26	8 (1)	0	2	0	10 (1)	0
MCKECHNIE, Jack	25	17	2	2	0	19	2
MCLEAN, James	33	4 (2)	1	2	2	6 (2)	3
MCLEAN, Robert	26	14	5	3	0	17	5
MUNRO, Allan	33	11	0	3	0	14	0
MURRAY, James	32	7 (3)	6	3	0	10 (3)	6
PETRIE, Michael	33	1 (2)	0	-	-	1 (2)	0
PORTEOUS, Adam	25	2 (2)	0	-	-	2 (2)	0
SHEPHERD, Lewis	21	2 (1)	2	1 (1)	0	3 (2)	2
STEVEN, Grant	31	7	0	1	0	8	0
SUTHERLAND, Sandy	37	(8)	0	-	-	(8)	0
WILSON, Aaron	21	19	4	2	0	21	4
YUILL, Cameron (GK)	22	10	0	1	0	11	0

* Players with less than 3 appearances not displayed due to size of squad.

84

MATCH RESULTS 2022/23

Date	Opponent	Comp	Score	Scorers
Aug 20	Nairn County A (A)	LGE	4-2	G Aitkenhead, Coghill, Alexander, Shepherd
Aug 27	Halkirk United (A)	FTC R1	2-2ᵖ	Macgregor, J McLean
Sep 3	Fort William (H)	LGE	1-2	Murray
Sep 14	Halkirk United (A)	LGE	0-3	
Sep 17	St Duthus (H)	FTC QF	1-3	J McLean
Sep 24	Bonar Bridge (A)	LGE	5-1	Shepherd, J McLean, Wilson, Green, R McLean
Oct 1	Golspie Sutherland (H)	LGE	1-2	R McLean
Oct 8	Alness United (H)	LGE	0-5	
Oct 15	St Duthus (A)	LGE	1-3	Wilson
Oct 22	Orkney (H)	LGE	1-1	R McLean
Oct 29	Invergordon (A)	LGE	0-5	
Nov 5	Loch Ness (H)	LGE	0-0	
Nov 12	Inverness Athletic (A)	LGE	1-2	R McLean
Nov 19	Clachnacuddin A (H)	LGE	3-4	Kennedy, Innes, G Aitkenhead
Dec 3	Fort William (A)	LGE	0-6	
Dec 10	Orkney (A)	LGE	2-0	Murray, Hardwick
Jan 7	Golspie Sutherland (A)	LGE	1-2	Murray
Jan 14	Invergordon (H)	NCC R1	0-7	
Jan 28	St Duthus (H)	LGE	3-5	A Gunn (2), R McLean
Feb 11	Bonar Bridge (H)	LGE	10-0	B Gunn (3), Hale, Green, Wilson (2), J McKechnie (2), E Monaghan o.g.
Feb 18	Loch Ness (A)	LGE	0-2	
Feb 25	Invergordon (H)	LGE	1-5	A Gunn
Mar 4	Inverness Athletic (H)	LGE	1-2	B Gunn
Mar 18	Clachnacuddin A (A)	LGE	0-7	
Mar 25	Alness United (A)	LGE	2-9	Murray (2)
Apr 7	Halkirk United (H)	LGE	0-0	
Apr 15	Nairn County A (H)	LGE	1-2	Murray

LATE MILLER BRACE SETS INVERGORDON ON THEIR WAY FOR SEASON DOUBLE

Invergordon secured the first of two trophies during the 2022-23 when they won the Football Times Cup. Andrew Miller netted twice late on again St Duthus to win it.   Photo: Niall Harkiss

The destination of the North Caledonian FA's first trophy of the 2022-23 season was decided by two late strikes on November 12, with Invergordon pipping local rivals St Duthus in the final at Golspie.

The teams were originally scheduled to meet on North Caledonian League duty on the same fixture day, but their fate as finalists was sealed after St Duthus secured their place with a semi-final penalties win over Clachnacuddin, and Invergordon beat league leader Loch Ness 3-1 in close fought win at Fortrose.

In front of a packed crowd at King George V Park, Invergordon dominated in the early going, and unsurprisingly broke the deadlock after five minutes with a goal from Ken Morrison, who side footed home from ten yards.

Gary Campbell's men were unable to extend their advantage in the first period though, thanks to a man of the match performance from William Godding in the Saints goal, who kept his aggressors at bay valiantly.

On 18 minutes, a foul on Jordan Knight inside the area led to a penalty award for Invergordon – but the eventual kick from Ben Kelly was saved by Godding, who reacted superbly to palm the ball away to safety.

Things were more even upon the restart, and less than ten minutes in, St Duthus notched a surprise leveller through Bradi Hulme, the plucky striker hitting a first time shot beyond Slaney after a run into the box from Finn As-Chainey.

There were chances at either end to take the lead throughout the peak of the second period, with Sam Ross of St Duthus most notably heading over the bar from 5 yards out.

With their only substitute of the game, Invergordon completely undid the locks on the St Duthus defence, and placed one hand on the cup with goal on 83 minutes.

A long free kick was nodded down by Charlie MacDonald and first to the ball, Andrew Miller prodded the ball into the net.

The wind swept out of the Saints' sails and just minutes later Miller added a second to send Invergordon supporters into celebration, finishing well with a low driven stike after being played in behind the defence by Kelly.

Post-match, Man of the Match William Godding was presented with an engraved hip flask, before league secretary Sandy Stephen called forward the winning captain, Jack Mackay, up to collect the trophy.

Mr Stephen thanked both participating clubs and their committees, the cup final match officials, hosts Golspie Sutherland and sponsors Inverness Trophy Centre for

Invergordon captain Jack Mackay collects the trophy from league secretary Sandy Stephen.

a well attended final.

A paying crowd of 108 watched the final, with a gate of £540 raised towards two charities of the clubs' choosing.

INVERGORDON..............................3 (1)
K Morrison 5, Miller 83, 87
ST DUTHUS...1 (0)
Hulme 54

Invergordon: Slaney, Docherty, Laidlaw, Macdonald, B Morrison, Mason, Knight (Miller 70), Mackay, Kelly, K Morrison, Smith Not used: Murray, Patience, Sutherland, Kerr

St Duthus: Godding, W Ross, S Ross (K Mackenzie 87), JW Skinner, Davidson (A Allan 69), Mackay, MacRitchie, J Skinner (Marshall 52), Hulme (Campbell 69), Gair (Voigt 87), As-Chainey

Referee: D Alexander

CHARLIE MAC FIRES BACK WITH DOUBLE DECIDER

Invergordon made it two out of two cups despite missing out on this year's league championship.
Photo: Sandy Stephen

Invergordon completed a cup double with a 2-1 win over hosts Golspie Sutherland to bring the curtain down on a long season, capturing the North Caledonian Cup for a third time.

But Gary Campbell's Invergordon side had to come back from a goal down to secure the trophy, after youngster Gary Pullen had fired Golspie into the lead after 20 minutes.

The equaliser arrived towards the end of a frenetic first half, with Ben Kelly notching on 39 minutes to make it 1-1.

The winner was reserved for central defender Charlie Macdonald who popped up to put Invergordon into the lead just two minutes into the second period.

INVERGORDON...........................2 (1)
Kelly 39, C Macdonald 47
GOLSPIE SUTHERLAND..............1 (1)
Pullen 20

Invergordon: Slaney, T Sutherland, Patience, Duff, C Macdonald, K Morrison, Docherty, Mackay, Miller (Goller 85), Kelly, Maclean (Gow 58). Not used: Murray, Knight, Laidlaw

Golspie Sutherland: Renwick, C Sutherland, J Sutherland (M Mackay 85), A Sutherland, Harrold, S Mackay (C Ross 61), Pullen, J Ross, B Cairns, Urquhart, Murray (Macpherson 77). Not used: M Mackenzie, R Sutherland

Referee: G Morrison

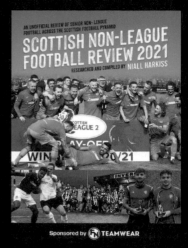

BANCHORY ST TERNAN J.F.C.
Milton Park, Banchory

	Age	LEAGUE Apps	LEAGUE Goals	CUPS Apps	CUPS Goals	ALL Apps	ALL Goals
ABOLFATHI, Aryia	18	13 (1)	0	7	0	20 (1)	0
AIRENS, Joey	21	4 (2)	0	1	0	5 (2)	0
ANDERSON, Calan	19	21 (3)	3	7	2	28 (3)	5
BOYLAN, Jamie	20	10 (9)	1	1 (5)	0	11 (14)	1
CAMPBELL, Neil	19	14 (6)	0	3 (1)	0	17 (7)	0
CHILAKA, Ndouma	31	(3)	0	-	-	(3)	0
CLARK, Rhys	20	1	0	1	0	2	0
DLUGOSZ, Alexsander	19	5 (4)	1	2 (2)	1	7 (6)	2
DONALDSON, Dean	19	(5)	0	-	-	(5)	0
DUTHIE, Blair	25	13	0	1	1	14	1
FINDLAY, Brett	19	18 (7)	6	5 (2)	0	23 (9)	6
GASSAMA, Adrian	24	4 (4)	0	-	-	4 (4)	0
GOVE, Conall	19	1 (5)	0	1 (1)	0	2 (6)	0
HENDERSON, Charlie	18	4 (2)	0	-	-	4 (2)	0
HENDERSON, Dean	27	21 (1)	2	5	1	26 (1)	3
IBAZEBO, David	21	4 (1)	1	-	-	4 (1)	1
LECHNER, Christian	26	3 (1)	0	1	0	4 (1)	0
LEIPER, Lewis (GK)	18	14	0	3	0	17	0
LINTON, Aidan (GK)	18	2	0	-	-	2	0
MACGREGOR, Scott	34	2	0	-	-	2	0
MAY, Liam	19	9 (3)	0	2 (1)	0	11 (4)	0
MILNE, Greg	19	16 (6)	1	1 (5)	1	17 (11)	2
MILNE, Lee	27	(3)	1	1	0	1 (3)	1
MONKS, Jamie	20	2	0	(1)	0	2 (1)	0
NAPIER, Connor	19	1 (3)	0	(1)	0	1 (4)	0
OTTO, Joseph	20	5	0	-	-	5	0
PARK, Ryan	19	20 (5)	3	5 (1)	1	25 (6)	4
PASZKIEWICZ, Brunon	19	1 (1)	0	(2)	0	1 (3)	0
PAUL, Ewan (GK)	19	5	0	4	0	9	0
RENNIE, Jamie	23	1 (3)	0	-	-	1 (3)	0
ROBERTSON, Josh	30	23 (2)	0	6	0	29 (2)	0
ROSS, Ben	23	1	0	2	0	3	0
STEPHEN, Archie (GK)	18	5	0	-	-	5	0
STEWART, Andy	30	17	2	5	0	22	2
THOMPSON, Murray	19	7	2	4	1	11	3
TRAVERS, Steven	33	2	0	1	0	3	0
TUREK, Kurtis	22	2 (2)	0	-	-	2 (2)	0
WHYTE, James	19	12	0	6	0	18	0
WOOD, Finlay	22	3 (1)	0	2	0	5 (1)	0

* Players with less than 1 full appearance not displayed due to size of squad.

MATCH RESULTS 2022/23

Date	Opponent	Comp	Score	Scorers
Jul 30	Bridge of Don Thistle (A)	GLC GRP	0-7	
Aug 6	Nairn St. Ninian (H)	LGE	4-3	G Milne, D Henderson, Findlay, L Milne
Aug 9	East End (H)	GLC GRP	0-2	
Aug 13	Ellon United (A)	LGE	1-2	Boylan
Aug 16	Stoneywood Parkvale (A)	LGE	0-6	
Aug 20	East End (H)	LGE	1-3	Findlay
Aug 23	Culter (H)	LGE	0-4	
Aug 27	Vale of Leven (A)	SJC R1	4-2	Anderson, Park, G Milne, Thompson
Sep 3	Maud (A)	LGE	0-1	
Sep 24	Gartcairn (H)	SJC R2	1-6	D Henderson
Oct 1	Montrose Roselea (H)	LGE	2-0	Thompson (2)
Oct 8	Bridge of Don Thistle (A)	LGE	1-4	Anderson
Oct 15	Dyce (H)	LGE	1-5	Dlugosz
Oct 22	Stonehaven (A)	LGE	1-2	Ibazebo
Oct 29	Colony Park (H)	LGE	2-4	Findlay, D Henderson
Nov 5	Newmachar United (H)	NRC R1	2-4	Anderson, Dlugosz
Nov 12	Montrose Roselea (A)	IRC R1	0-4	
Nov 19	Hermes (A)	LGE	0-1	
Nov 26	Dufftown (A)	LGE	1-3	Stewart
Jan 7	Nairn St. Ninian (A)	LGE	1-4	Findlay
Jan 14	Maud (H)	LGE	0-0	
Jan 28	Colony Park (A)	LGE	0-3	
Feb 4	Stoneywood Parkvale (H)	LGE	1-4	Park
Feb 11	Montrose Roselea (A)	LGE	0-2	
Feb 18	Culter (H)	McL R1	1-4	Duthie
Feb 25	Stonehaven (H)	LGE	0-4	
Mar 4	Bridge of Don Thistle (H)	LGE	1-1	Stewart
Mar 18	Culter (A)	LGE	1-4	Findlay
Mar 25	Dyce (A)	LGE	0-3	
Apr 1	Ellon United (H)	LGE	3-3	Park (2), Anderson
Apr 8	East End (A)	LGE	0-5	
Apr 15	Hermes (H)	LGE	0-5	
May 6	Dufftown (H)	LGE	2-0	Anderson, Findlay

PLAYING SQUAD & STATISTICS 2022/23

BRIDGE OF DON THISTLE J.F.C.
Aberdeen Sports Village

	Age	LEAGUE		CUPS		ALL	
		Apps	Goals	Apps	Goals	Apps	Goals
AHMANACHE, Mourad	21	1 (8)	0	(1)	0	1 (9)	0
BAIN, James	35	2 (8)	5	(2)	1	2 (10)	6
BOOTH, David	36	10 (7)	2	3 (3)	0	13 (10)	2
BOWDEN, Cameron	33	22	1	10	0	32	1
BURNETT, Jack	21	1 (3)	0	(1)	0	1 (4)	0
BURNETT, Liam	26	24	4	10	1	34	5
CLOSE, Andrew	30	3 (6)	0	3 (3)	1	6 (9)	1
CLUBB, Harris	18	15	0	7	0	22	0
COWLING, Robbie	-	(1)	0	-	-	(1)	0
DEANS, Bradley	31	5 (13)	0	3 (4)	0	8 (17)	0
FORBES, Darren	29	22 (1)	0	8	0	30 (1)	0
FORSYTH, Ross	37	17 (1)	1	10	1	27 (1)	2
GAULD, Kyle	28	21 (4)	1	6 (3)	2	27 (7)	3
GORDON, Nicky	40	2	0	-	-	2	0
HAY, Chris	26	7 (1)	0	3	0	10 (1)	0
HOLT, Darren	28	13 (2)	0	4 (3)	0	17 (5)	0
JOJI, Adam	23	6 (14)	7	3 (3)	3	9 (17)	10
LAKSIR, Yassine	25	3 (2)	1	(1)	0	3 (3)	1
MCKEOWN, Craig	38	3	0	2	0	5	0
MILNE, Declan	26	5 (5)	2	1 (4)	0	6 (9)	2
MITCHELL, Toby	-	(1)	0	-	-	(1)	0
MUIRHEAD, Lewis	57	(1)	0	-	-	(1)	0
MUIRHEAD, Sam	31	20	24	8	8	28	32
MUNRO, Grant	31	1 (7)	1	(2)	0	1 (9)	1
MURPHY, Kyle	19	19 (4)	0	5 (4)	0	24 (8)	0
NAPIER, Paul	36	17 (2)	1	5 (2)	0	22 (4)	1
RENNIE, Stewart	25	20	7	7 (2)	1	27 (2)	8
ROBERTSHAW, Keith (GK)	23	26	0	10	0	36	0
ROBERTSON, Sam	24	1 (3)	0	2 (3)	1	3 (6)	1
SHAW, Dylan	-	(1)	0	(1)	0	(2)	0

MATCH RESULTS 2022/23

Date	Opponent	Comp	Score	Scorers
Jul 30	Banchory St. Ternan (H)	GLC GRP	7-0	Close, S Muirhead (2), Gauld, L May o.g., Bain, Robertson
Aug 2	East End (A)	GLC GRP	0-1	
Aug 6	Stonehaven (H)	LGE	2-3	L Burnett, Bain
Aug 13	Montrose Roselea (A)	LGE	1-0	Joji
Aug 16	East End (A)	LGE	1-2	Napier
Aug 20	Dufftown (H)	LGE	6-0	S Muirhead (3), Booth, Gauld, Bain
Aug 23	Colony Park (A)	LGE	3-0	Joji, Bowden, Rennie
Aug 27	Wishaw (A)	SJC R1	1-2	
Sep 3	Nairn St. Ninian (A)	LGE	0-2	
Sep 17	Ellon United (H)	LGE	1-0	Bain
Sep 24	Maud (A)	LGE	6-0	S Muirhead (3), Rennie, Bain (2)
Oct 1	Stoneywood Parkvale (A)	LGE	4-0	Booth, Rennie, S Muirhead, Joji
Oct 8	Banchory St. Ternan (H)	LGE	4-1	Rennie, S Muirhead (3)
Oct 14	Hermes (A)	LGE	1-1	S Muirhead
Oct 22	Culter (H)	LGE	0-3	
Nov 5	Maud (A)	NRC R1	3-2	Joji (2), S Muirhead
Nov 12	Lossiemouth United (H)	IRC R1	1-0	Gauld
Dec 3	Colony Park (A)	NRC R2	4-0	L Burnett, S Muirhead (2), Joji
Jan 7	Buchanhaven Hearts (H)	IRC R2	3-0	Rennie, S Muirhead (2)
Jan 14	Nairn St. Ninian (H)	LGE	1-1	S Muirhead
Jan 28	Ellon United (A)	LGE	3-0	Rennie, L Burnett, S Muirhead
Feb 4	Dyce (H)	LGE	0-2	
Feb 11	Carnoustie Panmure (A)	IRC R3	2-3	Unknown
Feb 18	Hermes (H)	LGE	2-2	S Muirhead, Milne
Feb 25	Montrose Roselea (A)	NRC QF	1-2	S Muirhead
Mar 4	Banchory St. Ternan (A)	LGE	1-1	Joji
Mar 18	East End (H)	McL QF	1-1p	Forsyth
Mar 25	Colony Park (H)	LGE	5-1	S Muirhead (3), Rennie, L Burnett
Apr 1	Dyce (A)	LGE	2-2	S Muirhead, Forsyth
Apr 8	Montrose Roselea (H)	LGE	4-0	S Muirhead (2), Rennie, L Burnett
Apr 11	Stonehaven (A)	LGE	0-0	
Apr 15	Stoneywood Parkvale (H)	LGE	5-0	S Muirhead, Joji (3), Laksir
Apr 18	Culter (A)	LGE	0-6	
Apr 22	Dufftown (A)	LGE	1-0	Milne
Apr 29	Maud (H)	LGE	0-3	
May 6	East End (H)	LGE	4-5	S Muirhead (3), Munro

COLONY PARK J.F.C.
Colony Park/Davidson Park, Inverurie

	Age	LEAGUE		CUPS		ALL	
		Apps	Goals	Apps	Goals	Apps	Goals
ANDERSON, J	-	(1)	0	-	-	(1)	0
ANGUS, Aaron	20	19 (1)	1	6 (2)	0	25 (3)	1
BRAILSFORD, Jamie	22	20	1	7 (1)	0	27 (1)	1
BYRES, Josh	20	20 (5)	3	8	0	28 (5)	3
CHAUVIN, Anton	18	12 (6)	1	6 (2)	3	18 (8)	4
CLELLAND, Ross	20	10 (7)	2	1 (5)	0	11 (12)	2
COULL, Scott	19	20 (3)	0	8 (1)	1	28 (4)	1
DORRAT, Craig	34	1	0	-	-	1	0
DORRAT, Greg	31	18	2	6	0	24	2
DUNCAN, Callum	18	18 (6)	3	10	6	28 (6)	9
DURNO, Ross	33	11 (5)	0	3 (1)	0	14 (6)	0
FORSYTH, Scott	26	1 (5)	1	6 (1)	0	7 (6)	1
GERRARD, Corey	19	19	0	4 (2)	1	23 (2)	1
GORDON, Adam	18	3 (6)	1	(8)	1	3 (14)	2
GORDON, Kyle	26	5	2	1	1	6	3
LIVINGSTONE, Stevie	18	5 (6)	1	1	0	6 (6)	1
LYNCH, Jordan	20	7	0	2	1	9	1
MACKIE, Thomas (GK)	21	26	0	8	0	34	0
MARR, Campbell	24	4	1	4	2	8	3
MASON, Taylor	18	9 (2)	0	7 (2)	1	16 (4)	1
MATHERS, Keigan	19	(2)	0	-	-	(2)	0
MCKENZIE, Blair	22	2 (4)	1	3	2	5 (4)	3
MCKEOWN, Nathan	21	2	1	3	0	5	1
MCTAVISH, Michael	31	5 (4)	0	-	-	5 (4)	0
MORRISON, Adam	31	8 (1)	1	7	2	15 (1)	3
PETERMANN, Matthew	19	3 (1)	0	-	-	3 (1)	0
RODDIE, Calvin	28	(1)	0	-	-	(1)	0
SIMOND, Andrew	21	2 (3)	0	-	-	2 (3)	0
SKINNER, Ewan	19	2 (3)	0	-	-	2 (3)	0
STRACHAN, Conor	24	13 (2)	0	3 (3)	2	16 (5)	2
STRACHAN, Jack	34	10	4	3	2	13	6
THOMSON, Reigan	23	10	2	1	0	11	2
WILSON, Rian	23	1 (7)	0	-	-	1 (7)	0

MATCH RESULTS 2022/23

Date	Opponent	Comp	Score	Scorers
Jul 30	Longside (A)	GLC GRP	6-3	Marr, Duncan, Morrison (2), D McCouaig o.g., Chauvin
Aug 2	Buchanhaven Hearts (A)	GLC GRP	2-0	McKenzie, Coull
Aug 6	Ellon United (H)	LGE	0-0	
Aug 9	Cruden Bay (H)	GLC GRP	6-0	McKenzie, Duncan (2), Chauvin, Marr, A Gordon
Aug 13	East End (A)	LGE	2-2	Chauvin, A Gordon
Aug 16	Hermes (H)	LGE	0-7	
Aug 20	Maud (A)	LGE	4-3	Forsyth, J Strachan (2), Marr
Aug 23	Bridge of Don Thistle (H)	LGE	0-3	
Aug 27	Bellshill Athletic (H)	SJC R1	3-4	Mason, C Strachan (2)
Sep 3	New Elgin (H)	GLC QF	3-0	Duncan, Chauvin, Gerrard
Sep 17	East End (H)	GLC SF	0-4	
Sep 24	Nairn St. Ninian (H)	LGE	1-3	Brailsford
Oct 1	Dufftown (H)	LGE	3-1	K Gordon, G Dorrat, Clelland
Oct 8	Dyce (A)	LGE	0-5	
Oct 15	Stonehaven (H)	LGE	0-3	
Oct 22	Montrose Roselea (H)	LGE	0-2	
Oct 29	Banchory St. Ternan (A)	LGE	4-2	Byres, G Dorrat, K Gordon, McKeown
Nov 5	Ellon United (A)	NRC R1	2-0	Duncan, K Gordon
Nov 12	East End (H)	IRC R1	2-2	J Strachan, Lynch
Nov 19	Culter (A)	LGE	0-8	
Nov 26	Nairn St. Ninian (A)	LGE	1-1	Morrison
Dec 3	Bridge of Don Thistle (H)	NRC R2	0-4	
Jan 7	Montrose Roselea (A)	LGE	0-0	
Jan 28	Banchory St. Ternan (H)	LGE	3-0	Thomson, J Strachan (2)
Feb 4	Hermes (A)	LGE	0-4	
Feb 11	Dufftown (A)	LGE	0-1	
Feb 18	Nairn St. Ninian (H)	McL R1	2-2	Duncan, J Strachan
Feb 25	Ellon United (A)	LGE	2-1	Byres, Livingstone
Mar 4	Dyce (H)	LGE	2-2	Clelland, Duncan
Mar 25	Bridge of Don Thistle (A)	LGE	1-5	Duncan
Apr 1	Stoneywood Parkvale (H)	LGE	0-3	
Apr 8	Stoneywood Parkvale (A)	LGE	1-4	McKenzie
Apr 11	East End (H)	LGE	0-1	
Apr 25	Culter (H)	LGE	0-3	
May 2	Maud (H)	LGE	4-2	Thomson, Byres, Angus, Duncan
May 6	Stonehaven (A)	LGE	0-3	

CULTER J.F.C.
Crombie Park, Peterculter

		LEAGUE		CUPS		ALL	
	Age	Apps	Goals	Apps	Goals	Apps	Goals
ADAM, Mark	30	18	2	11 (1)	0	29 (1)	2
CHEYNE, Jay	28	17 (5)	1	15 (1)	1	32 (6)	2
CLARK, Ross	23	21 (3)	18	15 (1)	12	36 (4)	30
DIMOV, Danail	23	6 (6)	0	4 (1)	2	10 (7)	2
DUNBAR, Callum	30	10 (10)	5	11 (4)	5	21 (14)	10
EMSLIE, Keller (GK)	24	4	0	3	0	7	0
FAWCETT, Luke	23	5 (6)	0	4 (2)	0	9 (8)	0
FRASER, Cameron	24	23 (1)	33	16 (1)	14	39 (2)	47
HUTCHISON, Lewis	-	(4)	1	(1)	0	(5)	1
KEMLO, Finn	20	(3)	0	(1)	1	(4)	1
MACASKILL, Craig	28	10 (5)	2	6 (2)	4	16 (7)	6
MATHERS, Willie	29	10 (4)	1	5 (5)	4	15 (9)	5
MCGREGOR, Ben	30	21 (4)	0	13 (1)	1	34 (5)	1
MCTAVISH, Neal	31	24	2	12 (1)	1	36 (1)	3
PETRIE, Richie	26	21 (2)	1	16	0	37 (2)	1
ROSS, Kai	28	2 (2)	0	(3)	0	2 (5)	0
RUSSELL, Gordon	34	9 (7)	1	6 (7)	0	15 (14)	1
SMART, Ryan	27	17 (8)	10	8 (10)	9	25 (18)	19
STEWART, Ryan	28	10 (7)	0	11 (3)	0	21 (10)	0
TAIT, Peter (GK)	26	22	0	15	0	37	0
TODD, Liam	35	6 (12)	0	4 (7)	0	10 (19)	0
WALLACE, Ryan	32	5 (4)	1	6 (5)	1	11 (9)	2
WILSON, Graeme	32	21 (1)	3	13 (1)	1	34 (2)	4
WOZNIAK, Nikolas	26	4 (17)	7	3 (11)	4	7 (28)	11

MATCH RESULTS 2022/23

Date	Opponent	Comp	Score	Scorers
Jul 30	Glentanar (A)	GLC GRP	6-0	Fraser, Smart, Wilson, Mathers, Wozniak (2)
Aug 2	Sunnybank (H)	GLC GRP	7-1	Fraser (2), Clark, Wozniak, Smart (2), Dunbar
Aug 6	Montrose Roselea (H)	LGE	4-0	Adam, Smart, Fraser, Dunbar
Aug 9	Hermes (A)	GLC GRP	2-1	Fraser, Clark
Aug 13	Dufftown (A)	LGE	2-0	Fraser, Wallace
Aug 16	Maud (A)	LGE	2-1	Mathers, Wozniak
Aug 20	Nairn St. Ninian (H)	LGE	3-1	Wozniak (2), Hutchison
Aug 23	Banchory St. Ternan (A)	LGE	4-0	Wozniak (2), Clark (2)
Aug 27	Dundee Violet (A)	SJC R1	4-1	Fraser (2), Smart (2)
Sep 3	Stoneywood Parkvale (A)	GLC QF	2-0	Clark, Fraser
Sep 17	Rothie Rovers (A)	GLC SF	2-0	Clark, Mathers
Sep 24	Stonehaven (A)	SJC R2	1-1ᵖ	Mathers
Oct 2	East End (N)	GLC Final	5-1	Dunbar, Fraser, Mathers, Clark, Cheyne
Oct 8	Hermes (H)	LGE	4-1	Fraser (2), Dunbar, Clark
Oct 15	Stoneywood Parkvale (A)	LGE	3-1	Dunbar (2), Wilson
Oct 22	Bridge of Don Thistle (A)	LGE	3-0	McTavish, Wilson, Clark
Oct 29	Dyce (H)	LGE	1-1	Fraser
Nov 5	New Elgin (A)	NRC R1	8-1	Wozniak, Fraser, Dunbar, Clark (3), Wallace, Smart
Nov 12	Stoneywood Parkvale (A)	IRC R1	1-2	McGregor
Nov 19	Colony Park (H)	LGE	8-0	Fraser (4), Clark, Smart, Wozniak (2)
Nov 26	Stonehaven (A)	LGE	2-0	Fraser, Clark
Dec 3	Fraserburgh United (H)	NRC R2	1-0	McTavish
Jan 7	Dufftown (H)	LGE	8-2	Smart (2), Fraser (3), Clark, Wilson, S Black o.g.
Jan 14	Ellon United (H)	LGE	6-1	Smart (2), Fraser (2), Clark (2)
Jan 28	East End (A)	LGE	1-0	Fraser
Feb 4	Maud (H)	LGE	3-1	Smart, Fraser (2)
Feb 10	Dyce (A)	LGE	3-1	Fraser (2), Dunbar
Feb 18	Banchory St. Ternan (A)	McL R1	4-1	MacAskill, Dimov, Dunbar, Kemlo
Feb 25	Hermes (A)	NRC QF	3-0	Dimov, Fraser, Smart
Mar 3	Hermes (A)	LGE	0-2	
Mar 18	Banchory St. Ternan (H)	LGE	4-1	Clark (2), Russell, Fraser
Mar 21	Hermes (A)	McL QF	2-0	Dunbar, MacAskill
Mar 25	Nairn St. Ninian (A)	LGE	4-1	Smart, Fraser, Petrie, Clark
Apr 1	East End (H)	NRC SF	5-1	Clark (3), Smart, Fraser
Apr 8	Ellon United (A)	LGE	4-0	Fraser (2), Smart, Clark
Apr 12	Montrose Roselea (A)	LGE	2-1	Fraser, Clark
Apr 15	Stonehaven (H)	LGE	3-0	Fraser (3)
Apr 18	Bridge of Don Thistle (H)	LGE	6-0	Fraser (3), Cheyne, Clark, Adam
Apr 22	Maud (A)	McL SF	4-1	Fraser (2), Smart, MacAskill
Apr 25	Colony Park (A)	LGE	3-0	C Gerrard o.g., MacAskill, Clark
Apr 29	East End (H)	LGE	2-1	MacAskill, Clark
May 2	Stoneywood Parkvale (H)	LGE	5-1	Fraser (2), McTavish, Smart, Clark
May 5	Rothie Rovers (N)	NRC Final	2-0	Clark, MacAskill
May 12	Stonehaven (N)	McL Final	1-0	Fraser

DUFFTOWN J.F.C.
Westburn Park, Dufftown

	Age	LEAGUE		CUPS		ALL	
		Apps	Goals	Apps	Goals	Apps	Goals
ANDERSON, Aaron	21	1 (1)	0	1 (1)	0	2 (2)	0
BLACK, Stewart (GK)	28	22	0	5	0	27	0
BOWIE, Scott	30	7 (2)	0	1	0	8 (2)	0
CAMERON, Shaun	20	25	5	5 (1)	1	30 (1)	6
CHRISTIE, Charlie (GK)	21	2	0	2	0	4	0
CLARK, Callum	26	9 (4)	0	5 (1)	1	14 (5)	1
COOK, Matthew (GK)	-	2	0	-	-	2	0
CRAIB, Jack	22	12 (1)	0	1 (1)	0	13 (2)	0
DUNCAN, Kris	34	11	1	1	0	12	1
DUNN, Michael	33	14 (1)	0	4	1	18 (1)	1
ELDER, Ross	32	(4)	0	-	-	(4)	0
EWEN, Michael	37	2	0	-	-	2	0
GAIR, Shaun	29	13 (4)	0	3 (1)	0	16 (5)	0
GRANT, Cameron	25	7 (1)	0	4 (2)	0	11 (3)	0
GRANT, Logan	18	2 (1)	0	3 (2)	0	5 (3)	0
HARRIS, Karl	32	14 (4)	1	3 (1)	0	17 (5)	1
LOGAN, Jake	24	4 (8)	1	2 (1)	0	6 (9)	1
MAIN, Kelvin	34	15	0	4	0	19	0
MITCHELL, Darren	33	(5)	0	-	-	(5)	0
MORRISON, Bruce	27	12 (2)	1	3	0	15 (2)	1
MURISON, Owen	22	4 (2)	0	-	-	4 (2)	0
RATTRAY, Steve	47	1	0	-	-	1	0
REID, Murdo	18	5 (3)	1	1	0	6 (3)	1
ROYAN, Jack	19	9	1	4 (1)	0	13 (1)	1
SIMPSON, Euan	22	15 (7)	1	5 (1)	3	20 (8)	4
STABLES, Finlay	29	25	5	7	0	32	5
STABLES, James	30	20 (2)	4	5 (1)	1	25 (3)	5
TAWSE, Richard	29	2	0	1	0	3	0
THOMSON, Mark	24	15 (4)	0	3 (1)	0	18 (5)	0
WATT, Craig	27	12 (3)	1	2	0	14 (3)	1
WINCHESTER, Marc	22	4 (6)	0	2 (2)	0	6 (8)	0

MATCH RESULTS 2022/23

Date	Opponent	Comp	Score	Scorers
Jul 30	Nairn St. Ninian (A)	GLC GRP	1-3	Simpson
Aug 2	Forres Thistle (H)	GLC GRP	1-1	Simpson
Aug 6	Hermes (A)	LGE	0-7	
Aug 9	New Elgin (H)	GLC GRP	4-5	Cameron, Dunn, Simpson, J Stables
Aug 13	Culter (H)	LGE	0-2	
Aug 20	Bridge of Don Thistle (A)	LGE	0-6	
Aug 23	Nairn St. Ninian (A)	LGE	2-2	Reid, Harris
Aug 27	Maryhill (H)	SJC R1	0-3	
Sep 3	Ellon United (A)	LGE	0-2	
Sep 17	Stonehaven (A)	LGE	1-1	F Stables
Sep 24	Dyce (H)	LGE	1-1	J Stables
Oct 1	Colony Park (A)	LGE	1-3	F Stables
Oct 8	Ellon United (H)	LGE	1-2	J Stables
Oct 15	East End (A)	LGE	0-3	
Oct 22	Maud (H)	LGE	1-2	F Stables
Oct 29	Montrose Roselea (H)	LGE	1-5	F Stables
Nov 12	Dyce (A)	IRC R1	1-4	Clark
Nov 26	Banchory St. Ternan (H)	LGE	3-1	Cameron (2), Morrison
Dec 3	Newmachar United (A)	NRC R2	0-4	
Jan 7	Culter (A)	LGE	2-8	J Stables, Royan
Jan 14	Dyce (A)	LGE	0-2	
Jan 28	Stonehaven (H)	LGE	0-3	
Feb 4	Montrose Roselea (A)	LGE	1-2	Cameron
Feb 11	Colony Park (H)	LGE	1-0	F Stables
Feb 25	Nairn St. Ninian (H)	LGE	1-1	J Stables
Mar 4	Stoneywood Parkvale (H)	LGE	1-1	Simpson
Apr 1	Stonehaven (H)	McL R1	0-3	
Apr 8	Hermes (H)	LGE	0-5	
Apr 15	Maud (A)	LGE	2-1	Watt, Cameron
Apr 22	Bridge of Don Thistle (H)	LGE	0-1	
Apr 29	Stoneywood Parkvale (A)	LGE	1-4	Duncan
May 6	Banchory St. Ternan (A)	LGE	0-2	
May 13	East End (H)	LGE	2-2	Cameron, Logan

DYCE J.F.C.
Ian Mair Park, Dyce

		LEAGUE		CUPS		ALL	
	Age	Apps	Goals	Apps	Goals	Apps	Goals
BARBOSA, Gui	18	9 (4)	2	5 (5)	2	14 (9)	4
BRUCE, Mikey	26	1 (17)	2	2 (4)	1	3 (21)	3
BUIRDS, Jake	19	12 (4)	1	6 (2)	0	18 (6)	1
BYARS, Gavin	21	13 (6)	8	5 (3)	3	18 (9)	11
CAMPBELL, Robbie	20	3 (10)	4	(3)	0	3 (13)	4
COCHRANE, Graeme	23	18 (2)	1	4 (5)	0	22 (7)	1
COLLINS, Damon	18	(5)	0	-	-	(5)	0
CONNON, Ross	18	(2)	0	-	-	(2)	0
COOK, Morgan (GK)	24	26	0	11	0	37	0
CUMMING, Dylan	20	2 (5)	1	3 (1)	0	5 (6)	1
DONALD, Glen	25	23	1	12	3	35	4
DOUGLAS, Kyle	19	21 (3)	0	9 (1)	0	30 (4)	0
GARNHAM, Sam	20	15 (5)	3	3 (4)	1	18 (9)	4
JOHNSTON, Blair	32	11 (1)	0	6	0	17 (1)	0
KEIR, Lyall	20	19 (1)	9	9 (2)	8	28 (3)	17
LEITH, Ian	32	5	0	4	0	9	0
MACKIE, Craig	26	17	3	12	0	29	3
MCDONALD, Craig	19	11 (1)	0	1 (1)	0	12 (2)	0
MCDONALD, Dean	29	6 (7)	3	5 (2)	0	11 (9)	3
MEAD, George	25	1	0	-	-	1	0
PATERSON, Arran	-	(1)	0	-	-	(1)	0
PETER, Craig	26	6 (4)	0	6 (3)	0	12 (7)	0
REID, Darren	28	19 (2)	0	5 (3)	1	24 (5)	1
ROBERTSON, Sam	26	13 (1)	5	9	4	22 (1)	9
ROBERTSON, Scott	-	5 (2)	0	3 (1)	0	8 (3)	0
ROBERTSON*, Sam	24	8 (2)	1	1	0	9 (2)	1
WALKER, Jack	23	22 (1)	7	10 (1)	7	32 (2)	14

MATCH RESULTS 2022/23

Date	Opponent	Comp	Score	Scorers
Jul 27	Inverurie Locos (H)	AC R1	1-2	Sam Robertson
Jul 30	Aberdeen Uni. (A)	GLC GRP	5-0	Walker (2), Barbosa (2), Bruce
Aug 2	Ellon United (A)	GLC GRP	8-0	Keir (6), Reid, Walker
Aug 6	Stoneywood Parkvale (H)	LGE	2-0	Walker, Campbell
Aug 9	Montrose Roselea (H)	GLC GRP	1-0	Walker
Aug 13	Stonehaven (A)	LGE	1-2	Mackie
Aug 16	Ellon United (A)	LGE	1-0	Walker
Aug 20	Montrose Roselea (H)	LGE	0-1	
Aug 23	Maud (A)	LGE	4-0	Walker, Sam Robertson, Keir, Barbosa
Aug 27	Downfield (A)	SJC R1	2-3	Donald, Sam Robertson
Sep 3	Rothie Rovers (H)	GLC QF	3-7	Walker, Byars (2)
Sep 17	Nairn St. Ninian (H)	LGE	2-2	Garnham, D McDonald
Sep 24	Dufftown (A)	LGE	1-1	D McDonald
Oct 1	Ellon United (H)	LGE	2-0	Keir (2)
Oct 8	Colony Park (H)	LGE	5-0	Byars (2), Sam Robertson (2), D McDonald
Oct 12	Buckie Thistle (A)	AS R1	0-5	
Oct 15	Banchory St. Ternan (A)	LGE	5-1	Sam Robertson, Mackie, Buirds, Walker, D Henderson o.g.
Oct 21	Hermes (H)	LGE	1-2	Keir
Oct 29	Culter (A)	LGE	1-1	Sam Robertson
Nov 5	Stoneywood Parkvale (H)	NRC R1	4-2	Donald, Keir, Byars, Walker
Nov 12	Dufftown (H)	IRC R1	4-1	C Grant o.g., Sam Robertson, Keir, Donald
Dec 3	Montrose Roselea (A)	NRC R2	1-2	Walker
Jan 7	Islavale (H)	IRC R2	2-2	Garnham, Sam Robertson
Jan 14	Dufftown (H)	LGE	2-0	Donald, Garnham
Jan 21	Montrose Roselea (A)	LGE	1-1	Barbosa
Jan 28	Nairn St. Ninian (A)	LGE	5-2	Byars, Cochrane, Keir, Bruce, Cumming
Feb 4	Bridge of Don Thistle (A)	LGE	2-0	Byars, Garnham
Feb 10	Culter (H)	LGE	1-3	Byars
Feb 18	East End (A)	McL R1	0-1	
Feb 25	Maud (H)	LGE	2-0	Walker, Mackie
Mar 4	Colony Park (A)	LGE	2-2	Walker, Byars
Mar 18	Hermes (A)	LGE	0-7	
Mar 21	East End (H)	LGE	4-1	Campbell (2), Keir (2)
Mar 25	Banchory St. Ternan (H)	LGE	3-0	Keir (2), Campbell
Apr 1	Bridge of Don Thistle (H)	LGE	2-2	Walker, Byars
Apr 8	Stonehaven (H)	LGE	0-0	
Apr 11	Stoneywood Parkvale (A)	LGE	1-0	Byars
Apr 18	East End (A)	LGE	2-1	Sam Robertson*, Bruce

EAST END J.F.C.
New Advocates Park, Aberdeen

		LEAGUE		CUPS		ALL	
	Age	Apps	Goals	Apps	Goals	Apps	Goals
AKINDILENI, Timmy	-	(1)	0	-	-	(1)	0
BOLTON, Josh	24	9	8	10 (1)	5	19 (1)	13
CHOUMAN, Ross	24	15 (1)	0	6 (6)	1	21 (7)	1
CLARK, Jordan	26	3 (5)	0	3 (6)	1	6 (11)	1
CORBETT, Grant	-	(1)	0	-	-	(1)	0
CORTHALS, Ryan	23	17	1	14	0	31	1
ELLIS, Zack (GK)	23	20	0	15	0	35	0
FINDLAY, Tim (GK)	20	1	0	-	-	1	0
HENDRY, Aiden	18	2 (1)	0	-	-	2 (1)	0
IBAZEBO, David	21	2	0	(2)	0	2 (2)	0
JOHNSTON, Finlay	24	1 (4)	0	4 (1)	0	5 (5)	0
KELLER, Mikey	27	19	2	17	1	36	3
KERR, Scott	23	17 (2)	6	12 (3)	2	29 (5)	8
MACKIE, Craig	25	16 (1)	5	12 (4)	3	28 (5)	8
MANSON, Bradley	25	23 (1)	5	16	2	39 (1)	7
MASSON, Lewis	25	25	7	18	6	43	13
MATTHEW, Cai	22	19 (1)	4	9 (2)	3	28 (3)	7
MCALLISTER, Lee	23	9 (6)	1	4 (4)	1	13 (10)	2
ODLIN, Jack	24	18 (5)	0	10 (5)	0	28 (10)	0
REID, Max	22	2	1	-	-	2	1
RITCHIE, Callum (GK)	26	2	0	(1)	0	2 (1)	0
RITCHIE, Craig	33	4 (10)	1	6 (10)	0	10 (20)	1
SHARP, Clark	17	(3)	1	-	-	(3)	1
STEWART, Matthew	24	23 (2)	0	16 (2)	0	39 (4)	0
WHYTE, Gregor	22	8 (4)	0	5 (2)	0	13 (6)	0
WHYTE, James	19	3 (8)	0	1 (1)	0	4 (9)	0
WILSON, Caleb (GK)	23	4 (1)	0	3 (1)	0	7 (2)	0
WOOD, Connor	23	2	2	2	0	4	2
WOOD, Finlay	22	7 (7)	0	2 (1)	0	9 (8)	0
WOODS, Harry	19	3 (4)	0	4 (8)	1	7 (12)	1
YOUNGSON, Andy	24	12 (1)	4	9 (2)	5	21 (3)	9

MATCH RESULTS 2022/23

Date	Opponent	Comp	Score	Scorers
Aug 2	Bridge of Don Thistle (H)	GLC GRP	1-0	Masson
Aug 6	Maud (A)	LGE	2-0	C Wood, Keller
Aug 9	Banchory St. Ternan (A)	GLC GRP	2-0	Masson, Youngson
Aug 13	Colony Park (H)	LGE	2-2	Bolton, Mackie
Aug 16	Bridge of Don Thistle (H)	LGE	2-1	Bolton, C Wood
Aug 20	Banchory St. Ternan (A)	LGE	3-1	Youngson (2), Bolton
Aug 23	Stonehaven (A)	LGE	2-2	Ross Mitchell o.g., Youngson
Aug 27	Lanark United (H)	SJC R1	5-3	
Sep 3	Lossiemouth United (A)	GLC QF	3-0	Youngson, McAllister, T Corrin o.g.
Sep 17	Colony Park (A)	GLC SF	4-0	Clark, Youngson, Masson, Keller
Sep 24	Sunnybank (H)	SJC R2	2-2	Bolton (2)
Oct 2	Culter (N)	GLC Final	1-5	Masson
Oct 8	Montrose Roselea (A)	LGE	4-3	Kerr, Bolton (3)
Oct 15	Dufftown (H)	LGE	3-0	Kerr, Bolton (2)
Oct 22	Nairn St. Ninian (A)	LGE	5-1	Matthew, Corthals, Masson, Keller, A Maclean o.g.
Oct 29	Newmachar United (H)	SJC R3	3-1	Bolton, Matthew, Chouman
Nov 5	Longside (H)	NRC R1	2-0	Kerr, Woods
Nov 12	Colony Park (A)	IRC R1	2-2	Bolton (2)
Nov 26	Stoneywood Parkvale (H)	LGE	1-3	Mackie
Dec 3	Larkhall (A)	SJC R4	1-1ᵖ	M Craig o.g.
Jan 7	Hermes (A)	IRC R2	0-4	
Jan 28	Culter (H)	LGE	0-1	
Feb 4	Burghead Thistle (A)	NRC R2	5-0	Matthew (2), Mackie, Youngson, Masson
Feb 11	Ellon United (A)	LGE	4-1	Masson, Kerr, Mackie, Matthew
Feb 18	Dyce (H)	McL R1	1-0	Mackie
Feb 25	Newmachar United (H)	NRC QF	3-1	Mackie, Manson, Masson
Mar 4	Montrose Roselea (H)	LGE	2-3	Matthew, Sharp
Mar 18	Bridge of Don Thistle (A)	McL QF	1-1	Manson
Mar 21	Dyce (A)	LGE	1-4	C Ritchie
Mar 25	Stoneywood Parkvale (A)	LGE	0-1	
Mar 28	Hermes (A)	LGE	0-0	
Apr 1	Culter (A)	NRC SF	1-5	Ross Clark o.g.
Apr 8	Banchory St. Ternan (H)	LGE	5-0	Manson (2), Masson, Youngson, Kerr
Apr 11	Colony Park (A)	LGE	1-0	Manson
Apr 15	Nairn St. Ninian (H)	LGE	3-0	Liam Robinson o.g., McAllister, Masson
Apr 18	Dyce (H)	LGE	1-2	Manson
Apr 22	Ellon United (H)	LGE	2-2	Masson, Mackie
Apr 25	Stonehaven (A)	McL SF	2-2	Youngson, Kerr
Apr 29	Culter (A)	LGE	1-2	Masson
May 2	Hermes (H)	LGE	0-2	
May 6	Bridge of Don Thistle (A)	LGE	5-4	Reid, Kerr (2), Harris Clubb o.g., Matthew
May 13	Dufftown (A)	LGE	2-2	Mackie, Manson
May 16	Stonehaven (H)	LGE	1-2	Masson
May 20	Maud (H)	LGE	0-1	

ELLON UNITED J.F.C.
The Meadows, Ellon

		LEAGUE		CUPS		ALL	
	Age	Apps	Goals	Apps	Goals	Apps	Goals
AIRENS, Joey	21	7 (9)	2	3 (3)	1	10 (12)	3
BAIN, James	35	2 (5)	1	(2)	0	2 (7)	1
FARQUHAR, Dillon	19	13 (8)	2	7 (3)	0	20 (11)	2
GILL, Fraser	24	13 (9)	1	4 (4)	0	17 (13)	1
GRAY, Scott	23	16 (2)	6	5	1	21 (2)	7
GRAY, Stewart (GK)	37	19	1	7	0	26	1
HARRISON, Sam	28	18 (3)	2	5 (1)	0	23 (4)	2
HAY, Aaron	20	(1)	1	-	-	(1)	1
IRVINE, Calum	34	16 (1)	1	6 (1)	0	22 (2)	1
IRVINE, Neil	33	21 (1)	0	6	1	27 (1)	1
JOHNSON, Lenny	30	13 (5)	2	7 (2)	1	20 (7)	3
MACKAY, Archie (GK)	19	7	0	3	0	10	0
MCDONALD, Craig	-	6 (1)	0	4 (1)	1	10 (2)	1
MCDONALD, Dean	29	6 (3)	1	1	0	7 (3)	1
MCINTOSH, Calum	21	14 (3)	0	6 (1)	0	20 (4)	0
MISACAS, Andreas	29	3 (5)	0	4 (3)	0	7 (8)	0
MORRICE, Jordan	32	20 (1)	0	5 (1)	1	25 (2)	1
MORRIS, Owen	19	18 (4)	3	7 (1)	0	25 (5)	3
SHAND, Ryan	27	5 (4)	1	2	0	7 (4)	1
SMITH, Lucas	19	20 (2)	0	10	0	30 (2)	0
STUART, Connor	18	9 (2)	0	4 (2)	0	13 (4)	0
THOMSON, Fraser	31	18 (4)	2	6 (2)	1	24 (6)	3
TREMAINE, Callum	29	22 (3)	14	7 (1)	4	29 (4)	18

MATCH RESULTS 2022/23

Date	Opponent	Comp	Score	Scorers
Jul 30	Montrose Roselea (H)	GLC GRP	3-1	Johnson, Tremaine (2)
Aug 2	Dyce (H)	GLC GRP	0-8	
Aug 6	Colony Park (A)	LGE	0-0	
Aug 9	Aberdeen Uni. (A)	GLC GRP	1-0	Morrice
Aug 13	Banchory St. Ternan (H)	LGE	2-1	F Thomson, Tremaine
Aug 16	Dyce (H)	LGE	0-1	
Aug 20	Hermes (A)	LGE	1-5	Morris
Aug 23	Montrose Roselea (H)	LGE	3-2	Farquhar, Tremaine (2)
Aug 27	Carluke Rovers (A)	SJC R1	1-1	C Mcdonald
Sep 3	Dufftown (H)	LGE	2-0	Gill, Tremaine
Sep 17	Bridge of Don Thistle (A)	LGE	0-1	
Sep 24	Bathgate Thistle (H)	SJC R2	1-1	Airens
Oct 1	Dyce (A)	LGE	0-2	
Oct 8	Dufftown (A)	LGE	2-1	Tremaine (2)
Oct 15	Nairn St. Ninian (H)	LGE	3-1	Tremaine (2), S Gray
Oct 22	Stoneywood Parkvale (H)	LGE	4-0	Tremaine, Harrison, S Gray, Morris
Oct 29	East Craigie (A)	SJC R3	1-3	S Gray
Nov 5	Colony Park (H)	NRC R1	0-2	
Nov 12	Aberdeen Uni. (H)	IRC R1	4-1	Tremaine (2), N Irvine, F Thomson
Nov 26	Maud (H)	LGE	4-1	Tremaine, L Kinsella o.g., S Gray, Airens
Dec 3	Stoneywood Parkvale (A)	LGE	3-3	S Gray, Tremaine (2)
Jan 7	Maud (H)	IRC R2	0-4	
Jan 14	Culter (A)	LGE	1-6	Tremaine
Jan 28	Bridge of Don Thistle (H)	LGE	0-3	
Feb 11	East End (H)	LGE	1-4	Tremaine
Feb 18	Maud (A)	McL R1	0-1	
Feb 25	Colony Park (H)	LGE	1-2	Harrison
Mar 4	Nairn St. Ninian (A)	LGE	3-0	S Gray, Johnson, C Irvine
Mar 18	Stonehaven (A)	LGE	2-1	Farquhar, Hay
Mar 25	Maud (A)	LGE	1-2	F Thomson
Apr 1	Banchory St. Ternan (A)	LGE	3-3	Morris, S Gray, Shand
Apr 8	Culter (H)	LGE	0-4	
Apr 11	Hermes (H)	LGE	1-3	D McDonald
Apr 15	Montrose Roselea (A)	LGE	1-2	Bain
Apr 22	East End (A)	LGE	2-2	Airens, Johnson
May 2	Stonehaven (H)	LGE	1-0	S Gray

HERMES J.F.C.
Lochside Park, Bridge of Don

	Age	LEAGUE		CUPS		ALL	
		Apps	Goals	Apps	Goals	Apps	Goals
BARBOUR, Luke	34	22 (1)	6	11	2	33 (1)	8
BEGG, Ryan	29	3 (2)	0	2 (1)	0	5 (3)	0
BURR, Joe	27	19 (6)	7	14	5	33 (6)	12
CAIRNS, James	30	2 (4)	0	3 (2)	1	5 (6)	1
CRAIG, Jack	28	24 (2)	16	15	13	39 (2)	29
DAVIDSON, Andrew	26	11 (7)	1	2 (7)	1	13 (14)	2
DAWSON, Michael	34	(1)	0	-	-	(1)	0
ESSLEMONT, Paul	25	14 (9)	7	6 (6)	4	20 (15)	11
GIBBON, Ross	26	4 (8)	1	1 (5)	0	5 (13)	1
INNES, Callum	34	10 (12)	2	1 (7)	0	11 (19)	2
MCKENZIE, Connor	31	22	3	14	1	36	4
MCMAHON, James	25	10 (14)	7	7 (6)	2	17 (20)	9
MILNE, Cameron	25	18 (1)	0	12 (1)	0	30 (2)	0
MITCHELL, Grant	34	22 (1)	4	12 (1)	0	34 (2)	4
OTTO, Jacob (GK)	23	1	0	1	0	2	0
PASZKIEWICZ, Brunon	19	1 (9)	6	(2)	0	1 (11)	6
RAE, Dominic	29	17 (2)	2	10 (1)	1	27 (3)	3
REID, Jordan	30	10 (3)	6	4 (5)	3	14 (8)	9
SIMPSON, Greg (GK)	35	25	0	13	0	38	0
TAIT, Jack	26	16 (4)	6	11 (1)	1	27 (5)	7
WHYTE, Steven	35	14 (6)	0	6 (3)	0	20 (9)	0
YOUNGSON, Callum	25	21 (2)	18	15	2	36 (2)	20

MATCH RESULTS 2022/23

Date	Opponent	Comp	Score	Scorers
Jul 27	Deveronvale (H)	AC R1	1-1ᵖ	Craig
Jul 30	Sunnybank (A)	GLC GRP	4-0	Barbour, Craig, Burr, Cairns
Aug 2	Glentanar (A)	GLC GRP	7-0	Craig (3), Tait, McMahon, Esslemont, Barbour
Aug 6	Dufftown (H)	LGE	7-0	Reid, Youngson, McKenzie (2), Craig (2), Esslemont
Aug 9	Culter (H)	GLC GRP	1-2	Esslemont
Aug 13	Nairn St. Ninian (H)	LGE	6-0	McMahon (2), Innes, Esslemont, McKenzie, Tait
Aug 16	Colony Park (A)	LGE	7-0	Barbour, Craig, Tait, Reid, Youngson (2), Paszkiewicz
Aug 20	Ellon United (H)	LGE	5-1	Tait, Craig, Mitchell, Barbour, McMahon
Aug 23	Stoneywood Parkvale (A)	LGE	2-0	Craig, Youngson
Aug 27	Lesmahagow (A)	SJC R1	2-1	Craig, Reid
Sep 17	Maud (H)	LGE	6-1	Tait (2), Barbour (2), Craig, Esslemont
Sep 24	Beith Juniors (A)	SJC R2	0-2	
Oct 1	Stonehaven (H)	LGE	1-0	Craig
Oct 8	Culter (A)	LGE	1-4	Youngson
Oct 11	Formartine United (H)	AS R1	0-2	
Oct 14	Bridge of Don Thistle (H)	LGE	1-1	McMahon
Oct 21	Dyce (A)	LGE	2-1	Esslemont, Youngson
Oct 29	Maud (A)	LGE	5-0	Craig (2), Youngson, McMahon, Mitchell
Nov 5	Stonehaven (H)	NRC R1	4-0	Craig, Esslemont, Burr (2)
Nov 19	Banchory St. Ternan (H)	LGE	1-0	Craig
Nov 26	Montrose Roselea (A)	LGE	1-1	Youngson
Dec 3	Sunnybank (A)	NRC R2	7-1	Craig (3), Youngson, McKenzie, Davidson, McMahon
Jan 7	East End (H)	IRC R2	4-0	Craig, Rae, Burr, Reid
Jan 28	Montrose Roselea (H)	LGE	5-2	Mitchell, C Doan o.g., Youngson (2), Esslemont
Feb 4	Colony Park (H)	LGE	4-0	Reid (2), Youngson, Burr
Feb 11	Kirriemuir Thistle (H)	IRC R3	2-0	Unknown o.g., Reid
Feb 18	Bridge of Don Thistle (A)	LGE	2-2	Burr, Mitchell
Feb 25	Culter (H)	NRC QF	0-3	
Mar 3	Culter (H)	LGE	2-0	Rae, Craig
Mar 14	Glentanar (H)	IRC QF	4-1	Esslemont, Craig, Youngson, Burr
Mar 18	Dyce (H)	LGE	7-0	Davidson, Esslemont (2), Youngson, Burr, Paszkiewicz (2)
Mar 21	Culter (H)	McL QF	0-2	
Mar 28	East End (H)	LGE	0-0	
Apr 1	Nairn St. Ninian (A)	LGE	8-1	Rae, Reid (2), Craig (2), Barbour, Burr, Paszkiewicz
Apr 4	Stoneywood Parkvale (H)	LGE	1-1	Youngson
Apr 8	Dufftown (A)	LGE	5-0	Barbour, Youngson (3), McMahon
Apr 11	Ellon United (A)	LGE	3-1	Youngson, Craig, Innes
Apr 15	Banchory St. Ternan (A)	LGE	5-0	McMahon, Paszkiewicz, Burr, Craig (2)
Apr 22	Stonehaven (A)	LGE	5-0	Cameron Cook o.g., Burr (2), Tait, Paszkiewicz
Apr 29	Dundee North End (A)	IRC SF	1-2	Craig
May 2	East End (A)	LGE	2-0	Youngson, Gibbon

MAUD J.F.C.
Pleasure Park, Maud

	Age	LEAGUE Apps	LEAGUE Goals	CUPS Apps	CUPS Goals	ALL Apps	ALL Goals
ANYAEGBUNAM, Ebube	18	11 (2)	0	3 (5)	1	14 (7)	1
ARTHUR, Josh	26	1 (1)	0	-	-	1 (1)	0
BEATTIE, Lewis	23	3	1	1 (1)	0	4 (1)	1
BEGG, Matthew	19	1 (1)	0	2	0	3 (1)	0
CHRISTIE, Ryan	38	(1)	0	-	-	(1)	0
COLLIN, Aiden	19	8 (6)	0	3 (5)	2	11 (11)	2
COWIE, Jack	18	1	0	1	0	2	0
D'AMBRUOSO, Luca	19	19 (3)	0	7 (2)	0	26 (5)	0
ESSON, Murray	22	23	1	7	0	30	1
GOODLAD, Steven	26	4 (3)	1	2 (3)	0	6 (6)	1
INGLIS, Sam (GK)	-	4	0	1	0	5	0
KEITH, Matthew	20	16 (8)	0	9 (2)	3	25 (10)	3
KINSELLA, Luke	20	14	3	4	1	18	4
KNOX, Alfie	18	11 (11)	5	5 (4)	1	16 (15)	6
LINTON, Aidan (GK)	18	1	0	-	-	1	0
LOWDEN, Craig	38	13 (2)	1	6	0	19 (2)	1
MACKINTOSH, Owen	19	14 (7)	2	6 (4)	1	20 (11)	3
MACLELLAN, Jamie	19	25	5	9	0	34	5
MCCREDIE, Kian	20	8 (6)	0	5 (1)	0	13 (7)	0
MCDONALD, Jake	19	17 (6)	1	7 (2)	0	24 (8)	1
MCDONALD, Matthew	28	23 (2)	6	10 (1)	5	33 (3)	11
MCLENNAN, Austin	22	5 (12)	1	1 (3)	1	6 (15)	2
MOAR, Cameron	21	12 (7)	0	8 (2)	0	20 (9)	0
MOIR, Callum	18	3 (2)	2	2 (1)	0	5 (3)	2
MOWAT, Ross (GK)	22	22	0	10	0	32	0
NICOL, Callum	19	2 (3)	0	-	-	2 (3)	0
RAE, Michael	35	1	0	-	-	1	0
STAINTON, Mark	31	9 (4)	1	5 (2)	0	14 (6)	1
WHELAN, Scott	31	15 (2)	0	7	1	22 (2)	1

MATCH RESULTS 2022/23

Date	Opponent	Comp	Score	Scorers
Jul 30	Rothie Rovers (H)	GLC GRP	2-3	Keith, Knox
Aug 2	Fraserburgh United (H)	GLC GRP	2-1	M McDonald, Whelan
Aug 6	East End (H)	LGE	0-2	
Aug 9	Deveronside (A)	GLC GRP	2-1	Mackintosh, M McDonald
Aug 13	Stoneywood Parkvale (A)	LGE	1-0	Mackintosh
Aug 16	Culter (H)	LGE	1-2	Mackintosh
Aug 20	Colony Park (H)	LGE	3-4	Moir (2), Maclellan
Aug 23	Dyce (H)	LGE	0-4	
Aug 27	Montrose Roselea (A)	SJC R1	2-3	McLennan, Anyaegbunam
Sep 3	Banchory St. Ternan (H)	LGE	1-0	M McDonald
Sep 17	Hermes (A)	LGE	1-6	Goodlad
Sep 24	Bridge of Don Thistle (H)	LGE	0-6	
Oct 1	Nairn St. Ninian (H)	LGE	3-5	Beattie, Maclellan, M McDonald
Oct 8	Stonehaven (A)	LGE	1-2	M McDonald
Oct 15	Montrose Roselea (H)	LGE	3-2	McLennan, Esson, Lowden
Oct 22	Dufftown (A)	LGE	2-1	Kinsella, Maclellan
Oct 29	Hermes (H)	LGE	0-5	
Nov 5	Bridge of Don Thistle (H)	NRC R1	2-3	M McDonald (2)
Nov 12	Cruden Bay (H)	IRC R1	1-0	Collin
Nov 26	Ellon United (A)	LGE	1-4	Maclellan
Dec 3	Nairn St. Ninian (A)	LGE	0-1	
Jan 7	Ellon United (A)	IRC R2	4-0	
Jan 14	Banchory St. Ternan (A)	LGE	0-0	
Jan 28	Stoneywood Parkvale (H)	LGE	1-2	M McDonald
Feb 4	Culter (A)	LGE	1-3	Knox
Feb 11	Downfield (H)	IRC R3	0-1	
Feb 18	Ellon United (H)	McL R1	1-0	M McDonald
Feb 25	Dyce (A)	LGE	0-2	
Mar 4	Stonehaven (H)	LGE	0-0	
Mar 25	Ellon United (H)	LGE	2-1	J McDonald, Kinsella
Apr 1	Montrose Roselea (A)	LGE	2-2	Maclellan, Knox
Apr 8	Nairn St. Ninian (H)	McL QF	3-1	Keith (2), Kinsella
Apr 15	Dufftown (H)	LGE	1-2	Kinsella
Apr 22	Culter (H)	McL SF	1-4	Collin
Apr 29	Bridge of Don Thistle (A)	LGE	3-0	Knox, M McDonald (2)
May 2	Colony Park (A)	LGE	2-4	Knox, Stainton
May 20	East End (A)	LGE	1-0	Knox

PLAYING SQUAD & STATISTICS 2022/23

MONTROSE ROSELEA J.F.C.
Links Park Stadium, Montrose

	Age	LEAGUE		CUPS		ALL	
		Apps	Goals	Apps	Goals	Apps	Goals
BAILEY, Liam	26	18 (2)	2	6 (1)	1	24 (3)	3
BEEDIE, David	29	24 (2)	2	11 (1)	0	35 (3)	2
BROADHURST, Ryan	37	1	0	-	-	1	0
BURGOYNE, Jacob	20	20 (3)	0	8 (1)	1	28 (4)	1
DAVIDSON, Adam	23	7 (5)	3	4 (2)	1	11 (7)	4
DOAN, Chulainn	19	21 (4)	1	10 (2)	0	31 (6)	1
EDGAR, Eric	33	11 (2)	1	4 (1)	0	15 (3)	1
GAMMIE, Harry	-	(2)	0	-	-	(2)	0
GILL, Tayler	24	1 (3)	0	(4)	0	1 (7)	0
GREIG, Stephen	33	8 (4)	3	5	0	13 (4)	3
GRIGGS, Dylan	19	4 (8)	3	(6)	0	4 (14)	3
JAMIESON, Fraser	20	5 (1)	1	3 (1)	1	8 (2)	2
KINNAIRD, Murray (GK)	30	1	0	1	0	2	0
MARTIN, Aulay	18	3	0	-	-	3	0
MARTIN, Duncan	24	1 (1)	0	3 (1)	3	4 (2)	3
MCCORMACK, Kade (GK)	24	14	0	9	0	23	0
MCCORMICK, Jack	20	4	0	3	0	7	0
MCDONALD, Dylan	20	13 (10)	0	5 (6)	0	18 (16)	0
MCLEAN, Neil	42	1	0	-	-	1	0
MCLEOD, R (GK)	-	1	0	-	-	1	0
MIDDLETON, Cameron (GK)	18	2	0	-	-	2	0
MITCHELL, Connor	27	10 (5)	1	1 (5)	0	11 (10)	1
REOCH, Jordan	31	16 (1)	3	11	2	27 (1)	5
ROBERTSON, Conlan	24	14 (4)	3	5 (3)	0	19 (7)	3
SHINGLER, Jamie (GK)	19	3	0	1	0	4	0
SIMPSON, Stewart	19	2 (5)	0	1 (1)	0	3 (6)	0
SOUTAR, Murray	24	16 (1)	2	9	2	25 (1)	4
STEPHEN, Blair	28	22 (1)	1	11 (1)	2	33 (2)	3
TAYLOR, Ryan	29	14 (3)	0	8	1	22 (3)	1
THOMSON, Kieran	23	18 (1)	12	9	7	27 (1)	19
TWEED, Gregor (GK)	21	4	0	-	-	4	0
WATSON, Calum	39	(2)	0	1 (2)	0	1 (4)	0
WATSON, Eric	41	7 (6)	2	2 (2)	0	9 (8)	2

Date	Opponent	Comp	Score	Scorers
Jul 30	Ellon United (A)	GLC GRP	1-3	D Martin
Aug 3	Aberdeen Uni. (H)	GLC GRP	4-1	D Martin (2), Thomson, Stephen
Aug 6	Culter (A)	LGE	0-4	
Aug 9	Dyce (A)	GLC GRP	0-1	
Aug 13	Bridge of Don Thistle (H)	LGE	0-1	
Aug 20	Dyce (A)	LGE	1-0	Jamieson
Aug 23	Ellon United (A)	LGE	2-3	Robertson, Bailey
Aug 27	Maud (H)	SJC R1	3-2	Thomson (2), Jamieson
Sep 3	Stonehaven (H)	LGE	2-2	Thomson (2)
Sep 17	Stoneywood Parkvale (H)	LGE	2-2	Bailey, Edgar
Sep 24	Shotts Bon Accord (H)	SJC R2	1-2	Reoch
Oct 1	Banchory St. Ternan (A)	LGE	0-2	
Oct 8	East End (H)	LGE	3-4	Reoch, E Watson, Thomson
Oct 15	Maud (A)	LGE	2-3	Thomson (2)
Oct 22	Colony Park (A)	LGE	2-0	Thomson, Davidson
Oct 29	Dufftown (A)	LGE	5-1	E Watson, Davidson, Reoch, Soutar, Thomson
Nov 5	Forres Thistle (A)	NRC R1	3-1	Thomson, Stephen, Reoch
Nov 12	Banchory St. Ternan (H)	IRC R1	4-0	Soutar, Thomson, Bailey, Taylor
Nov 19	Nairn St. Ninian (H)	LGE	2-0	J Maclean o.g., Thomson
Nov 26	Hermes (H)	LGE	1-1	Griggs
Dec 3	Dyce (H)	NRC R2	2-1	Davidson, Thomson
Dec 10	Rothie Rovers (H)	IRC R2	1-2	Burgoyne
Jan 7	Colony Park (H)	LGE	0-0	
Jan 14	Stonehaven (A)	LGE	1-2	Soutar
Jan 21	Dyce (H)	LGE	1-1	Doan
Jan 28	Hermes (A)	LGE	2-5	Beedie (2)
Feb 4	Dufftown (H)	LGE	2-1	Davidson, Thomson
Feb 11	Banchory St. Ternan (H)	LGE	2-0	Stephen, Mitchell
Feb 18	Stoneywood Parkvale (A)	McL R1	1-4	Thomson
Feb 25	Bridge of Don Thistle (H)	NRC QF	2-1	C Hay o.g., Soutar
Mar 4	East End (A)	LGE	3-2	Thomson (2)
Mar 11	Nairn St. Ninian (A)	LGE	4-3	Griggs (2), Reoch, Thomson
Mar 18	Stoneywood Parkvale (A)	LGE	0-3	
Mar 25	Rothie Rovers (A)	NRC SF	0-1	
Apr 1	Maud (H)	LGE	2-2	Greig (2)
Apr 8	Bridge of Don Thistle (A)	LGE	0-4	
Apr 12	Culter (H)	LGE	1-2	Greig
Apr 15	Ellon United (H)	LGE	2-1	Robertson (2)

PLAYING SQUAD & STATISTICS 2022/23

NAIRN ST NINIAN J.F.C.
The Showfield, Nairn

	Age	LEAGUE		CUPS		ALL	
		Apps	Goals	Apps	Goals	Apps	Goals
ANDERSON, Jack	28	23 (1)	1	6	0	29 (1)	1
ANDREW, Jordan	22	16 (2)	2	1 (2)	1	17 (4)	3
BARTON, Reece	26	(3)	0	(3)	0	(6)	0
BROWN, Cailean	19	(1)	0	-	-	(1)	0
CHAMBERS, David	41	6 (7)	1	5 (2)	2	11 (9)	3
CHISHOLM, Gavin	38	3 (4)	1	2 (1)	1	5 (5)	2
CRICHTON, Adam (GK)	22	15	0	1	0	16	0
DAVIDSON, Angus	22	11 (7)	0	5 (3)	0	16 (10)	0
DUNCAN, Jason	35	9	0	2	1	11	1
FONWEBAN, Charlie	38	24 (1)	14	7 (1)	5	31 (2)	19
FRASER, Kieran	24	15	0	6	0	21	0
GRANT, Mervyn	32	16 (2)	2	5	0	21 (2)	2
GRIMM, Kyle	19	3 (11)	0	(2)	0	3 (13)	0
HEPBURN, Ross (GK)	26	9	0	7	0	16	0
HOATH, Cameron	19	16 (1)	0	7	0	23 (1)	0
HUTTON, Connor (GK)	27	2	0	-	-	2	0
MACDONALD, Marc	36	15	1	6	0	21	1
MACDONALD, Robert	32	11 (5)	3	5 (1)	0	16 (6)	3
MACLEAN, Andrew	24	20	0	3	0	23	0
MACLEAN, Jack	26	9 (3)	0	3 (1)	1	12 (4)	1
MAIN, Glenn	38	12	3	2	0	14	3
MUNRO, Craig	25	5 (6)	1	2	0	7 (6)	1
ROBINSON, Liam	29	13 (8)	5	5 (1)	0	18 (9)	5
TAYLOR, Lewis	25	13 (2)	2	3	0	16 (2)	2
WALKER, Sam	27	18 (1)	2	4 (1)	1	22 (2)	3
YOUNG, Shaun	19	2 (8)	0	1 (4)	0	3 (12)	0

MATCH RESULTS 2022/23

Date	Opponent	Comp	Score	Scorers
Jul 30	Dufftown (H)	GLC GRP	3-1	Walker, Chambers, Fonweban
Aug 2	New Elgin (A)	GLC GRP	2-3	Fonweban, Chambers
Aug 6	Banchory St. Ternan (A)	LGE	3-4	Robinson, Fonweban, R Macdonald
Aug 9	Forres Thistle (H)	GLC GRP	1-1	J Maclean
Aug 13	Hermes (A)	LGE	0-6	
Aug 20	Culter (A)	LGE	1-3	Grant
Aug 23	Dufftown (H)	LGE	2-2	Robinson, Munro
Aug 27	Petershill (A)	SJC R1	0-4	
Sep 3	Bridge of Don Thistle (H)	LGE	2-0	Chisholm, Fonweban
Sep 17	Dyce (A)	LGE	2-2	Walker, Fonweban
Sep 24	Colony Park (A)	LGE	3-1	Robinson, R Macdonald, Fonweban
Oct 1	Maud (A)	LGE	5-3	Fonweban, Anderson, M Macdonald, Taylor, Robinson
Oct 15	Ellon United (A)	LGE	1-3	Taylor
Oct 22	East End (H)	LGE	1-5	Robinson
Oct 29	Stoneywood Parkvale (H)	LGE	1-2	Grant
Nov 5	Burghead Thistle (A)	NRC R1	2-2	Fonweban (2)
Nov 12	Sunnybank (A)	IRC R1	1-3	Fonweban
Nov 19	Montrose Roselea (A)	LGE	0-2	
Nov 26	Colony Park (H)	LGE	1-1	Fonweban
Dec 3	Maud (H)	LGE	1-0	Fonweban
Jan 7	Banchory St. Ternan (H)	LGE	4-1	Andrew, Fonweban (2), Main
Jan 14	Bridge of Don Thistle (A)	LGE	1-1	Andrew
Jan 28	Dyce (H)	LGE	2-5	Main, Chambers
Feb 4	Stonehaven (A)	LGE	0-1	
Feb 11	Stoneywood Parkvale (A)	LGE	1-4	Walker
Feb 18	Colony Park (A)	McL R1	2-2	Duncan, Andrew
Feb 25	Dufftown (A)	LGE	1-1	Fonweban
Mar 4	Ellon United (H)	LGE	0-3	
Mar 11	Montrose Roselea (H)	LGE	3-4	Fonweban (2), R Macdonald
Mar 25	Culter (H)	LGE	1-4	Main
Apr 1	Hermes (H)	LGE	1-8	Fonweban
Apr 8	Maud (A)	McL QF	1-3	Chisholm
Apr 15	East End (A)	LGE	0-3	
Apr 29	Stonehaven (H)	LGE	1-2	Fonweban

STONEHAVEN J.F.C.
Glenury Park, Stonehaven

		LEAGUE		CUPS		ALL	
	Age	Apps	Goals	Apps	Goals	Apps	Goals
ANDERSON, Danny	30	21 (4)	8	11 (2)	4	32 (6)	12
BAILLIE, David	32	1 (4)	2	3 (1)	1	4 (5)	3
BARRON, Wayne	33	11 (4)	2	6 (6)	1	17 (10)	3
BEATTIE, Cameron	22	14 (2)	2	6 (2)	0	20 (4)	2
BOYLAN, Derek	33	11	0	7	0	18	0
BURGOYNE, Jacob	20	2 (2)	0	-	-	2 (2)	0
CHALMERS, Thomas	18	(3)	1	-	-	(3)	1
CHRISTIE, Josh	23	15 (3)	5	6 (2)	2	21 (5)	7
COOK, Cameron	22	13 (3)	0	9 (3)	0	22 (6)	0
DUNCAN, Reece (GK)	25	24	0	14	0	38	0
DUTHIE, Blair	25	2 (8)	1	1 (4)	0	3 (12)	1
FRASER, Steven (GK)	36	2	0	-	-	2	0
GOMES, James	21	1 (1)	0	-	-	1 (1)	0
GORDON, Nicky	40	8 (1)	1	2 (1)	0	10 (2)	1
GUNN, Ian	35	(1)	0	(1)	0	(2)	0
HORNE, Keith	36	17 (2)	6	14	10	31 (2)	16
INGRAM, Harry	21	4 (2)	1	-	-	4 (2)	1
JOLLY, Chris	31	1 (1)	0	(1)	0	1 (2)	0
KIDD, Lewis	29	11 (3)	2	6 (2)	0	17 (5)	2
LESLIE, Jay	19	1	0	-	-	1	0
MACLENNAN, Adam	24	13 (5)	2	7 (2)	1	20 (7)	3
MASSON, Findlay	31	10 (4)	0	6 (1)	3	16 (5)	3
MASSON, Ronan	22	19 (1)	1	13	0	32 (1)	1
MCDONALD, Caie	21	7 (9)	1	1 (7)	0	8 (16)	1
MEARNS, Daniel	29	3 (1)	0	1 (2)	0	4 (3)	0
METELSKI, Ludwik	41	21 (2)	1	8 (2)	0	29 (4)	1
MITCHELL, Ross	26	22 (3)	1	13	2	35 (3)	3
PETERS, Josh	23	2 (4)	1	2 (4)	2	4 (8)	3
ROBERTSON, Clark	31	9 (2)	0	9	0	18 (2)	0
ROLLO, Martyn	41	1	0	-	-	1	0
SALSBURY, Lee	23	1 (6)	0	1 (3)	0	2 (9)	0
TAGGART, Lee	20	19 (2)	4	5 (5)	3	24 (7)	7
WILSON, Reece	21	(3)	0	2	0	2 (3)	0

MATCH RESULTS 2022/23

Date	Opponent	Comp	Score	Scorers
Jul 30	Banks o' Dee Juniors (H)	GLC GRP	4-3	Horne (2), Peters, Baillie
Aug 2	Newmachar United (A)	GLC GRP	3-2	Horne, Anderson, Taggart
Aug 6	Bridge of Don Thistle (A)	LGE	3-2	Christie, Baillie, Anderson
Aug 9	Stoneywood Parkvale (H)	GLC GRP	0-0	
Aug 13	Dyce (H)	LGE	2-1	Horne, Peters
Aug 20	Stoneywood Parkvale (H)	LGE	1-2	Barron
Aug 23	East End (H)	LGE	2-2	Duthie, R Masson
Aug 27	Blairgowrie (A)	SJC R1	6-0	F Masson, Barron, Anderson (2), Peters, Horne
Sep 3	Montrose Roselea (A)	LGE	2-2	Anderson, Christie
Sep 17	Dufftown (H)	LGE	1-1	Baillie
Sep 24	Culter (H)	SJC R2	1-1ᵖ	Horne
Oct 1	Hermes (A)	LGE	0-1	
Oct 8	Maud (H)	LGE	2-1	Kidd, Horne
Oct 15	Colony Park (A)	LGE	3-0	Mitchell, Kidd, Christie
Oct 22	Banchory St. Ternan (H)	LGE	2-1	Barron, A MacLennan
Oct 29	St Rochs (H)	SJC R3	1-4	Horne
Nov 5	Hermes (A)	NRC R1	0-4	
Nov 12	Deveronside (H)	IRC R1	2-2	Christie, A MacLennan
Nov 26	Culter (H)	LGE	0-2	
Jan 7	Forres Thistle (A)	IRC R2	4-1	F Masson, Horne (2), Christie
Jan 14	Montrose Roselea (H)	LGE	2-1	Anderson, Beattie
Jan 28	Dufftown (A)	LGE	3-0	Gordon, Christie, Horne
Feb 4	Nairn St. Ninian (H)	LCE	1-0	Anderson
Feb 11	Dundee North End (H)	IRC R3	0-3	
Feb 25	Banchory St. Ternan (A)	LGE	4-0	Metelski, Horne (2), Christie
Mar 4	Maud (A)	LGE	0-0	
Mar 18	Ellon United (H)	LGE	1-2	Taggart
Apr 1	Dufftown (A)	McL R1	3-0	F Masson, Taggart, Horne
Apr 8	Dyce (A)	LGE	0-0	
Apr 11	Bridge of Don Thistle (H)	LGE	0-0	
Apr 15	Culter (A)	LGE	0-3	
Apr 18	Stoneywood Parkvale (H)	McL QF	3-0	Horne, Anderson, Mitchell
Apr 22	Hermes (H)	LGE	0-5	
Apr 25	East End (H)	McL SF	2-2	Mitchell, Taggart
Apr 29	Nairn St. Ninian (A)	LGE	2-1	Anderson, A MacLennan
May 2	Ellon United (A)	LGE	0-1	
May 6	Colony Park (H)	LGE	3-0	Taggart, Horne, Anderson
May 9	Stoneywood Parkvale (A)	LGE	8-0	Kyle Wood o.g., Ingram, Beattie, Anderson, Taggart (2), Chalmers
May 12	Culter (N)	McL Final	0-1	
May 16	East End (A)	LGE	2-1	McDonald, Anderson

STONEYWOOD-PARKVALE J.F.C.
Arjowiggins Stoneywood Park, Aberdeen

	Age	LEAGUE		CUPS		ALL	
		Apps	Goals	Apps	Goals	Apps	Goals
AGNEW, Daniel	21	20 (2)	10	5 (1)	2	25 (3)	12
AMANN, Louis (GK)	18	21	0	6	0	27	0
BAIN, Liam	32	15 (5)	1	6	0	21 (5)	1
BENNETT, Jackson	18	1 (2)	0	1 (4)	1	2 (6)	1
DAVIDSON, Adam	28	5 (4)	0	1	0	6 (4)	0
DAVIDSON, Neale	32	24 (1)	4	9	2	33 (1)	6
GALASHAN, Mark	37	23	1	6 (1)	0	29 (1)	1
GREIG, Nathan	28	22 (1)	0	8 (1)	0	30 (2)	0
ISAKOV, Yehor	20	(1)	0	1	0	1 (1)	0
KANE, Curtis	28	2 (16)	2	3 (4)	1	5 (20)	3
MARSHALL, Craig	27	22	1	9 (1)	1	31 (1)	2
MCHARDY, Sean	22	10 (10)	1	5 (5)	1	15 (15)	2
MCKENZIE, Liam (GK)	27	5 (1)	0	3 (1)	0	8 (2)	0
MCKENZIE, Owen	18	1 (16)	0	(6)	0	1 (22)	0
MILNE, Daniel	34	21	2	10	0	31	2
OLUMOFE, James	22	(1)	0	-	-	(1)	0
PAUL, Martyn	40	14 (2)	0	6	0	20 (2)	0
PETERS, Josh	23	13 (2)	11	2 (1)	0	15 (3)	11
PETERS, Stephen	18	2 (2)	0	1	0	3 (2)	0
REID, Calum	26	(1)	0	2 (1)	1	2 (2)	1
REID, Jordan	24	20 (3)	0	7 (1)	0	27 (4)	0
RITCHIE, Cory	24	20 (1)	3	8 (1)	0	28 (2)	3
SHAND, Aaron	32	1 (8)	2	2 (3)	0	3 (11)	2
STILL, Dean	27	13 (5)	7	8	4	21 (5)	11
WILSON, K	-	(1)	0	-	-	(1)	0
WOOD, Kyle	-	11 (4)	0	1 (2)	0	12 (6)	0

Date	Opponent	Comp	Score	Scorers
Jul 30	Newmachar United (H)	GLC GRP	3-0	Marshall, Bennett, C Reid
Aug 2	Banks o' Dee Juniors (A)	GLC GRP	2-1	Still (2)
Aug 6	Dyce (A)	LGE	0-2	
Aug 9	Stonehaven (A)	GLC GRP	0-0	
Aug 13	Maud (H)	LGE	0-1	
Aug 16	Banchory St. Ternan (H)	LGE	6-0	Still, N Davidson, Marshall, Shand (2), Agnew
Aug 20	Stonehaven (A)	LGE	2-1	Danny Anderson o.g., Kane
Aug 23	Hermes (H)	LGE	0-2	
Sep 3	Culter (H)	GLC QF	0-2	
Sep 17	Montrose Roselea (A)	LGE	2-2	Agnew, Still
Oct 1	Bridge of Don Thistle (H)	LGE	0-4	
Oct 8	Bellshill Athletic (H)	SJC R2	1-2	Kane
Oct 15	Culter (H)	LGE	1-3	Ritchie
Oct 22	Ellon United (A)	LGE	0-4	
Oct 29	Nairn St. Ninian (A)	LGE	2-1	Agnew, Jack Anderson o.g.
Nov 5	Dyce (A)	NRC R1	2-4	Agnew, Still
Nov 12	Culter (H)	IRC R1	2-1	N Davidson (2)
Nov 26	East End (A)	LGE	3-1	N Davidson, J Peters (2)
Dec 3	Ellon United (H)	LGE	3-3	J Peters, Still, L Bain
Jan 7	Glentanar (A)	IRC R2	1-1	
Jan 28	Maud (A)	LGE	2-1	Milne, J Peters
Feb 4	Banchory St. Ternan (A)	LGE	4-1	J Peters, Agnew (2), Kane
Feb 11	Nairn St. Ninian (H)	LGE	4-1	Agnew, J Peters (2), Still
Feb 18	Montrose Roselea (H)	McL R1	4-1	Blair Stephen o.g., McHardy, Still, Agnew
Mar 4	Dufftown (A)	LGE	1-1	Agnew
Mar 18	Montrose Roselea (H)	LGE	3-0	Still (2), Agnew
Mar 25	East End (H)	LGE	1-0	Still
Apr 1	Colony Park (A)	LGE	3-0	N Davidson, Agnew, McHardy
Apr 4	Hermes (A)	LGE	1-1	J Peters
Apr 8	Colony Park (H)	LGE	4-1	J Peters (3), Ritchie
Apr 11	Dyce (H)	LGE	0-1	
Apr 15	Bridge of Don Thistle (A)	LGE	0-5	
Apr 18	Stonehaven (A)	McL QF	0-3	
Apr 29	Dufftown (H)	LGE	4-1	N Davidson, Milne, Ritchie, Agnew
May 2	Culter (A)	LGE	1-5	Galashan
May 9	Stonehaven (H)	LGE	0-8	

FIVE STAR PERFORMANCE FROM CLINICAL CULTER

Culter secured the Grill League Cup in style with five goals to East End's one.
Photo: Craig B Duff Photography/Dee Media

It was all one-way traffic at Lochside Park in the North Region Juniors Grill League Cup final of Saturday October 2, as Culter coasted to a 5–1 win over East End to lift the association's first trophy of the season.

It took the Crombie Park men just seven minutes to break the deadlock when Callum Dunbar pounced on a rebound off the bar to send the ball past East End goalkeeper Zack Ellis.

The dream start continued when Culter were awarded a penalty for a foul on Ross Clark by Ryan Corthals, and Cammy Fraser made no mistake with the spot kick from 12 yards.

It was 3–0 shortly before the half hour mark when Willie Mathers netted from close range.

A fourth before the interval put the game beyond East End, Clark adding his name to the scoresheet adding the finishing touch to a long ball from Fraser.

With Culter already in a celebratory mood, there was little to suggest a comeback might be on the cards and the game was put to bed with a Jay Cheyne goal on 56 minutes.

East End did manage to bag a goal with eight minutes left on the clock; Lewis Masson finding the net to reduce the scoreline to 5–1 – but it served as a mere consolation as there was no sign of a comeback.

Adding to the losing side's misery, manager Stuart Whicher was shown his marching orders for comments made to referee Kevin Murray.

CULTER...5 (4)
Dunbar 9, Fraser pen 14, Mathers 28, Clark 45, Cheyne 56
EAST END...1 (0)
Masson 82
Culter: Tait, Russell (Wozniak), Cheyne, Adam, McTavish, Wilson, Clark, Stewart (Ross), Fraser (Wallace), Dunbar (Todd), Mathers (Smart). Not used: Carroll, Emslie
East End: Ellis, Masson, Cortals, Keller, Johnston (Ritchie), Stewart, Odlin (Woods), Manson (Chouman), Mackie (Matthew), Bolton, Kerr (Mcallister). Not used: Whyte, Wilson
Referee: K Murray

CULTER COMPLETE TRIO OF TROPHIES

Winning the second of three cup competitions in 2022-23, Culter beat Rothie Rovers to lift the North Regional Cup. Photo: Craig B Duff Photography/Dee Media

Two first half goals secured the North Regional Cup for Culter as they extended their trophy haul to a tremendous treble for 2022-23.

Ross Clark broke the deadlock in front of a packed crowd at Davidson Park in Inverurie to give his side the lead on the half hour mark.

It was the 30th goal of the season for the Culter striker.

Just eight minutes later, Culter were 2-0 to the good, as Craig MacAskill found the net.

Both sides had chances to add to the scoring during a more evenly contested second half, but Culter held their lead to secure the trophy.

CULTER...2 (2)
Clark 30, MacAskill 38
ROTHIE ROVERS.............................0 (0)
Culter: Tait, Cheyne, Adam, Petrie, McTavish, Wilson, MacAskill (Mathers 90), Clark, Fraser (Stewart 87), Dunbar (Smart 73), McGregor (Fawcett 73). Not used: Russell, Dimov, Emslie
Rothie Rovers: Milne, Chalmers (Mcalley 86), Smith, R Walker (K Walker 63), Wood (Gray 73), Mair (Cormack 63), Hendry (Faskin 86), Stewart, Hodge, Thompson. Not used: Reid, Findlay
Referee: L Brown

EAST REGION MIDLANDS FOOTBALL LEAGUE

ARBROATH VICTORIA J.F.C.
Ogilvy Park, Arbroath

	Age	LEAGUE		CUPS		ALL	
		Apps	Goals	Apps	Goals	Apps	Goals
BASTOW, Jonathon	25	13 (4)	0	3	0	16 (4)	0
BELL, Bradley	21	15 (13)	0	1 (4)	1	16 (17)	1
CHALMERS, Josh	27	12	2	4	0	16	2
CLARK, Sam	25	28 (1)	5	3 (1)	0	31 (2)	5
CONNOR, Steven (GK)	24	1 (1)	0	-	-	1 (1)	0
DUFF, Euan	30	29 (3)	6	4 (1)	3	33 (4)	9
DURNO, Kevin	42	(2)	0	-	-	(2)	0
DYE, John	26	9 (4)	0	3	0	12 (4)	0
FERRIES, Robbie	27	27	1	6	0	33	1
FILLIE, Alex	33	(2)	0	-	-	(2)	0
FINDLAY, Ross	25	29 (4)	12	4	2	33 (4)	14
GRAY, Connor	30	17 (6)	0	4 (1)	0	21 (7)	0
GRAY, R (GK)	-	2	0	-	-	2	0
GRIBBEN, Jack	31	20 (5)	0	2 (1)	0	22 (6)	0
HARDIE, Dean	27	17 (5)	1	2 (3)	0	19 (8)	1
KEOGH, Matt	28	20 (2)	0	3 (1)	0	23 (3)	0
LYALL, Arran (GK)	22	25	0	4	0	29	0
MARTIN, Fraser	19	2 (2)	0	1	0	3 (2)	0
MARTIN, Kieran	20	2 (1)	0	1 (1)	0	3 (2)	0
MATHER, Jamie	-	3 (5)	0	(1)	0	3 (6)	0
MCFARLANE, Connor	20	26 (7)	16	3 (2)	4	29 (9)	20
MILNE, Scott	25	15 (1)	5	4	3	19 (1)	8
RAMSAY, Kyle	24	(2)	0	-	-	(2)	0
RIDDELL, Dale	34	23 (1)	0	5	0	28 (1)	0
ROBB, Ryan	26	1 (6)	0	-	-	1 (6)	0
SIVEWRIGHT, Lewis	20	(8)	0	(2)	0	(10)	0
SMITH, Morgan	26	26 (2)	0	4 (1)	3	30 (3)	3
STEPHEN, Aaron	27	2 (4)	0	(1)	0	2 (5)	0
STURROCK, David	40	(3)	0	-	-	(3)	0
WALKER, Marc	30	(3)	2	-	-	(3)	2
WATT, Jamie (GK)	22	2 (1)	0	-	-	2 (1)	0
WHITTON, Jack (GK)	27	5	0	1	0	6	0
WILLIAMS, Mitchell	-	3 (8)	0	(1)	0	3 (9)	0
WOOD, Calvin	22	20 (11)	5	4 (2)	3	24 (13)	8
YULE, Fraser	-	(6)	0	(1)	0	(7)	0

* Players with less than 2 appearances not displayed due to size of squad.

Date	Opponent	Comp	Score	Scorers
Jul 23	Lochee United (A)	LGE	1-1	Mcfarlane
Jul 27	Dundee St James (H)	LGE	4-1	Duff, Findlay (2), Milne
Jul 30	Forfar West End (H)	LGE	2-2	Milne (2)
Aug 3	Dundee North End (A)	LGE	0-0	
Aug 6	Scone Thistle (A)	LGE	1-2	Clark
Aug 10	Letham (H)	LGE	0-1	
Aug 13	Coupar Angus (H)	LGE	0-1	
Aug 17	Lochee Harp (H)	LGE	2-0	Milne, Mcfarlane
Aug 20	Tayport (A)	LGE	1-3	Clark
Aug 27	Lossiemouth United (A)	SJC R1	6-0	Wood, Duff, Milne (3), Mcfarlane
Sep 3	Tayport (H)	LGE	2-2	Milne, Wood
Sep 17	Dundee Violet (A)	LGE	1-0	Duff
Sep 24	Kilsyth Rangers (H)	SJC R2	2-1	Findlay, Mcfarlane
Oct 1	East Craigie (H)	LGE	0-3	
Oct 8	Lochee United (A)	IRC R1	0-3	
Oct 15	Kirriemuir Thistle (H)	LGE	2-1	Clark, Walker
Oct 22	Downfield (A)	LGE	2-4	Mcfarlane, Duff
Oct 29	Hurlford United (H)	SJC R3	0-0p	
Nov 5	Blairgowrie (H)	LGE	5-1	Chalmers, Findlay (2), Mcfarlane, Walker
Nov 12	Brechin Victoria (A)	LGE	4-0	Duff (2), Chalmers, Wood
Nov 19	Broughty Athletic (H)	LGE	0-2	
Nov 26	Lochee United (H)	LGE	0-0	
Dec 3	Forfar United (A)	LGE	3-1	Wood, Findlay, Mcfarlane
Jan 14	Scone Thistle (H)	LGE	3-0	Findlay, Mcfarlane (2)
Jan 21	Letham (A)	LGE	1-0	Findlay
Jan 28	Blairgowrie (A)	LGE	2-2	Duff, Findlay
Feb 4	Forfar United (H)	LGE	1-2	Wood
Feb 11	Dundee St James (A)	LGE	2-2	Mcfarlane (2)
Feb 18	Forfar West End (H)	ELC R2	9-0	Wood, Duff (2), M Smith (2), Findlay, Bell, Mcfarlane (2)
Feb 25	Broughty Athletic (A)	LGE	0-8	
Mar 4	Carnoustie Panmure (A)	LGE	0-5	
Mar 11	Dundee Violet (H)	LGE	1-4	Findlay
Mar 25	Coupar Angus (A)	LGE	3-2	Mcfarlane, Findlay (2)
Apr 1	Kirriemuir Thistle (A)	LGE	2-4	Mcfarlane, Findlay
Apr 8	Downfield (H)	LGE	1-2	Mcfarlane
Apr 15	Forfar West End (A)	LGE	3-2	Mcfarlane, Clark, L Stephen o.g.
Apr 22	Brechin Victoria (H)	LGE	1-2	Hardie
Apr 26	Dundee North End (H)	LGE	1-6	Luc Bollan o.g.
Apr 29	Lochee Harp (A)	LGE	3-1	Wood, Clark, Mcfarlane
May 6	Carnoustie Panmure (H)	LGE	2-3	Mcfarlane (2)
May 10	Dundee North End (H)	ELC QF	2-6	Wood, M Smith
May 17	East Craigie (A)	LGE	1-3	Ferries

BLAIRGOWRIE J.F.C.
Davie Park, Blairgowrie

		LEAGUE		CUPS		ALL	
	Age	Apps	Goals	Apps	Goals	Apps	Goals
ADAM, Matthew	30	24 (1)	13	2	0	26 (1)	13
AXWORTHY, Gary	32	30 (1)	15	3	1	33 (1)	16
BEEDIE, Ryan	24	10 (2)	0	2	0	12 (2)	0
BROWN, Kaisey	-	30 (5)	3	2 (1)	1	32 (6)	4
BROWN, Stefan	24	(3)	0	-	-	(3)	0
CORMACK, Dean	19	1	0	-	-	1	0
CRUICKSHANK, Allan	34	1 (2)	0	-	-	1 (2)	0
CUSSICK, Brodie	18	21 (5)	0	2	0	23 (5)	0
DONNAN, Connar	21	1	0	-	-	1	0
FLEMING, Jay	20	(5)	0	(1)	0	(6)	0
GEDDES, Blair	25	27	2	2	0	29	2
GEMINE, Lewis	23	13 (3)	2	1	0	14 (3)	2
JOHNSTONE, Cameron (GK)	27	35	0	3	0	38	0
LAW, Stefan	26	2	0	-	-	2	0
MCCOMBIE, Gary	28	(2)	0	-	-	(2)	0
MCILVENNY, Evan	28	1	0	-	-	1	0
MCLELLEN, Craig	18	34	1	3	0	37	1
MCMANUS, Cameron	27	26 (4)	7	3	2	29 (4)	9
MCPHERSON, Liam	28	1 (3)	0	1	0	2 (3)	0
MITCHELL, Lawrie	24	13 (3)	2	1 (1)	0	14 (4)	2
NICOLL, Stewart	37	1	0	-	-	1	0
PIRIE, Gordan	35	10 (5)	0	1	0	11 (5)	0
PLENDERLEITH, Ian	32	26 (6)	0	-	-	26 (6)	0
REILLY, Keir	28	1	0	-	-	1	0
ROBERTSON, D	-	2	0	-	-	2	0
SCOBBIE, Kurt	27	1	0	-	-	1	0
SCOTT, Paul	24	22 (2)	0	3	0	25 (2)	0
SIMPSON, James	30	27	0	2	0	29	0
THOMS, Logan	20	15 (1)	1	2	0	17 (1)	1
WALLACE, Harley	25	3	0	-	-	3	0
WATSON, Harry	-	3 (14)	0	(2)	0	3 (16)	0
WATSON, Robbie	-	4 (21)	1	(2)	0	4 (23)	1
WHITTET, Harrison	18	(2)	0	-	-	(2)	0

* Players with less than 1 full appearance not displayed due to size of squad.

MATCH RESULTS 2022/23

Date	Opponent	Comp	Score	Scorers
Jul 23	Dundee Violet (H)	LGE	0-2	
Jul 27	East Craigie (A)	LGE	1-2	Thoms
Jul 30	Kirriemuir Thistle (A)	LGE	2-3	Adam (2)
Aug 3	Forfar United (H)	LGE	2-0	Adam, Axworthy
Aug 6	Downfield (H)	LGE	3-3	Axworthy (2), Adam
Aug 13	Broughty Athletic (H)	LGE	0-7	
Aug 17	Brechin Victoria (A)	LGE	3-0	Mitchell (2), Axworthy
Aug 20	Dundee St James (H)	LGE	3-1	McManus, Axworthy (2)
Aug 22	Lochee United (A)	LGE	1-8	McManus
Aug 27	Stonehaven (H)	SJC R1	0-6	
Sep 3	Dundee North End (A)	LGE	3-4	McManus (3)
Sep 17	Forfar West End (H)	LGE	0-1	
Sep 24	Brechin Victoria (H)	LGE	1-1	Axworthy
Oct 1	Scone Thistle (A)	LGE	1-0	Axworthy
Oct 8	Broughty Athletic (H)	IRC R1	1-1ᵖ	McManus
Oct 15	Lochee Harp (A)	LGE	1-4	Axworthy
Oct 21	Coupar Angus (H)	LGE	1-4	Adam
Oct 29	Downfield (A)	LGE	0-4	
Nov 5	Arbroath Victoria (A)	LGE	1-5	D Hardie o.g.
Nov 12	Tayport (H)	LGE	0-2	
Nov 26	Dundee Violet (A)	LGE	3-4	Adam, Gemine, Geddes
Dec 3	Letham (H)	LGE	1-1	Gemine
Jan 14	Lochee Harp (H)	LGE	2-4	Adam, Axworthy
Jan 28	Arbroath Victoria (H)	LGE	2-2	Axworthy (2)
Feb 3	Broughty Athletic (A)	LGE	0-6	
Feb 11	Forfar United (A)	LGE	4-0	Axworthy (3), Adam
Feb 18	Lochee United (H)	LGE	1-5	Adam
Feb 22	Dundee North End (H)	ELC R1	3-4	Axworthy, K Brown, McManus
Feb 25	Dundee St James (A)	LGE	1-2	Adam
Mar 4	Dundee North End (H)	LGE	0-5	
Mar 15	Carnoustie Panmure (H)	LGE	0-5	
Mar 18	Kirriemuir Thistle (H)	LGE	0-2	
Mar 24	Letham (A)	LGE	1-4	Adam
Apr 15	Coupar Angus (A)	LGE	3-0	Adam, McLellen, K Brown
Apr 22	East Craigie (H)	LGE	1-6	Adam
Apr 29	Forfar West End (A)	LGE	5-1	K Brown (2), McManus (2), Geddes
May 13	Tayport (A)	LGE	0-5	
May 27	Carnoustie Panmure (A)	LGE	1-8	R Watson

BRECHIN VICTORIA J.F.C.
Victoria Park, Brechin

	Age	LEAGUE		CUPS		ALL	
		Apps	Goals	Apps	Goals	Apps	Goals
ARCHER, Zac	29	2 (7)	2	-	-	2 (7)	2
BARCLAY, Steven	33	1 (4)	0	(2)	0	1 (6)	0
BARKWORTH, Callum (GK)	24	1	0	-	-	1	0
BLACK, Scott	35	1 (5)	0	(1)	0	1 (6)	0
CROSBY, Charlie	22	1 (7)	1	-	-	1 (7)	1
CROSBY, Jamie	19	4 (9)	0	-	-	4 (9)	0
CROWE, Douglas	24	18 (3)	0	1 (1)	0	19 (4)	0
CROWE, Fraser	29	2 (1)	0	-	-	2 (1)	0
DONALD, Chris	26	13 (7)	0	(1)	0	13 (8)	0
DUNCAN, Bob (GK)	-	1	0	-	-	1	0
ELDER, Darren	25	33 (2)	1	4	0	37 (2)	1
FARQUHAR, Dugald	-	14	1	1	0	15	1
FLIGHT, Ross	23	8 (1)	0	1 (1)	0	9 (2)	0
HARRISON, Lewis (GK)	21	1	0	1	0	2	0
HILL, Corey	18	14 (5)	0	2	0	16 (5)	0
HOLMES, Ben	21	31 (1)	3	4	0	35 (1)	3
LAWSON, Colin	31	10 (5)	0	3	0	13 (5)	0
LIEPER, Daniel	32	18 (6)	8	2 (1)	0	20 (7)	8
LONGMUIR, Kieran	21	25 (2)	1	2	0	27 (2)	1
MCINTOSH, Aulay	20	1	0	-	-	1	0
MOONEY, Ben	24	13 (1)	2	1 (1)	0	14 (2)	2
MORRISON, Aaron (GK)	22	20	0	2	0	22	0
NAGLIK, Dominic	19	12	0	-	-	12	0
PATERSON, Josh	20	9 (7)	1	3	0	12 (7)	1
PATERSON, Ross	25	26 (1)	0	3	0	29 (1)	0
RAUSCH, Jordan	28	3 (1)	2	1	0	4 (1)	2
RENILSON, Lewis	22	20 (3)	0	3 (1)	0	23 (4)	0
SMITH, Mitchell	21	27 (2)	3	3 (1)	1	30 (3)	4
SMITH, Murray	26	19 (4)	9	3	2	22 (4)	11
SMITH, Steven	31	11	0	-	-	11	0
STEWART, Evan	-	(5)	0	-	-	(5)	0
WILL, Jordan	28	9	1	1	0	10	1
WINTER, Cameron (GK)	22	13 (1)	0	1	0	14 (1)	0
WOOD, Sam	25	15 (8)	1	2 (1)	1	17 (9)	2

* Players with less than 1 full appearance not displayed due to size of squad.

MATCH RESULTS 2022/23

Date	Opponent	Comp	Score	Scorers
Jul 23	Carnoustie Panmure (H)	LGE	0-5	
Jul 27	Dundee Violet (H)	LGE	1-1	Mooney
Jul 30	Forfar United (A)	LGE	0-4	
Aug 3	East Craigie (H)	LGE	0-3	
Aug 6	Kirriemuir Thistle (H)	LGE	2-4	Will, Mooney
Aug 10	Downfield (A)	LGE	2-5	Rausch (2)
Aug 17	Blairgowrie (H)	LGE	0-3	
Aug 20	Lochee United (H)	LGE	0-5	
Aug 24	Broughty Athletic (A)	LGE	0-4	
Aug 27	Maybole (H)	SJC R1	0-5	
Sep 3	Dundee St James (A)	LGE	0-4	
Sep 17	Dundee North End (H)	LGE	1-2	Lieper
Sep 24	Blairgowrie (A)	LGE	1-1	Lieper
Oct 1	Forfar West End (A)	LGE	0-2	
Oct 8	East Craigie (H)	IRC R2	1-2	Murray Smith
Oct 15	Letham (A)	LGE	1-2	Murray Smith
Oct 22	Lochee Harp (H)	LGE	2-2	Elder, Mitchell Smith
Oct 29	Scone Thistle (H)	LGE	3-3	Mitchell Smith, Holmes, Lieper
Nov 5	Coupar Angus (A)	LGE	2-2	Murray Smith, Lieper
Nov 12	Arbroath Victoria (H)	LGE	0-4	
Nov 26	Carnoustie Panmure (A)	LGE	2-6	Murray Smith (2)
Dec 3	Scone Thistle (A)	ELC R2	3-0	Mitchell Smith, Wood, Murray Smith
Jan 7	Forfar United (H)	LGE	1-3	Farquhar
Jan 28	Lochee Harp (A)	LGE	3-2	Lieper (2), Murray Smith
Feb 11	Tayport (H)	LGE	1-3	Archer
Feb 18	Broughty Athletic (H)	LGE	0-3	
Feb 25	Lochee United (A)	LGE	0-3	
Mar 4	Dundee St James (H)	LGE	1-2	Murray Smith
Mar 18	Forfar West End (H)	LGE	5-1	Lieper, Holmes, Murray Smith, J Paterson, C Crosby
Mar 25	Scone Thistle (A)	LGE	1-1	Murray Smith
Apr 1	Letham (H)	LGE	1-2	Wood
Apr 8	Kirriemuir Thistle (A)	LGE	1-2	Lieper
Apr 15	Dundee Violet (A)	LGE	1-0	Murray Smith
Apr 19	East Craigie (A)	LGE	0-3	
Apr 22	Arbroath Victoria (A)	LGE	2-1	Mitchell Smith, Holmes
Apr 29	Tayport (A)	LGE	0-1	
May 10	Downfield (H)	LGE	0-1	
May 13	Dundee North End (A)	LGE	0-2	
May 17	Broughty Athletic (H)	ELC QF	0-2	
May 20	Coupar Angus (H)	LGE	2-2	Longmuir, Archer

PLAYING SQUAD & STATISTICS 2022/23 *

BROUGHTY ATHLETIC J.F.C.
Whitton Park, Broughty Ferry

		LEAGUE		CUPS		ALL	
	Age	Apps	Goals	Apps	Goals	Apps	Goals
ALLAN, Matthew	27	4	1	-	-	4	1
ANDERSON, Gregor	28	1	0	-	-	1	0
ANDERSON, Louie	21	1 (13)	0	1 (3)	0	2 (16)	0
BAIRD, Finlay	22	4 (2)	1	-	-	4 (2)	1
BOYLAN, Lewis	18	21 (3)	1	4 (4)	0	25 (7)	1
BRANDER, Oliver	19	1 (8)	0	(1)	0	1 (9)	0
BUCHANAN, Cain	-	(5)	0	(3)	0	(8)	0
BURNETT, Fraser (GK)	21	7 (1)	0	2	0	9 (1)	0
CAIRNS, Argyle	22	(2)	0	(1)	0	(3)	0
DIAMOND, Sean (GK)	30	29	0	8	0	37	0
DONALDSON, Fraser	-	(1)	0	(1)	0	(2)	0
FARQUHARSON, John	37	4 (6)	0	1 (1)	0	5 (7)	0
FERGUSON, Ryan	29	28 (3)	1	9	2	37 (3)	3
FINDLAY, Mitchell	19	15 (19)	15	4 (5)	4	19 (24)	19
FRASER, Gary	37	1 (3)	0	(1)	0	1 (4)	0
FRASER, Lewis	21	29 (3)	4	7 (2)	0	36 (5)	4
GARRICK, Ben	20	3 (5)	1	-	-	3 (5)	1
GILLESPIE, Rikki	30	6 (1)	5	1 (1)	0	7 (2)	5
HENRY, Ruari	20	25 (8)	10	9 (1)	4	34 (9)	14
KESSON, Derryn	25	5 (2)	1	5	1	10 (2)	2
MACDONALD, Jay	-	(3)	0	-	-	(3)	0
MCCONNACHIE, Thomas	-	(1)	0	(1)	0	(2)	0
MCINNES, Ryan	18	5 (1)	3	-	-	5 (1)	3
MCNAUGHTON, Greig	25	31 (4)	2	9 (1)	1	40 (5)	3
MCNAUGHTON, Ross	20	(2)	0	-	-	(2)	0
MIDDLETON, Ben	28	29 (1)	3	8	2	37 (1)	5
PATERSON, Grant	24	2 (8)	0	(1)	0	2 (9)	0
REID, Jamie	29	28 (1)	1	9	0	37 (1)	1
SIVEWRIGHT, Ben	27	33 (1)	1	7 (2)	0	40 (3)	1
SKELLY, Josh	26	24	33	8	8	32	41
SMITH, Brad	26	28 (2)	16	6 (1)	4	34 (3)	20
STEWART, Ben	18	(5)	0	(3)	0	(8)	0
TOSH, Craig	22	25 (5)	14	8	6	33 (5)	20
WINTER, Ryan	28	7 (8)	2	4 (2)	2	11 (10)	4

* Players with less than 1 full appearance not displayed due to size of squad.

MATCH RESULTS 2022/23

Date	Opponent	Comp	Score	Scorers
Jul 23	Tayport (H)	LGE	2-0	Smith (2)
Jul 27	Carnoustie Panmure (A)	LGE	2-3	Tosh, Garrick
Jul 30	East Craigie (A)	LGE	0-0	
Aug 3	Dundee Violet (H)	LGE	2-0	Allan, Smith
Aug 6	Forfar United (H)	LGE	5-0	Henry, Baird, Smith (2), Boylan
Aug 10	Kirriemuir Thistle (A)	LGE	0-4	
Aug 13	Blairgowrie (A)	LGE	7-0	McInnes, Gillespie (3), Findlay (2), Middleton
Aug 17	Downfield (H)	LGE	3-1	Gillespie, McInnes (2)
Aug 24	Brechin Victoria (H)	LGE	4-0	Smith (2), D Crowe o.g., Gillespie
Aug 27	Kirriemuir Thistle (A)	SJC R1	4-2	Middleton, Smith (2), Henry
Sep 3	Lochee United (A)	LGE	2-2	Greg Kirk o.g., Smith
Sep 17	Dundee St James (H)	LGE	5-0	Skelly (2), Reid, Findlay (2)
Sep 24	East Craigie (A)	SJC R2	2-3	Ferguson, Skelly
Oct 1	Dundee North End (A)	LGE	2-1	L Fraser, Henry
Oct 8	Blairgowrie (A)	IRC R1	1-1ᵖ	Tosh
Oct 15	Scone Thistle (A)	LGE	4-0	Tosh, L Fraser, Skelly, Ferguson
Oct 22	Letham (H)	LGE	1-1	Skelly
Oct 29	Forfar West End (H)	LGE	5-0	Tosh, Middleton, Smith (2), G McNaughton
Nov 5	Lochee Harp (A)	LGE	3-1	Smith (2), Findlay
Nov 12	Coupar Angus (H)	LGE	1-1	Smith
Nov 19	Arbroath Victoria (A)	LGE	2-0	Winter (2)
Nov 26	Tayport (A)	LGE	3-0	Tosh (2), Sivewright
Dec 3	Tayport (H)	IRC R2	4-2	Findlay (2), Smith, Tosh
Dec 10	Carnoustie Panmure (H)	LGE	4-1	Henry, Tosh, Skelly, Middleton
Jan 7	East Craigie (H)	LGE	1-2	Skelly
Jan 21	Kirriemuir Thistle (H)	LGE	3-2	Tosh, R Beedie o.g., Findlay
Jan 28	Downfield (A)	LGE	1-3	Findlay
Feb 3	Blairgowrie (H)	LGE	6-0	Findlay, Skelly, Tosh (3), G McNaughton
Feb 11	Islavale (H)	IRC R3	6-0	G McNaughton, Winter (2), Tosh, Findlay, Ferguson
Feb 18	Brechin Victoria (A)	LGE	3-0	Henry (2), Skelly
Feb 25	Arbroath Victoria (H)	LGE	8-0	Findlay (2), Skelly (4), Tosh, L Fraser
Mar 4	Lochee United (H)	LGE	5-3	Skelly (2), Tosh (2), Findlay
Mar 18	Downfield (H)	IRC QF	2-3	Skelly, Findlay
Mar 25	Forfar West End (A)	LGE	9-0	H Taylor o.g., Smith (2), Skelly (3), Henry (2), Findlay
Apr 1	Dundee Violet (A)	LGE	2-1	Tosh, Skelly
Apr 8	Letham (A)	LGE	5-0	Skelly (3), L Fraser, Findlay
Apr 15	Dundee North End (H)	LGE	1-3	Henry
Apr 22	Lochee Harp (H)	LGE	4-1	M Kelly o.g., Skelly (3)
Apr 29	Coupar Angus (A)	LGE	2-1	Skelly (2)
May 3	Letham (A)	ELC R2	3-1	Skelly (2), Henry
May 6	Forfar United (A)	LGE	2-1	Kesson, Skelly
May 10	Dundee St James (A)	LGE	7-0	Henry (2), Skelly (2), E Smith o.g., Findlay (2)
May 17	Brechin Victoria (A)	ELC QF	2-0	Henry, Middleton
May 24	Forfar United (H)	ELC SF	7-2	Tosh, Henry, Kesson, Skelly (3), Smith
May 27	Scone Thistle (H)	LGE	5-2	Skelly (4), Smith
Jun 3	Carnoustie Panmure (A)	ELC Final	3-3ᵖ	Tosh (2), Skelly

CARNOUSTIE PANMURE J.F.C.
Laing Park, Carnoustie

	Age	LEAGUE		CUPS		ALL	
		Apps	Goals	Apps	Goals	Apps	Goals
BATCHELOR, Craig	27	9 (2)	8	-	-	9 (2)	8
BROWN, Hugo	19	1 (7)	0	(1)	0	1 (8)	0
CHALMERS, Jack	18	(6)	0	(1)	0	(7)	0
CLARK, Brian	35	9 (5)	3	7	1	16 (5)	4
CLARKSON, Darren (GK)	25	34	0	14	0	48	0
CONWAY, Kieran	24	6 (1)	1	-	-	6 (1)	1
CONWAY, Paddy	37	4 (3)	0	-	-	4 (3)	0
DIGNAN, Ryan	33	6 (2)	1	5 (2)	1	11 (4)	2
DOROVIC, Daniel	24	2 (15)	2	1 (2)	3	3 (17)	5
FRASER, Ross	22	32 (3)	14	13 (2)	2	45 (5)	16
GRANT, L	-	(1)	0	-	-	(1)	0
HAMILTON, Scott	18	(2)	0	-	-	(2)	0
HOON, Rhys	18	(2)	1	-	-	(2)	1
JOYCE, Louis	20	32 (1)	0	15 (1)	1	47 (2)	1
KEMLO, Finn	20	2	0	(2)	0	2 (2)	0
LEIPER, Arran	19	5 (3)	1	1 (1)	0	6 (4)	1
MACDONALD, Gordon	34	19 (8)	12	11 (5)	8	30 (13)	20
MARTIN, Pat	26	17 (9)	4	4 (5)	2	21 (14)	6
MCINNES, Ryan	18	3 (3)	1	(1)	0	3 (4)	1
MCWALTER, Kieran	28	9 (9)	0	6 (3)	0	15 (12)	0
MILLAR, Danny	35	13 (1)	2	9 (1)	1	22 (2)	3
REID, Dale	30	23 (6)	45	14 (1)	11	37 (7)	56
ROBERTSON, Aidan (GK)	22	1 (1)	0	-	-	1 (1)	0
ROCHE, Ryan	26	26	4	11	1	37	5
SIMPSON, Sam	28	23 (4)	8	10 (1)	2	33 (5)	10
SMITH, Pat	27	3 (4)	0	5 (1)	1	8 (5)	1
STEEL, Bailey	24	25 (2)	1	11 (1)	0	36 (3)	1
STEPHEN, Dylan	22	22 (2)	9	5 (3)	0	27 (5)	9
SUTTIE, Ryan	32	33	4	10	1	43	5
WARWICK, Greg	25	13 (5)	0	12 (2)	0	25 (7)	0
WINTER, Jamie	38	13 (8)	3	10 (4)	4	23 (12)	7

Date	Opponent	Comp	Score	Scorers
Jul 23	Brechin Victoria (A)	LGE	5-0	Martin, Fraser (2), Roche, Hoon
Jul 27	Broughty Athletic (H)	LGE	3-2	Fraser, Simpson, Suttie
Jul 30	Dundee St James (H)	LGE	4-0	MacDonald, Martin, D Reid, Fraser
Aug 3	Lochee United (A)	LGE	0-2	
Aug 6	Dundee North End (A)	LGE	2-2	Dignan, K Conway
Aug 10	Forfar West End (H)	LGE	4-1	Winter, Simpson, MacDonald, Fraser
Aug 13	Letham (H)	LGE	2-0	Simpson, Leiper
Aug 17	Scone Thistle (A)	LGE	4-0	Roche, D Reid (3)
Aug 20	Coupar Angus (H)	LGE	3-0	
Aug 24	Lochee Harp (H)	LGE	4-1	D Reid (2), Martin, Fraser
Aug 27	Hawick R.A. United (H)	SC PR.	1-1	Fraser
Sep 3	Hawick R.A. United (A)	SC PR.	3-0	Martin, Winter, D Reid
Sep 17	Rothes (H)	SC R1	3-1	MacDonald, D Reid (2)
Sep 24	West Calder United (H)	SJC R2	4-2	Simpson, Winter, MacDonald, D Reid
Oct 8	Forfar United (H)	IRC R2	2-1	Dignan, Roche
Oct 15	East Craigie (H)	LGE	3-0	D Reid (2), P Moran o.g.
Oct 22	Formartine United (H)	SC R2	1-2	Suttie
Oct 29	Petershill (A)	SJC R3	3-2	Winter, Millar, Simpson
Nov 5	Kirriemuir Thistle (H)	LGE	3-0	D Reid, Fraser, Millar
Nov 12	Downfield (A)	LGE	1-1	MacDonald
Nov 26	Brechin Victoria (H)	LGE	6-2	L Renilson o.g., D Reid (2), Simpson, MacDonald (2)
Dec 3	Glenafton Athletic (H)	SJC R4	1-3	MacDonald
Dec 10	Broughty Athletic (A)	LGE	1-4	Fraser
Jan 7	Dundee St James (A)	LGE	7-1	MacDonald (2), Fraser, Clark (2), D Reid (2)
Jan 14	Dundee North End (H)	LGE	4-0	D Reid, MacDonald (2), Winter
Jan 28	Scone Thistle (H)	LGE	5-1	D Reid (4), McInnes
Feb 4	Letham (A)	LGE	3-0	D Reid (2), Suttie
Feb 11	Bridge of Don Thistle (H)	IRC R3	3-2	Fraser, D Reid (2)
Feb 18	Lochee Harp (A)	LGE	7-2	Roche, D Reid (5), Fraser
Feb 25	Coupar Angus (A)	LGE	3-1	D Reid (3)
Mar 4	Arbroath Victoria (H)	LGE	5-0	F Martin o.g., MacDonald, Fraser (2), Simpson
Mar 11	Tayport (A)	LGE	3-0	Millar, Stephen, Suttie
Mar 15	Blairgowrie (A)	LGE	5-0	D Reid (5)
Mar 18	Lochee Harp (A)	IRC QF	6-1	Dorovic (3), MacDonald (2), Winter
Mar 25	Dundee Violet (H)	LGE	3-2	Fraser, Dorovic, Stephen
Apr 1	East Craigie (A)	LGE	1-1	Batchelor
Apr 8	Forfar United (H)	LGE	5-1	Batchelor (2), MacDonald, D Reid (2)
Apr 15	Tayport (H)	LGE	4-2	D Reid, Suttie, Simpson (2)
Apr 19	Kirriemuir Thistle (A)	LGE	0-0	
Apr 22	Downfield (H)	LGE	0-1	
Apr 29	Downfield (A)	IRC SF	3-0	Joyce, MacDonald (2)
May 3	Forfar United (A)	LGE	4-0	D Reid, Batchelor, Stephen (2)
May 6	Arbroath Victoria (A)	LGE	3-2	Batchelor (2), Roche
May 10	Dundee Violet (A)	LGE	9-1	Stephen (3), Martin, D Reid (3), MacDonald, Winter
May 13	Lochee United (H)	LGE	1-2	D Reid
May 15	Downfield (A)	ELC R2	1-0	D Reid
May 17	Forfar West End (A)	LGE	6-0	Dorovic, L Stephen o.g., Batchelor (2), Simpson, D Reid
May 20	Dundee North End (A)	IRC F	1-4	MacDonald
May 24	Kirriemuir Thistle (A)	ELC QF	2-0	D Reid, Martin
May 27	Blairgowrie (H)	LGE	8-1	Clark, D Reid (3), Stephen (2), Fraser, Steel
May 31	Dundee North End (H)	ELC SF	2-0	D Reid (2)
Jun 3	Broughty Athletic (H)	ELC Final	3-3ᵖ	Smith, Clark, D Reid

PLAYING SQUAD & STATISTICS 2022/23 *

COUPAR ANGUS J.F.C.
Foxhall Park, Coupar Angus

	Age	LEAGUE		CUPS		ALL	
		Apps	Goals	Apps	Goals	Apps	Goals
BELL, Aaron	19	10 (8)	0	1	0	11 (8)	0
BLACK, Scott	35	(2)	0	-	-	(2)	0
BLAIR, Dominic	29	28	7	3	0	31	7
BLAIR, Duncan	31	3 (1)	0	-	-	3 (1)	0
BUCHAN, Kevin	29	3	0	-	-	3	0
CONNELLY, Connaire	29	19 (5)	2	1 (1)	0	20 (6)	2
DANDIE, Jonathan	34	(2)	0	-	-	(2)	0
DOLAN, Kieron	19	9 (13)	5	1 (1)	0	10 (14)	5
EGAN, Kevin	36	7 (7)	1	(1)	0	7 (8)	1
EGAN, Liam	33	1 (1)	0	-	-	1 (1)	0
EWING, Lennard (GK)	31	27	0	3	0	30	0
FAIRFIELD, Dominic	19	(4)	0	(1)	0	(5)	0
FRASER, Jamie	-	11 (4)	1	1	0	12 (4)	1
GALLACHER, Ian	35	1 (2)	0	-	-	1 (2)	0
GREIG, Nairn	19	23 (7)	0	2 (1)	0	25 (8)	0
HAMILTON, Kai	18	1 (4)	2	(1)	0	1 (5)	2
HARRIS, Brian	21	10	3	2 (1)	0	12 (1)	3
HENRY, Paul	34	10	0	3	0	13	0
HUGHES, Frankie	18	1 (1)	0	-	-	1 (1)	0
HUNTER, Ryan	26	19 (2)	1	2 (1)	0	21 (3)	1
LAING, Max	-	1 (2)	0	-	-	1 (2)	0
LUKE, David (GK)	38	2	0	-	-	2	0
MACLEAN, Iain	36	4	0	1	0	5	0
MCDONALD, James	19	18 (9)	0	3	0	21 (9)	0
MCGREGOR, Ryan	19	3 (5)	0	(1)	0	3 (6)	0
MCINTOSH, Dale	36	16 (6)	0	3 (1)	0	19 (7)	0
MILLAR, Brad	41	1 (3)	0	-	-	1 (3)	0
MURDOCH, Lyall	33	5 (2)	1	1	0	6 (2)	1
NEAVE, Jack	26	28	2	3	0	31	2
NEAVE, Owen	29	3 (6)	2	1	0	4 (6)	2
NORRIE, Gordon	31	6 (1)	2	-	-	6 (1)	2
NORRIE, Robbie	28	26 (4)	10	3	1	29 (4)	11
OLD, Liam	18	1 (2)	0	-	-	1 (2)	0
PETERS, Ben (GK)	31	2	0	-	-	2	0
ROELEVELD, Lee	34	25	4	4	3	29	7
SMART, Jonathan	42	(3)	0	-	-	(3)	0
SMART, Wayne	-	4 (5)	0	-	-	4 (5)	0
TRONT, Stephen	34	8 (4)	0	1	0	9 (4)	0
TUCKER, Sean	32	27	12	2 (1)	0	29 (1)	12
VAN DER KUHL, Marc	36	19 (1)	1	2 (1)	0	21 (2)	1

* Players with less than 2 appearances not displayed due to size of squad.

MATCH RESULTS 2022/23

Date	Opponent	Comp	Score	Scorers
Jul 23	Dundee St James (A)	LGE	3-2	Roeleveld, Percy, Dolan
Jul 27	Dundee North End (H)	LGE	1-3	Harris
Jul 30	Scone Thistle (H)	LGE	2-4	Ross Loudon o.g., Dom Blair
Aug 3	Forfar West End (A)	LGE	2-3	Connelly, Tucker
Aug 6	Letham (A)	LGE	0-7	
Aug 10	Lochee Harp (H)	LGE	2-1	Murdoch, R Norrie
Aug 13	Arbroath Victoria (A)	LGE	1-0	O Neave
Aug 20	Carnoustie Panmure (A)	LGE	0-3	
Aug 24	Tayport (H)	LGE	0-2	
Aug 27	Beith Juniors (H)	SJC R1	0-8	
Sep 3	Dundee Violet (H)	LGE	2-4	Tucker, Connelly
Sep 17	East Craigie (A)	LGE	0-4	
Sep 24	Dundee Violet (A)	ELC R2	2-0	R Norrie, Roeleveld
Oct 1	Forfar United (H)	LGE	4-1	Dolan (2), Harris (2)
Oct 15	Downfield (H)	LGE	0-2	
Oct 21	Blairgowrie (A)	LGE	4-1	Roeleveld, Dom Blair (2), Dolan
Oct 29	Lochee Harp (H)	IRC R2	1-1p	Roeleveld
Nov 5	Brechin Victoria (H)	LGE	2-2	R Norrie (2)
Nov 12	Broughty Athletic (A)	LGE	1-1	Roeleveld
Nov 26	Dundee St James (H)	LGE	5-1	Hunter, Tucker (2), O Neave, R Norrie
Dec 3	Kirriemuir Thistle (A)	LGE	1-4	van der Kuhl
Jan 14	Letham (H)	LGE	2-3	Dom Blair, Tucker
Jan 21	Lochee Harp (A)	LGE	2-0	Dom Blair, Dolan
Feb 4	Kirriemuir Thistle (H)	LGE	2-2	Tucker (2)
Feb 11	Lochee United (H)	LGE	1-4	Tucker
Feb 18	Tayport (A)	LGE	1-5	Tucker
Feb 25	Carnoustie Panmure (H)	LGE	1-3	Tucker
Mar 4	Dundee Violet (A)	LGE	1-5	G Norrie
Mar 18	Forfar United (A)	LGE	2-2	Tucker, Dom Blair
Mar 25	Arbroath Victoria (H)	LGE	2-3	G Norrie, K Egan
Apr 1	Downfield (A)	LGE	0-2	
Apr 8	Dundee North End (A)	LGE	0-2	
Apr 15	Blairgowrie (H)	LGE	0-3	
Apr 19	Scone Thistle (A)	LGE	2-1	R Norrie (2)
Apr 22	Forfar West End (H)	LGE	4-1	R Norrie (2), Roeleveld, Dom Blair
Apr 26	Lochee United (A)	LGE	1-4	R Norrie
Apr 29	Broughty Athletic (H)	LGE	1-2	Fraser
May 6	East Craigie (H)	LGE	4-2	R Norrie, Tucker, Hamilton (2)
May 17	Forfar United (H)	ELC QF	1-2	Roeleveld
May 20	Brechin Victoria (A)	LGE	2-2	J Neave (2)

PLAYING SQUAD & STATISTICS 2022/23

DOWNFIELD J.F.C.
Downfield Park, Dundee

	Age	LEAGUE Apps	Goals	CUPS Apps	Goals	ALL Apps	Goals
BREEN, Greg	21	15 (3)	6	3	1	18 (3)	7
BROWNE, Ross	31	18 (3)	2	5	0	23 (3)	2
COLQUHOUN, Jordan	29	12 (7)	4	3	1	15 (7)	5
COUPE, Connor	24	24 (5)	15	3 (1)	2	27 (6)	17
FARQUHARSON, John	37	15 (5)	2	(1)	0	15 (6)	2
GARDEN, Jordan	26	4 (3)	4	(1)	0	4 (4)	4
GARDEN, Morgan	18	8 (13)	3	1 (2)	0	9 (15)	3
GRAY, Corey	27	26	0	4	2	30	2
HAWES, Brandon	25	4 (4)	0	1 (1)	0	5 (5)	0
HAY, Mitchell	24	9 (13)	1	4 (2)	0	13 (15)	1
HEARN, Bruce	24	28 (2)	3	4 (1)	0	32 (3)	3
IRVINE, Logan	24	2 (4)	0	-	-	2 (4)	0
LUMSDEN, Jayden	19	(2)	0	-	-	(2)	0
MACLEOD, Connor	28	7 (5)	1	1	0	8 (5)	1
MCARTHUR, Michael	22	5 (1)	0	1	0	6 (1)	0
MCARTNEY, Liam	31	30	36	4 (1)	4	34 (1)	40
MCCLEARY, Callum	22	13 (18)	7	2	0	15 (18)	7
MCPHEE, Steven	32	27	5	6	1	33	6
NORRIE, Gordon	31	(6)	1	1 (1)	0	1 (7)	1
ROBERTSON, Fergus (GK)	19	4 (1)	0	1	0	5 (1)	0
RODGER, Grant	22	28 (2)	3	5	0	33 (2)	3
ROY, Richard	36	3 (5)	1	(1)	0	3 (6)	1
SAMUEL, Smith (GK)	18	1	0	-	-	1	0
SMITH, Robert	38	25 (2)	1	3 (2)	0	28 (4)	1
SNOWDON, Jonny	34	1	0	-	-	1	0
SORLEY, Gavin (GK)	35	2	0	1	0	3	0
STEWART, Mark (GK)	37	24	0	4	0	28	0
STORRIER, Ross	31	11 (6)	0	1 (2)	0	12 (8)	0
THOMSON, Gavin	28	(1)	0	-	-	(1)	0
TIMMONS, Jordan	32	30 (1)	0	5	1	35 (1)	1
TURNER, Finlay	-	(1)	0	-	-	(1)	0
VAN DER TOORN, Kyler	19	16 (12)	9	3 (2)	1	19 (14)	10
WATT, Khaelem (GK)	22	4 (1)	0	-	-	4 (1)	0

MATCH RESULTS 2022/23

Date	Opponent	Comp	Score	Scorers
Jul 23	East Craigie (H)	LGE	2-1	Mcartney, McCleary
Jul 27	Forfar United (A)	LGE	5-1	Coupe (3), Mcartney (2)
Aug 3	Kirriemuir Thistle (H)	LGE	2-3	J Garden (2)
Aug 6	Blairgowrie (A)	LGE	3-3	Coupe, Colquhoun, Hearn
Aug 10	Brechin Victoria (H)	LGE	5-2	Mcartney (3), J Garden, Hearn
Aug 13	Lochee United (H)	LGE	0-0	
Aug 17	Broughty Athletic (A)	LGE	1-3	Roy
Aug 20	Dundee North End (H)	LGE	1-2	Mcartney
Aug 24	Dundee St James (A)	LGE	6-0	Mcartney, Coupe, J Garden, van der Toorn (2), McCleary
Aug 27	Dyce (H)	SJC R1	3-2	Colquhoun, Mcartney, van der Toorn
Sep 3	Forfar West End (A)	LGE	4-3	Rodger, Hearn, Coupe, Mcartney
Sep 17	Scone Thistle (H)	LGE	3-1	Coupe, Mcartney, Breen
Oct 1	Letham (A)	LGE	3-1	Coupe (2), McPhee
Oct 8	Dundee St James (H)	IRC R2	6-2	Coupe (2), Gray, Mcartney, Timmons, McPhee
Oct 15	Coupar Angus (A)	LGE	2-0	Breen, Mcartney
Oct 22	Arbroath Victoria (H)	LGE	4-2	Mcartney (3), van der Toorn
Oct 29	Blairgowrie (H)	LGE	4-0	Mcartney (2), van der Toorn, M Garden
Nov 5	Tayport (A)	LGE	4-0	Coupe, McPhee, Mcartney (2)
Nov 12	Carnoustie Panmure (H)	LGE	1-1	Mcartney
Nov 26	East Craigie (A)	LGE	3-0	Mcartney (3)
Dec 3	Lochee Harp (H)	LGE	2-1	Mcartney, Rodger
Jan 28	Broughty Athletic (H)	LGE	3-1	McPhee, Mcartney (2)
Feb 4	Lochee United (A)	LGE	3-1	Coupe, Mcartney (2)
Feb 11	Maud (A)	IRC R3	1-0	Gray
Feb 25	Dundee North End (A)	LGE	2-0	Mcartney (2)
Mar 4	Forfar West End (H)	LGE	9-0	Colquhoun (2), Rodger, Breen, Mcartney, van der Toorn, Farquharson, McCleary (2)
Mar 11	Scone Thistle (A)	LGE	5-1	Breen, van der Toorn (3), Farquharson
Mar 18	Broughty Athletic (A)	IRC QF	3-2	Mcartney (2), Breen
Mar 25	Lochee Harp (A)	LGE	6-1	McCleary (2), Browne (2), Breen, Colquhoun
Apr 1	Coupar Angus (H)	LGE	2-0	Mcartney, Breen
Apr 8	Arbroath Victoria (A)	LGE	2-1	van der Toorn, Coupe
Apr 15	Letham (H)	LGE	3-1	McPhee (2), Norrie
Apr 19	Forfar United (H)	LGE	2-4	Mcartney (2)
Apr 22	Carnoustie Panmure (A)	LGE	1-0	Coupe
Apr 26	Dundee Violet (A)	LGE	5-1	Coupe (2), Macleod, Mcartney, M Garden
Apr 29	Carnoustie Panmure (H)	IRC SF	0-3	
May 6	Tayport (H)	LGE	1-3	Mcartney
May 10	Brechin Victoria (A)	LGE	1-0	Hay
May 13	Kirriemuir Thistle (A)	LGE	0-1	
May 15	Carnoustie Panmure (H)	ELC R2	0-1	
May 17	Dundee Violet (H)	LGE	3-1	McCleary, M Garden, Smith
May 27	Dundee St James (H)	LGE	1-1	Mcartney

DUNDEE NORTH END J.F.C.
North End Park, Dundee

	Age	LEAGUE		CUPS		ALL	
		Apps	Goals	Apps	Goals	Apps	Goals
ALLAN, Jack	23	27 (5)	0	9 (2)	1	36 (7)	1
BALLANTINE, Andy	42	13	0	2	0	15	0
BELL, Aaron	19	1 (7)	0	-	-	1 (7)	0
BOLLAN, Luc	23	4 (4)	2	7	1	11 (4)	3
BRITTON, Ben	-	23 (4)	2	4 (1)	2	27 (5)	4
DEASLEY, Bryan	35	8 (2)	5	2 (1)	0	10 (3)	5
DEVINE, Frankie	26	29 (1)	16	9 (2)	1	38 (3)	17
EMMETT, David	18	(1)	0	-	-	(1)	0
FERRIE, Neal (GK)	42	3	0	4	0	7	0
GARDEN, Jordan	26	16 (5)	13	5 (3)	3	21 (8)	16
GIBB, Liam	25	25	1	10	1	35	2
GIBSON, Millar	-	8 (9)	2	2 (1)	1	10 (10)	3
JAMIESON, Ross	23	28 (2)	3	8 (2)	0	36 (4)	3
LAW, Stefan	26	9 (9)	6	1 (2)	0	10 (11)	6
LORNIE, R	-	1 (2)	0	-	-	1 (2)	0
LUNAN, Paul	41	3	0	1	0	4	0
MACLEOD, Connor	28	7 (1)	4	2 (1)	0	9 (2)	4
MALONE, Robert	33	2 (2)	0	-	-	2 (2)	0
MCCABE, Owen	26	12 (12)	4	2 (6)	3	14 (18)	7
MCCORD, J	-	1 (1)	0	-	-	1 (1)	0
MCCORD, Ryan	34	14 (3)	0	8	1	22 (3)	1
MCKELVIE, Aidan	19	9 (4)	0	2 (1)	0	11 (5)	0
MCKENNA, Stuart	24	(1)	0	-	-	(1)	0
MCLAUGHLIN, Josh	22	13 (6)	12	4 (4)	3	17 (10)	15
MCNAUGHTON, Kevin	41	2 (1)	0	-	-	2 (1)	0
MONTGOMERY, Jamie	27	17 (4)	8	9 (1)	5	26 (5)	13
RICE, Brian	23	28	3	10	3	38	6
RICHARDSON, Jamie	18	8 (1)	7	5	2	13 (1)	9
RITCHIE, Reece	32	3 (4)	2	2 (1)	1	5 (5)	3
ROLLO, Kris	36	22 (2)	1	2 (2)	0	24 (4)	1
SMITH, Ryan	24	24 (8)	2	4 (4)	1	28 (12)	3
THAIN, Gary (GK)	36	33 (1)	0	7	0	40 (1)	0
THOMAS, Archie	24	3	1	-	-	3	1
TOSHNEY, Lewis	31	(2)	0	-	-	(2)	0

MATCH RESULTS 2022/23

Date	Opponent	Comp	Score	Scorers
Jul 23	Lochee Harp (H)	LGE	2-1	Law, B Mudie o.g.
Jul 27	Coupar Angus (A)	LGE	3-1	Macleod (2), Devine
Jul 30	Tayport (A)	LGE	2-1	Law, Devine
Aug 3	Arbroath Victoria (H)	LGE	0-0	
Aug 6	Carnoustie Panmure (H)	LGE	2-2	Britton, Thomas
Aug 10	Dundee Violet (H)	LGE	8-0	Deasley (3), Gibb, Law (2), McCabe, Devine
Aug 13	Forfar United (A)	LGE	4-2	Deasley, Devine, Gibson, L Godfrey o.g.
Aug 17	East Craigie (H)	LGE	1-2	Rollo
Aug 20	Downfield (A)	LGE	2-1	Devine (2)
Aug 24	Kirriemuir Thistle (H)	LGE	1-3	Deasley
Aug 27	Deveronside (H)	SJC R1	1-0	McLaughlin
Sep 3	Blairgowrie (H)	LGE	4-3	Garden (2), Macleod, McLaughlin
Sep 17	Brechin Victoria (A)	LGE	2-1	Jamieson, Montgomery
Sep 24	Kirkintilloch Rob Roy (A)	SJC R2	0-3	
Oct 1	Broughty Athletic (H)	LGE	1-2	Macleod
Oct 8	Tayport (H)	LGE	1-0	Devine
Oct 15	Dundee St James (H)	LGE	4-0	Rice (2), Garden, Smith
Oct 22	Forfar United (H)	LGE	6-1	Devine (3), Montgomery (2), Garden
Oct 29	Lochee United (A)	IRC R2	4-3	Montgomery, Garden, Devine, Smith
Nov 5	Forfar West End (A)	LGE	2-1	Montgomery, McLaughlin
Nov 12	Scone Thistle (H)	LGE	11-3	McLaughlin (4), Garden (4), Law, McCabe (2)
Nov 19	Letham (A)	LGE	2-1	Jamieson, Garden
Nov 26	Lochee Harp (A)	LGE	4-0	McLaughlin, Devine, Montgomery, Ritchie
Dec 3	Lochee United (A)	LGE	1-3	D Higgins o.g.
Jan 14	Carnoustie Panmure (A)	LGE	0-4	
Jan 28	East Craigie (A)	LGE	2-2	Devine (2)
Feb 4	Forfar West End (H)	LGE	3-0	Montgomery, Law, Devine
Feb 11	Stonehaven (A)	IRC R3	3-0	Rice, Montgomery, Gibb
Feb 18	Kirriemuir Thistle (A)	LGE	2-1	Devine, Montgomery
Feb 22	Blairgowrie (A)	ELC R1	4-3	Ritchie, Gibson, Montgomery, Allan
Feb 25	Downfield (H)	LGE	0-2	
Mar 4	Blairgowrie (A)	LGE	5-0	McLaughlin (2), McCabe, Bollan, Gibson
Mar 18	East Craigie (H)	IRC QF	3-1	McCabe, McLaughlin, R McCord
Mar 25	Lochee United (H)	LGE	4-1	McLaughlin (3), Garden
Apr 1	Dundee St James (A)	LGE	0-0	
Apr 8	Coupar Angus (H)	LGE	2-0	Richardson, Ritchie
Apr 15	Broughty Athletic (A)	LGE	3-1	Garden, Devine, Richardson
Apr 19	Dundee Violet (A)	LGE	4-0	Garden, Rice, Jamieson, Richardson
Apr 22	Scone Thistle (A)	LGE	1-2	Richardson
Apr 26	Arbroath Victoria (A)	LGE	6-1	Richardson (2), Montgomery, Garden, Smith, Bollan
Apr 29	Hermes (H)	IRC SF	2-1	Bollan, Richardson
May 3	Lochee United (H)	ELC R2	2-0	McCabe, Richardson
May 6	Letham (H)	LGE	0-1	
May 10	Arbroath Victoria (A)	ELC QF	6-2	Rice, Montgomery (2), Britton (2), Garden
May 13	Brechin Victoria (H)	LGE	2-0	Britton, Richardson
May 20	Carnoustie Panmure (H)	IRC F	4-1	Garden, McCabe, Rice, McLaughlin
May 31	Carnoustie Panmure (A)	ELC SF	0-2	

DUNDEE ST JAMES J.F.C.
Fairfield Park, Dundee

	Age	LEAGUE Apps	LEAGUE Goals	CUPS Apps	CUPS Goals	ALL Apps	ALL Goals
ABBOT, Steven	22	23 (3)	7	1	0	24 (3)	7
ADAM, Grant (GK)	32	3	0	-	-	3	0
ADEMUWAGUN, Jomi	23	4 (6)	0	2	0	6 (6)	0
AKINSOLA, Abdul Martin	21	5 (5)	0	(2)	0	5 (7)	0
BISGROVE, Connor	19	5 (10)	1	2 (1)	0	7 (11)	1
BOYLAN, David (GK)	20	4	0	1	0	5	0
BUCHAN, Sandy	20	35 (1)	6	3	0	38 (1)	6
BURRY, Ryan	26	14 (1)	1	-	-	14 (1)	1
CARLYLE, Richard	32	5	0	-	-	5	0
CARNEGIE, Ross	31	3	0	-	-	3	0
CLARK, Stephen	28	6 (1)	0	-	-	6 (1)	0
CORBITT, Ryan	21	3	0	-	-	3	0
COVENTRY, Sy	19	3	1	-	-	3	1
CUSHNIE, Greig	34	5	0	-	-	5	0
DE FRANCO, Chris	30	(8)	0	-	-	(8)	0
DOBBIE, Jackson	21	3	0	-	-	3	0
FERGUSON, Zain	20	27 (2)	1	3	0	30 (2)	1
HEGGIE, Barry	40	1 (4)	0	-	-	1 (4)	0
HIGGINS, Dylan	21	6	3	-	-	6	3
ILUPEJCI, Clinton	23	(4)	0	1	0	1 (4)	0
KELLY, Sean	31	6 (2)	0	2	0	8 (2)	0
KENNETH, Ryan	30	9	0	3	0	12	0
MARTIN, Alex	35	1 (5)	0	-	-	1 (5)	0
MARTIN, Steve	32	4 (3)	0	-	-	4 (3)	0
MCCANN, Jamie	20	13 (3)	7	2	0	15 (3)	7
MCCORMACK, Cameron	21	8 (7)	2	1	0	9 (7)	2
MCCRORY, Mark	21	30	2	3	0	33	2
MCLAREN, Cavan	20	7 (8)	4	(2)	0	7 (10)	4
MCLAUGHLIN, Josh	22	6	3	-	-	6	3
MCMILLAN-COLLETT, Jacob	19	4 (1)	0	-	-	4 (1)	0
MITCHELL, Callum	26	14 (1)	2	2	3	16 (1)	5
MORRIS, Joe	19	1 (11)	0	(3)	0	1 (14)	0
MURRAY, Keir	21	17 (3)	1	1	0	18 (3)	1
NSIMBI, Ivan	23	4 (5)	0	-	-	4 (5)	0
PIGGOT, Logan	20	24 (2)	2	1	0	25 (2)	2
RITCHIE, Scott	32	6 (2)	0	(1)	0	6 (3)	0
SKENE, Robert	32	19 (1)	0	3	0	22 (1)	0
SMITH, Dan	32	3	0	-	-	3	0
SMITH, Elliot (GK)	24	28	0	2 (1)	0	30 (1)	0
SMITH, Pat	27	4	0	-	-	4	0
TAYLOR, Jay	22	13	0	-	-	13	0
WIGHTON, Drew	22	9 (1)	0	-	-	9 (1)	0
WILLIAMS, Lawrence	20	2 (7)	0	-	-	2 (7)	0

* Players with less than 3 appearances not displayed due to size of squad.

Date	Opponent	Comp	Score	Scorers
Jul 23	Coupar Angus (H)	LGE	2-3	McLaughlin, S Buchan
Jul 27	Arbroath Victoria (A)	LGE	1-4	McLaughlin
Jul 30	Carnoustie Panmure (A)	LGE	0-4	
Aug 3	Tayport (H)	LGE	0-3	
Aug 6	Dundee Violet (H)	LGE	3-4	McLaughlin, Abbot (2)
Aug 10	East Craigie (A)	LGE	0-3	
Aug 13	Kirriemuir Thistle (A)	LGE	1-3	J McCann
Aug 17	Forfar United (H)	LGE	4-0	Abbot, J McCann (2), Piggot
Aug 20	Blairgowrie (A)	LGE	1-3	Ian Plenderleith o.g.
Aug 24	Downfield (H)	LGE	0-6	
Aug 27	St Anthonys (H)	SJC R1	0-5	
Sep 3	Brechin Victoria (H)	LGE	4-0	McCrory, Abbot, J McCann, Ferguson
Sep 17	Broughty Athletic (A)	LGE	0-5	
Sep 24	Kirriemuir Thistle (H)	ELC R2	1-4	Mitchell
Oct 1	Lochee United (H)	LGE	1-3	J McCann
Oct 8	Downfield (A)	IRC R2	2-6	Mitchell (2)
Oct 15	Dundee North End (A)	LGE	0-4	
Oct 22	Forfar West End (H)	LGE	1-0	S Buchan
Oct 29	Kirriemuir Thistle (H)	LGE	3-6	McLaren (3)
Nov 5	Scone Thistle (A)	LGE	1-3	J McCann
Nov 12	Letham (H)	LGE	1-4	McCrory
Nov 19	Lochee Harp (A)	LGE	1-1	McLaren
Nov 26	Coupar Angus (A)	LGE	1-5	Dale McIntosh o.g.
Jan 7	Carnoustie Panmure (H)	LGE	1-7	Bisgrove
Feb 4	Lochee Harp (H)	LGE	3-1	Mitchell, S Buchan, Burry
Feb 11	Arbroath Victoria (H)	LGE	2-2	Coventry, J McCann
Feb 18	Scone Thistle (H)	LGE	2-2	S Buchan, Murray
Feb 25	Blairgowrie (H)	LGE	2-1	Abbot, S Buchan
Mar 4	Brechin Victoria (A)	LGE	2-1	Piggot, McCormack
Mar 18	Lochee United (A)	LGE	2-4	Mitchell, Murdoch
Apr 1	Dundee North End (H)	LGE	0-0	
Apr 8	Forfar West End (A)	LGE	3-1	Higgins, Abbot, McCormack
Apr 15	Forfar United (A)	LGE	2-2	Abbot, S Buchan
Apr 19	Tayport (A)	LGE	1-0	Higgins
Apr 22	Letham (A)	LGE	0-3	
Apr 29	Dundee Violet (A)	LGE	1-1	Higgins
May 10	Broughty Athletic (H)	LGE	0-7	
May 13	East Craigie (H)	LGE	0-2	
May 27	Downfield (A)	LGE	1-1	M Cavin

DUNDEE VIOLET J.F.C.
Glenesk Park, Dundee

	Age	LEAGUE		CUPS		ALL	
		Apps	Goals	Apps	Goals	Apps	Goals
ADAMS, Jamie (GK)	-	8 (1)	0	1	0	9 (1)	0
BEATTIE, D (GK)	-	3	0	-	-	3	0
BENVIE, Aidan	25	20 (8)	10	2	0	22 (8)	10
BOYLE, Paddy	20	3 (6)	2	-	-	3 (6)	2
BREEN, Greg	21	10	8	1	0	11	8
BURNETT, Fraser (GK)	21	9	0	-	-	9	0
CUNNINGHAM, Thomas	18	11 (8)	5	(1)	1	11 (9)	6
DEWAR, Angus	19	7 (1)	2	1 (1)	1	8 (2)	3
HARKIN, Jay	19	6 (2)	2	-	-	6 (2)	2
HEGGIE, Bradie	27	12	0	-	-	12	0
HORNSHAW, Lewis	18	22 (7)	0	3	0	25 (7)	0
HOUSTON, Greg	31	11 (6)	4	1 (2)	0	12 (8)	4
IRANKUNDA, Patrick (GK)	28	13	0	1	0	14	0
IRONS, Robbie	28	10 (4)	2	1 (1)	0	11 (5)	2
IRVINE, Logan	24	21 (4)	1	2	0	23 (4)	1
JOHNSTON, Derek	23	25 (2)	1	2	0	27 (2)	1
KELLY, Andy	24	28 (2)	9	2 (1)	0	30 (3)	9
KELLY, Callum	-	1 (2)	0	-	-	1 (2)	0
LAWRIE, James	22	22 (8)	0	2	0	24 (8)	0
LOCKHART, Aiden	18	7 (22)	1	(2)	0	7 (24)	1
LORENTE, Aidan	20	16	1	1	0	17	1
MADDISON, Rhys	-	2 (1)	0	-	-	2 (1)	0
MCLAUGHLIN, Paul	-	1 (5)	0	-	-	1 (5)	0
MCQUILLAN, Ruari	20	1 (2)	0	-	-	1 (2)	0
MILLER, Lewis (GK)	-	2	0	1	0	3	0
RONAN, Brad	28	8 (2)	0	1	0	9 (2)	0
ROSS, Cammy	22	19 (2)	7	1 (1)	0	20 (3)	7
SCOBIE, Ryan	23	19 (1)	1	2 (1)	0	21 (2)	1
SMITH, Kyle	19	3 (3)	0	(1)	0	3 (4)	0
SMITH, Thomas	-	3 (3)	1	-	-	3 (3)	1
SZPAK, Jayce	-	1 (9)	0	-	-	1 (9)	0
TAYLOR, Jay	22	7 (5)	0	1 (1)	0	8 (6)	0
TENNANT, Christopher	-	13 (8)	0	2	0	15 (8)	0
TIMMONS, Jamie	21	26 (2)	3	3	0	29 (2)	3
WILL, Greg	20	2 (1)	0	(1)	0	2 (2)	0
WILSON, Barry	27	21 (8)	2	2	0	23 (8)	2

* Players with less than 3 appearances not displayed due to size of squad.

Date	Opponent	Comp	Score	Scorers
Jul 23	Blairgowrie (A)	LGE	2-0	Breen (2)
Jul 27	Brechin Victoria (A)	LGE	1-1	Breen
Jul 30	Lochee United (A)	LGE	0-0	
Aug 3	Broughty Athletic (A)	LGE	0-2	
Aug 6	Dundee St James (A)	LGE	4-3	B Wilson, Breen (3)
Aug 10	Dundee North End (A)	LGE	0-8	
Aug 13	Scone Thistle (H)	LGE	1-0	Cunningham
Aug 17	Forfar West End (A)	LGE	1-2	Breen
Aug 20	Lochee Harp (H)	LGE	3-0	Timmons (2), Irons
Aug 27	Culter (H)	SJC R1	1-4	
Sep 3	Coupar Angus (A)	LGE	4-2	Scobie, Brian Harris o.g., Irons, Breen
Sep 17	Arbroath Victoria (H)	LGE	0-1	
Sep 24	Coupar Angus (H)	ELC R2	0-2	
Oct 1	Tayport (A)	LGE	2-2	Ross, Houston
Oct 8	Scone Thistle (H)	IRC R2	6-3	
Oct 22	East Craigie (A)	LGE	1-5	Lockhart
Oct 29	Letham (A)	LGE	0-2	
Nov 5	Forfar United (H)	LGE	1-3	A Kelly
Nov 12	Kirriemuir Thistle (A)	LGE	3-8	Ross, Dewar, Gary Archibald o.g.
Nov 26	Blairgowrie (H)	LGE	4-3	A Kelly, Houston (2), Logan Thoms o.g.
Dec 3	Forfar West End (H)	LGE	3-2	Houston, Dewar, Lorente
Jan 28	Forfar United (A)	LGE	2-6	Irvine, A Kelly
Feb 4	Scone Thistle (A)	LGE	3-1	A Kelly (3)
Feb 11	Glentanar (H)	IRC R3	3-3ᵖ	Dewar, Cunningham
Feb 18	Letham (H)	LGE	1-7	Benvie
Feb 25	Lochee Harp (A)	LGE	5-2	Benvie (3), B Wilson, A Kelly
Mar 4	Coupar Angus (H)	LGE	5-1	Johnston, Ross, A Kelly (2), Benvie
Mar 11	Arbroath Victoria (A)	LGE	4-1	Benvie (2), Ross, Timmons
Mar 25	Carnoustie Panmure (A)	LGE	2-3	Ross, Harkin
Apr 1	Broughty Athletic (H)	LGE	1-2	Ross
Apr 8	East Craigie (H)	LGE	1-3	Benvie
Apr 15	Brechin Victoria (H)	LGE	0-1	
Apr 19	Dundee North End (H)	LGE	0-4	
Apr 22	Kirriemuir Thistle (H)	LGE	3-3	T Smith, Cunningham (2)
Apr 26	Downfield (H)	LGE	1-5	Ross
Apr 29	Dundee St James (H)	LGE	1-1	Harkin
May 6	Lochee United (H)	LGE	1-3	Boyle
May 10	Carnoustie Panmure (H)	LGE	1-9	Benvie
May 17	Downfield (A)	LGE	1-3	Benvie
May 27	Tayport (H)	LGE	3-3	Boyle, Cunningham (2)

PLAYING SQUAD & STATISTICS 2022/23

EAST CRAIGIE J.F.C.
Craigie Park, Dundee

	Age	LEAGUE		CUPS		ALL	
		Apps	Goals	Apps	Goals	Apps	Goals
BAH, Mohamed	19	1 (1)	0	(1)	0	1 (2)	0
BELL, Ross	23	4 (3)	0	-	-	4 (3)	0
BLACKLEY, Ben	18	(1)	0	-	-	(1)	0
BROWN, Adam	24	32 (1)	8	9	0	41 (1)	8
CAMERON, Lee	27	29 (4)	7	10	3	39 (4)	10
CHRISTIE, Cameron	22	29 (4)	2	8 (1)	0	37 (5)	2
CONSTABLE, Paul	38	12 (5)	5	5 (4)	2	17 (9)	7
CONWAY, Jordan	22	23 (4)	10	5 (3)	2	28 (7)	12
COVENTRY, Sy	19	2 (13)	3	-	-	2 (13)	3
DAVIE, Aaron	23	(4)	0	-	-	(4)	0
DUGUID, Jude	18	(3)	0	-	-	(3)	0
DUNN, Liam (GK)	26	35	0	10	0	45	0
FAULKNER, Rory	24	29	23	10	5	39	28
FORSYTH, Callum (GK)	18	(1)	0	-	-	(1)	0
GARRICK, Ben	20	10 (5)	8	3 (2)	1	13 (7)	9
HARRIS, Brian	21	1 (3)	0	-	-	1 (3)	0
HOWETT, Conan	26	2	0	-	-	2	0
MARSHALL, Aidan	20	27 (1)	0	7 (2)	0	34 (3)	0
MCCAFFERTY, Elliot	19	(2)	0	-	-	(2)	0
MCCONNACHIE, Stewart	42	22 (7)	12	7 (1)	1	29 (8)	13
MCDONALD, Andrew	36	19 (7)	0	4 (2)	1	23 (9)	1
MCNAUGHTON, Ross	20	24 (7)	7	7 (1)	2	31 (8)	9
MORAN, Jamie	18	10 (9)	2	(2)	0	10 (11)	2
MORAN, Paul	25	31 (3)	1	9	1	40 (3)	2
MUDIE, Chris	21	32 (1)	4	9	1	41 (1)	5
PATULLO, Dylan	19	(5)	0	-	-	(5)	0
REEKIE, Josh	18	6 (3)	1	2	0	8 (3)	1
ROLLO, Jack	20	15 (1)	0	5	0	20 (1)	0
ROSS, Iain (GK)	39	1	0	-	-	1	0

Date	Opponent	Comp	Score	Scorers
Jul 23	Downfield (A)	LGE	1-2	Cameron
Jul 27	Blairgowrie (H)	LGE	2-1	Cameron, McConnachie
Jul 30	Broughty Athletic (H)	LGE	0-0	
Aug 3	Brechin Victoria (A)	LGE	3-0	Conway, Coventry, J Moran
Aug 6	Lochee United (A)	LGE	3-5	Conway, Faulkner (2)
Aug 10	Dundee St James (H)	LGE	3-0	Brown, Faulkner, McNaughton
Aug 13	Forfar West End (H)	LGE	2-1	Conway, Faulkner
Aug 17	Dundee North End (A)	LGE	2-1	Brown, Faulkner
Aug 20	Letham (H)	LGE	3-1	Faulkner, P Moran, Cameron
Aug 24	Scone Thistle (A)	LGE	2-0	Mudie, Faulkner
Aug 27	Cambuslang Rangers (H)	SJC R1	2-1	Constable, Faulkner
Sep 3	Lochee Harp (A)	LGE	10-1	Mudie, Constable, Faulkner (2), Cameron, McConnachie (4), Coventry
Sep 17	Coupar Angus (H)	LGE	4-0	Brown (2), Faulkner (2)
Sep 24	Broughty Athletic (H)	SJC R2	3-2	Faulkner (2), P Moran
Oct 1	Arbroath Victoria (A)	LGE	3-0	McConnachie, Faulkner, Brown
Oct 8	Brechin Victoria (A)	IRC R2	2-1	McNaughton, Cameron
Oct 15	Carnoustie Panmure (A)	LGE	0-3	
Oct 22	Dundee Violet (A)	LGE	5-1	Christie, Constable (2), Conway, Mudie
Oct 29	Ellon United (H)	SJC R3	3-1	Constable, Conway, Faulkner
Nov 12	Forfar United (A)	LGE	3-1	McConnachie, Brown, Faulkner
Nov 19	Kirriemuir Thistle (H)	LGE	3-1	Faulkner, Constable, McConnachie
Nov 26	Downfield (H)	LGE	0-3	
Dec 3	St Rochs (H)	SJC R4	1-1ᵖ	McDonald
Jan 7	Broughty Athletic (A)	LGE	2-1	B Sivewright o.g., Faulkner
Jan 14	Lochee United (H)	LGE	1-2	Faulkner
Jan 28	Dundee North End (H)	LGE	2-2	Constable, Garrick
Feb 4	Tayport (A)	LGE	1-0	McNaughton
Feb 11	Shotts Bon Accord (H)	SJC QF	2-1	Mudie, Faulkner
Feb 18	Sunnybank (A)	IRC R3	2-0	McNaughton, Conway
Feb 25	Letham (A)	LGE	2-0	Conway (2)
Mar 4	Lochee Harp (H)	LGE	5-1	Christie, Faulkner, Garrick (2), Reekie
Mar 15	Letham (A)	ELC R1	2-3	Cameron, Garrick
Mar 18	Dundee North End (A)	IRC QF	1-3	Cameron
Mar 25	Forfar United (H)	LGE	1-2	Faulkner
Apr 1	Carnoustie Panmure (H)	LGE	1-1	Cameron
Apr 8	Dundee Violet (A)	LGE	3-1	McNaughton, McConnachie, Garrick
Apr 16	Rutheglen Glencairn (A)	SJC SF	1-1ᵖ	McConnachie
Apr 19	Brechin Victoria (H)	LGE	3-0	McNaughton, Conway, Faulkner
Apr 22	Blairgowrie (A)	LGE	6-1	J Moran, Faulkner, McConnachie, Brown, McNaughton, Coventry
Apr 26	Tayport (H)	LGE	4-0	Cameron, Faulkner (2), Conway
Apr 29	Kirriemuir Thistle (A)	LGE	2-2	Faulkner, McConnachie
May 6	Coupar Angus (A)	LGE	2-4	Cameron, Garrick
May 10	Scone Thistle (H)	LGE	2-2	McConnachie, Mudie
May 13	Dundee St James (A)	LGE	2-0	McNaughton, Garrick
May 17	Arbroath Victoria (H)	LGE	3-1	Conway (2), Brown
May 20	Forfar West End (A)	LGE	3-3	Garrick (2), McNaughton

FORFAR UNITED J.F.C.
Guthrie Park, Forfar

	Age	LEAGUE		CUPS		ALL	
		Apps	Goals	Apps	Goals	Apps	Goals
BAILLIE, Liam	19	(2)	0	-		(2)	0
BALFOUR, Keir	19	20 (7)	2	4	0	24 (7)	2
BELL, Ross	23	11 (2)	2	3	1	14 (2)	3
BIRSE, Connor	29	23 (3)	15	3	2	26 (3)	17
BOATH, Calum	25	7 (5)	1	(2)	0	7 (7)	1
CAMERON, Adam (GK)	20	2 (2)	0	1	0	3 (2)	0
CLARK, Kyle	25	3	0	-	-	3	0
CRIGHTON, Kieren	25	26 (2)	9	2	2	28 (2)	11
CRIGHTON, Rory	34	10 (2)	0	(1)	0	10 (3)	0
CROWE, Jamie	23	21 (1)	0	2	0	23 (1)	0
DAVIDSON, Robbie	22	9 (7)	0	1 (3)	0	10 (10)	0
FISHER, Guy	20	10 (5)	0	3	0	13 (5)	0
FLETCHER, Dean	30	8 (2)	1	2	0	10 (2)	1
FLETCHER, Jake	18	1 (8)	0	(1)	0	1 (9)	0
FLETCHER, Nick	20	22 (4)	6	3 (1)	1	25 (5)	7
FOTHERINGHAM, Blair	25	3	0	-	-	3	0
GODFREY, Liam	32	13 (4)	1	2	0	15 (4)	1
GOKALP, Cemi	18	1 (4)	0	1 (2)	1	2 (6)	1
GORDON, Josh	20	10 (9)	1	4	0	14 (9)	1
HOWIE, Cammy	30	1	0	-	-	1	0
KEMP, Fraser	22	6 (7)	5	1	0	7 (7)	5
KIDD, Evan	20	15 (9)	0	3 (1)	0	18 (10)	0
MITCHELL, Aaron	25	21 (10)	7	3	1	24 (10)	8
NISBET, Gary	37	23	0	2 (1)	0	25 (1)	0
RANSTEAD, Ben	22	18 (4)	0	1 (2)	0	19 (6)	0
REID, Fraser (GK)	26	2	0	1	0	3	0
REID, Max	27	23 (4)	2	2 (1)	0	25 (5)	2
SHAW, Jack (GK)	25	32	0	3	0	35	0
SIEVWRIGHT, Ross	35	6 (8)	0	1 (1)	0	7 (9)	0
SMITH, Danny	42	(1)	0	-	-	(1)	0
SMITH, Thomas	-	(2)	0	-	-	(2)	0
STIRTON, Ryan	26	20	0	3	0	23	0
WILLIAMS, Zack	27	22 (3)	0	4	0	26 (3)	0
YULE, Jay	21	7 (6)	7	-	-	7 (6)	7

Date	Opponent	Comp	Score	Scorers
Jul 23	Kirriemuir Thistle (A)	LGE	2-2	Kemp, K Crighton
Jul 27	Downfield (H)	LGE	1-5	K Crighton
Jul 30	Brechin Victoria (H)	LGE	4-0	Birse (2), D Fletcher, Yule
Aug 3	Blairgowrie (A)	LGE	0-2	
Aug 6	Broughty Athletic (A)	LGE	0-5	
Aug 10	Lochee United (H)	LGE	1-0	Birse
Aug 13	Dundee North End (H)	LGE	2-4	Birse, Gordon
Aug 17	Dundee St James (A)	LGE	0-4	
Aug 20	Scone Thistle (H)	LGE	4-2	W Laing o.g., Kemp (2), Mitchell
Aug 24	Forfar West End (A)	LGE	3-1	K Crighton (2), Birse
Aug 27	Lugar Boswell Th. (A)	SJC R1	2-3	Mitchell, Birse
Sep 3	Letham (A)	LGE	1-1	Boath
Sep 17	Lochee Harp (H)	LGE	2-1	Birse (2)
Sep 24	Forfar West End (H)	LGE	4-0	Mitchell, Godfrey, Balfour, R Hoon o.g.
Oct 1	Coupar Angus (A)	LGE	1-4	Kemp
Oct 8	Carnoustie Panmure (A)	IRC R2	1-2	Birse
Oct 15	Tayport (A)	LGE	0-8	
Oct 22	Dundee North End (A)	LGE	1-6	Balfour
Nov 5	Dundee Violet (A)	LGE	3-1	K Crighton, N Fletcher, Birse
Nov 12	East Craigie (H)	LGE	1-3	K Crighton
Nov 26	Kirriemuir Thistle (H)	LGE	1-5	Birse
Dec 3	Arbroath Victoria (H)	LGE	1-3	Birse
Jan 7	Brechin Victoria (A)	LGE	3-1	Yule (2), M Reid
Jan 21	Lochee United (A)	LGE	0-2	
Jan 28	Dundee Violet (H)	LGE	6-2	Yule, Mitchell, Bell, M Reid, K Crighton, Birse
Feb 4	Arbroath Victoria (A)	LGE	2-1	Yule, N Fletcher
Feb 11	Blairgowrie (H)	LGE	0-4	
Feb 25	Tayport (H)	ELC R1	1-0	N Fletcher
Mar 4	Letham (H)	LGE	2-2	Birse, N Fletcher
Mar 11	Lochee Harp (A)	LGE	1-3	Mitchell
Mar 18	Coupar Angus (H)	LGE	2-2	N Fletcher, Mitchell
Mar 25	East Craigie (A)	LGE	2-1	Kemp, Mitchell
Apr 1	Tayport (H)	LGE	2-4	K Crighton, Bell
Apr 8	Carnoustie Panmure (A)	LGE	1-5	Yule
Apr 15	Dundee St James (H)	LGE	2-2	Birse, N Fletcher
Apr 19	Downfield (A)	LGE	4-2	N Fletcher, K Crighton, Yule, Birse
Apr 29	Scone Thistle (A)	LGE	1-1	Birse
May 3	Carnoustie Panmure (H)	LGE	0-4	
May 6	Broughty Athletic (H)	LGE	1-2	Mitchell
May 17	Coupar Angus (A)	ELC QF	2-1	K Crighton (2)
May 24	Broughty Athletic (A)	ELC SF	2-7	Gokalp, Bell

PLAYING SQUAD & STATISTICS 2022/23 *

FORFAR WEST END J.F.C.
Strathmore Park, Forfar

	Age	LEAGUE		CUPS		ALL	
		Apps	Goals	Apps	Goals	Apps	Goals
ANDERSON, Rory	18	1 (8)	1	-	-	1 (8)	1
ARCHER, Zac	29	8 (3)	2	1	0	9 (3)	2
BRANDER, Oliver	19	9	0	-	-	9	0
BUIK, Kyle	23	13	0	(1)	0	13 (1)	0
CHALMERS, Jack	18	4 (5)	0	-	-	4 (5)	0
CLARK, L	-	2 (1)	0	1	0	3 (1)	0
CLARKE, Justin	18	7 (4)	1	-	-	7 (4)	1
COBB, Aidan	18	(6)	0	1	0	1 (6)	0
FINDLAY, Liam	20	16 (8)	0	1	0	17 (8)	0
FINNIS, Richard	35	7	2	-	-	7	2
FLIGHT, Ross	23	16	0	1	0	17	0
FLYNN, Robbie	20	18 (1)	1	1	0	19 (1)	1
FOTHERINGHAM, Michael	31	6 (5)	1	2	0	8 (5)	1
FRASER, Rhys	22	19 (2)	0	1	0	20 (2)	0
GOURLAY, Barrie	32	9 (1)	0	-	-	9 (1)	0
GRAY, Owen	20	6 (1)	2	-	-	6 (1)	2
HAMPTON, Brett	30	23 (5)	6	2	0	25 (5)	6
HARKIN, Jay	19	15 (6)	2	1 (1)	1	16 (7)	3
HOON, Rhys	18	10 (2)	0	1 (1)	0	11 (3)	0
JONES, Liam	22	18 (13)	6	2	0	20 (13)	6
LAIRD, Hayden	23	(4)	0	2	0	2 (4)	0
LOCKHART, Owen	18	18 (7)	1	2 (1)	0	20 (8)	1
MATTHEWS, Fraser	23	23	0	2	0	25	0
MATTHEWS, Ross (GK)	21	21	0	2	0	23	0
MCKENNA, Stuart	24	3	0	-	-	3	0
MCLAUCHLAN, Robbie	21	9 (5)	1	2	0	11 (5)	1
MITCHELL, Munro	21	1 (3)	0	-	-	1 (3)	0
PENMAN, Murray	25	17 (2)	0	1	0	18 (2)	0
SAMSON, Ethan	21	8 (2)	3	-	-	8 (2)	3
SANCHEZ, Samuel	30	7 (1)	0	-	-	7 (1)	0
SHAND, Kyle (GK)	19	9	0	1	0	10	0
STEPHEN, Dylan	22	11	4	1	0	12	4
STEPHEN, Logan	18	19 (4)	1	2	0	21 (4)	1
STEWART, Kieron	21	7	0	1	0	8	0
TAYLOR, Harrison	19	13 (3)	1	(2)	0	13 (5)	1
WILSON, Owen	24	5	0	-	-	5	0
WINTER, Cameron (GK)	22	5	0	-	-	5	0
WOODCOCK, Connor	21	1 (8)	0	1 (1)	0	2 (9)	0
ZINKO, Igor	19	4	0	(1)	0	4 (1)	0

* Players with less than 4 appearances not displayed due to size of squad.

MATCH RESULTS 2022/23

Date	Opponent	Comp	Score	Scorers
Jul 23	Letham (H)	LGE	1-2	D Stephen
Jul 27	Lochee Harp (H)	LGE	2-1	D Stephen, Flynn
Jul 30	Arbroath Victoria (A)	LGE	2-2	Jones, Fotheringham
Aug 3	Coupar Angus (H)	LGE	3-2	Samson, Jones, Harkin
Aug 6	Tayport (H)	LGE	0-3	
Aug 10	Carnoustie Panmure (A)	LGE	1-4	Hampton
Aug 13	East Craigie (A)	LGE	1-2	Samson
Aug 17	Dundee Violet (H)	LGE	2-1	Harkin, Samson
Aug 20	Kirriemuir Thistle (A)	LGE	0-4	
Aug 24	Forfar United (H)	LGE	1-3	Hampton
Aug 27	Kilsyth Rangers (H)	SJC R1	1-4	Harkin
Sep 3	Downfield (H)	LGE	3-4	McLauchlan, D Stephen (2)
Sep 17	Blairgowrie (A)	LGE	1-0	Archer
Sep 24	Forfar United (A)	LGE	0-4	
Oct 1	Brechin Victoria (H)	LGE	2-0	Jones, Hampton
Oct 8	Kirriemuir Thistle (H)	IRC R2	1-3	Unknown
Oct 15	Lochee United (H)	LGE	1-2	Taylor
Oct 22	Dundee St James (A)	LGE	0-1	
Oct 29	Broughty Athletic (A)	LGE	0-5	
Nov 5	Dundee North End (H)	LGE	1-2	Lockhart
Nov 26	Letham (A)	LGE	0-2	
Dec 3	Dundee Violet (A)	LGE	2-3	Clarke, Archer
Dec 10	Lochee Harp (A)	LGE	0-7	
Jan 14	Tayport (A)	LGE	1-4	Hampton
Feb 4	Dundee North End (A)	LGE	0-3	
Feb 11	Scone Thistle (A)	LGE	1-4	L Stephen
Feb 18	Arbroath Victoria (A)	ELC R2	0-9	
Feb 25	Kirriemuir Thistle (H)	LGE	2-5	Hampton, Aleksander
Mar 4	Downfield (A)	LGE	0-9	
Mar 18	Brechin Victoria (A)	LGE	1-5	Gray
Mar 25	Broughty Athletic (H)	LGE	0-9	
Apr 1	Lochee United (A)	LGE	0-5	
Apr 8	Dundee St James (H)	LGE	1-3	Anderson
Apr 15	Arbroath Victoria (H)	LGE	2-3	Hampton, Gray
Apr 22	Coupar Angus (A)	LGE	1-4	Finnis
Apr 29	Blairgowrie (H)	LGE	1-5	Finnis
May 6	Scone Thistle (H)	LGE	0-1	
May 17	Carnoustie Panmure (H)	LGE	0-6	
May 20	East Craigie (H)	LGE	3-3	Jones (3)

PLAYING SQUAD & STATISTICS 2022/23

KIRRIEMUIR THISTLE J.F.C.
Westview Park, Kirriemuir

		LEAGUE		CUPS		ALL	
	Age	Apps	Goals	Apps	Goals	Apps	Goals
ARCHIBALD, Gary	33	30 (3)	8	4 (1)	0	34 (4)	8
BATCHELOR, Craig	27	24	29	4	4	28	33
BEEDIE, Ryan	24	11 (1)	1	1	0	12 (1)	1
BROWN, Darren (GK)	35	3 (2)	0	-	-	3 (2)	0
BURNS, Darryl (GK)	31	13 (1)	0	3	0	16 (1)	0
CHEW, Nathan	19	5 (11)	1	(1)	0	5 (12)	1
COUTTS, Lewis (GK)	22	7	0	1	0	8	0
DEGERNIER, Nathan	28	30 (1)	2	3	0	33 (1)	2
DUELL, Bryan	42	13 (19)	14	1 (3)	1	14 (22)	15
DUELL, Liam	19	30 (2)	6	4	0	34 (2)	6
FRASER, Adam	28	8 (4)	2	1	0	9 (4)	2
FULLERTON, Scott	28	(4)	1	(1)	0	(5)	1
GALLACHER, Robbie	23	24 (3)	2	4	0	28 (3)	2
GEORGE, Robbie	31	12	0	2 (1)	0	14 (1)	0
GORDON, Josh	20	1	0	1	0	2	0
HART, Daniel	20	1 (4)	0	(1)	0	1 (5)	0
HUTCHISON, Chris (GK)	35	1	0	-	-	1	0
KERRIGAN, Ryan	24	31 (1)	4	4 (1)	0	35 (2)	4
KINNEAR, Calum	28	34	2	5	1	39	3
MCKENNA, Stuart	24	1	0	-	-	1	0
MCNALLY, Stephen	39	23 (9)	2	4	0	27 (9)	2
OGG, Marc	29	19 (6)	1	3 (1)	0	22 (7)	1
RENNIE, Callum	29	17 (6)	1	2	0	19 (6)	1
RUSSELL, Stewart	34	24 (4)	13	3	0	27 (4)	13
SMITH, Adam	-	1 (5)	0	-	-	1 (5)	0
SMITH, Andy (GK)	23	12	0	1	0	13	0
STARKEY, Ben	23	14 (13)	9	3	0	17 (13)	9
TAYLOR, Harrison	19	(7)	0	(1)	0	(8)	0
WALLS, Andy	30	6 (4)	0	1 (1)	0	7 (5)	0
WILSON, Ben	21	1 (9)	1	(2)	0	1 (11)	1

Date	Opponent	Comp	Score	Scorers
Jul 23	Forfar United (H)	LGE	2-2	B Duell (2)
Jul 30	Blairgowrie (H)	LGE	3-2	Kerrigan, Russell, Batchelor
Aug 3	Downfield (A)	LGE	3-2	J Garden o.g., B Duell, Batchelor
Aug 6	Brechin Victoria (A)	LGE	4-2	Batchelor, Kerrigan, B Duell (2)
Aug 10	Broughty Athletic (H)	LGE	4-0	Russell, Archibald, Kinnear, Batchelor
Aug 13	Dundee St James (H)	LGE	3-1	Ogg, Batchelor, Starkey
Aug 17	Lochee United (A)	LGE	5-5	Gallacher, Batchelor (2), Archibald (2)
Aug 20	Forfar West End (H)	LGE	4-0	Batchelor (3), Starkey
Aug 24	Dundee North End (A)	LGE	3-1	Batchelor (2), Degernier
Aug 27	Broughty Athletic (H)	SJC R1	2-4	Batchelor, B Duell
Sep 3	Scone Thistle (A)	LGE	4-0	Batchelor (2), L Duell, B Duell
Sep 17	Letham (H)	LGE	2-2	B Duell (2)
Sep 24	Dundee St James (A)	ELC R2	4-1	Batchelor (3), Kinnear
Oct 1	Lochee Harp (A)	LGE	3-3	L Duell, Kerrigan, B Duell
Oct 8	Forfar West End (A)	IRC R2	3-1	Unknown
Oct 15	Arbroath Victoria (A)	LGE	1-2	Batchelor
Oct 22	Tayport (H)	LGE	4-1	Batchelor (2), Archibald, Kinnear
Oct 29	Dundee St James (A)	LGE	6-3	L Duell, B Duell, Batchelor (4)
Nov 5	Carnoustie Panmure (A)	LGE	0-3	
Nov 12	Dundee Violet (H)	LGE	8-3	Batchelor (3), Russell (3), Archibald, Degernier
Nov 19	East Craigie (A)	LGE	1-3	Russell
Nov 26	Forfar United (A)	LGE	5-1	Gallacher, L Duell (2), Starkey, Wilson
Dec 3	Coupar Angus (H)	LGE	4-1	Batchelor (2), Starkey (2)
Jan 21	Broughty Athletic (A)	LGE	2-3	S Diamond o.g., Batchelor
Feb 4	Coupar Angus (A)	LGE	2-2	Batchelor (2)
Feb 11	Hermes (A)	IRC R3	0-2	
Feb 18	Dundee North End (H)	LGE	1-2	Fullerton
Feb 25	Forfar West End (A)	LGE	5-2	Rennie, Fraser, Beedie, Chew, L Clark o.g.
Mar 4	Scone Thistle (H)	LGE	3-1	Russell (3)
Mar 11	Letham (A)	LGE	2-2	B Duell, Russell
Mar 18	Blairgowrie (A)	LGE	2-0	Russell, Fraser
Mar 25	Tayport (A)	LGE	2-3	L Duell, Archibald
Apr 1	Arbroath Victoria (H)	LGE	4-2	Starkey (2), B Duell (2)
Apr 8	Brechin Victoria (H)	LGE	2-1	Russell (2)
Apr 15	Lochee United (H)	LGE	0-4	
Apr 19	Carnoustie Panmure (H)	LGE	0-0	
Apr 22	Dundee Violet (A)	LGE	3-3	Starkey, Archibald, S McNally
Apr 29	East Craigie (H)	LGE	2-2	Starkey, Archibald
May 6	Lochee Harp (H)	LGE	2-1	Kerrigan, S McNally
May 13	Downfield (H)	LGE	1-0	B Duell
May 24	Carnoustie Panmure (H)	ELC QF	0-2	

LETHAM J.F.C.
Seven Acres Park, Perth

	Age	LEAGUE		CUPS		ALL	
		Apps	Goals	Apps	Goals	Apps	Goals
ALLAN, Lewis	28	27 (6)	4	2 (2)	0	29 (8)	4
BRIGHT, Aidan (GK)	23	34	0	5	0	39	0
BRUCE, Calum	24	1 (1)	0	-	-	1 (1)	0
CUNNINGHAM, Alan	25	27	3	2	1	29	4
DAVIDSON, Lewis	19	3 (7)	0	(2)	0	3 (9)	0
DEANE, Patrick	33	15 (5)	5	2	0	17 (5)	5
EDWARDS, Aidan	23	25 (1)	8	4	0	29 (1)	8
FERRIE, Sean	34	1 (10)	2	-	-	1 (10)	2
GALLETLY, Aaron	29	26 (3)	2	5	0	31 (3)	2
GALLETLY, Connor	26	9 (10)	5	2 (1)	1	11 (11)	6
HOWGATE, Nathan	19	4 (4)	0	1 (1)	0	5 (5)	0
HUTCHISON, Jack	23	29	4	5	1	34	5
KELLY, Daniel	32	1 (2)	0	-	-	1 (2)	0
KENNEDY, Nathan	28	13 (12)	0	(2)	0	13 (14)	0
MACKENZIE, Andrew	26	11 (2)	1	4	0	15 (2)	1
MANN, Stephen	33	23 (3)	1	1	0	24 (3)	1
MCCONNACHIE, Paul	24	14 (2)	1	(1)	0	14 (3)	1
MCKENZIE, Jamie	37	3 (5)	0	1	0	4 (5)	0
NICOL, Stuart	37	30	3	5	2	35	5
NJIE, Abi	34	1 (1)	3	-	-	1 (1)	3
PRZESLICA, Kacper	18	14 (14)	7	(2)	0	14 (16)	7
SANCHEZ, Samuel	30	9 (1)	0	2	0	11 (1)	0
SHAW, Mark	28	9 (11)	3	1	0	10 (11)	3
SIMPSON, Shaun	24	22	2	3	0	25	2
SIMPSON, Zak (GK)	-	(1)	0	-	-	(1)	0
SMART, Dale	27	19 (2)	7	3 (1)	0	22 (3)	7
SPENCE, Darren	22	1 (3)	1	1	0	2 (3)	1
STORRAR, Adam	36	19 (5)	1	4	0	23 (5)	1
STRONG, Aidan	22	3 (8)	0	1	1	4 (8)	1
WHITWORTH, Sean	35	2 (6)	0	-	-	2 (6)	0
WHYTE, Lawrence	-	(5)	1	-	-	(5)	1
WILKIE, James	23	1 (6)	0	-	-	1 (6)	0

Date	Opponent	Comp	Score	Scorers
Jul 23	Forfar West End (A)	LGE	2-1	A Galletly, Smart
Jul 27	Scone Thistle (H)	LGE	5-1	Edwards, C Galletly (2), Allan, Ferrie
Jul 30	Lochee Harp (H)	LGE	1-1	Smart
Aug 6	Coupar Angus (H)	LGE	7-0	Hutchison, Edwards (2), McConnachie, Deane, Shaw, Przeslica
Aug 10	Arbroath Victoria (A)	LGE	1-0	Deane
Aug 13	Carnoustie Panmure (A)	LGE	0-2	
Aug 17	Tayport (H)	LGE	0-1	
Aug 20	East Craigie (A)	LGE	1-3	Shaw
Aug 27	Burghead Thistle (H)	SJC R1	1-1p	Nicol
Sep 3	Forfar United (H)	LGE	1-1	A Galletly
Sep 17	Kirriemuir Thistle (A)	LGE	2-2	Spence, C Galletly
Sep 24	Newmachar United (A)	SJC R2	0-2	
Oct 1	Downfield (H)	LGE	1-3	Przeslica
Oct 8	Lochee Harp (A)	IRC R1	1-2	Strong
Oct 15	Brechin Victoria (H)	LGE	2-1	Allan, Shaw
Oct 22	Broughty Athletic (A)	LGE	1-1	Edwards
Oct 29	Dundee Violet (H)	LGE	2-0	Storrar, Mann
Nov 5	Lochee United (H)	LGE	0-7	
Nov 12	Dundee St James (A)	LGE	4-1	Smart (2), Hutchison, A Cunningham
Nov 19	Dundee North End (H)	LGE	1-2	Allan
Nov 26	Forfar West End (H)	LGE	2-0	Hutchison, Deane
Dec 3	Blairgowrie (A)	LGE	1-1	Nicol
Jan 7	Lochee Harp (A)	LGE	1-1	S Simpson
Jan 14	Coupar Angus (A)	LGE	3-2	Edwards (2), Allan
Jan 21	Arbroath Victoria (H)	LGE	0-1	
Jan 28	Tayport (A)	LGE	0-1	
Feb 4	Carnoustie Panmure (H)	LGE	0-3	
Feb 18	Dundee Violet (A)	LGE	7-1	Smart, Przeslica (3), Mackenzie, Whyte, C Galletly
Feb 25	East Craigie (H)	LGE	0-2	
Mar 4	Forfar United (A)	LGE	2-2	Edwards, Przeslica
Mar 11	Kirriemuir Thistle (H)	LGE	2-2	Hutchison, Smart
Mar 15	East Craigie (H)	ELC R1	3-2	C Galletly, Hutchison, A Cunningham
Mar 24	Blairgowrie (H)	LGE	4-1	A Cunningham (2), Smart, Przeslica
Apr 1	Brechin Victoria (A)	LGE	2-1	Deane, Ferrie
Apr 8	Broughty Athletic (H)	LGE	0-5	
Apr 15	Downfield (A)	LGE	1-3	Edwards
Apr 22	Dundee St James (H)	LGE	3-0	Nicol (2), C Galletly
Apr 29	Lochee United (A)	LGE	2-3	S Simpson, Deane
May 3	Broughty Athletic (H)	ELC R2	1-3	Nicol
May 6	Dundee North End (A)	LGE	1-0	Njie
May 13	Scone Thistle (A)	LGE	2-0	Njie (2)

LOCHEE HARP J.F.C.
New Beechwood Park, Dundee

	Age	LEAGUE		CUPS		ALL	
		Apps	Goals	Apps	Goals	Apps	Goals
AFFLECK, Bryce	18	4 (1)	1	1	0	5 (1)	1
BLACK, Cameron	26	7 (2)	1	1	0	8 (2)	1
BROWN, Adam	19	17 (3)	1	3	0	20 (3)	1
BUIK, Kyle	23	10 (3)	1	2 (1)	0	12 (4)	1
BUTTER, Fraser (GK)	30	15	0	3	0	18	0
COBB, Aidan	18	(1)	0	-	-	(1)	0
CONWAY, Aaron	38	2 (4)	2	-	-	2 (4)	2
CONWAY, D	-	(1)	0	-	-	(1)	0
CORMACK, Dean	19	(2)	0	-	-	(2)	0
COUTTS, Lewis (GK)	22	12	0	1	0	13	0
DAVIDSON, Lewis	19	11 (6)	9	2	1	13 (6)	10
EDMONDS, Vincent	22	(5)	0	(2)	0	(7)	0
FLYNN, Kai	20	27 (3)	8	4	1	31 (3)	9
FYFFE, Blair	18	(1)	0	-	-	(1)	0
GAFFNEY, Nairn	18	1 (1)	0	-	-	1 (1)	0
GRAY, Owen	20	1 (8)	4	(1)	0	1 (9)	4
HART, Daniel	20	17 (4)	1	2 (2)	0	19 (6)	1
HOPKINS, Lewis	19	18 (8)	1	3	0	21 (8)	1
IRVINE, Murray	26	4 (3)	0	1	0	5 (3)	0
KELLY, Mark	33	23 (1)	0	4	0	27 (1)	0
KETTLES, B	-	(1)	0	-	-	(1)	0
KOLO, Ahmed	18	2 (4)	1	-	-	2 (4)	1
LOCKHART, Jamie (GK)	21	9	0	-	-	9	0
LOW, Craig	23	13 (6)	4	1 (1)	0	14 (7)	4
MADUGU, Imran	19	(3)	0	-	-	(3)	0
MCCABE, Jamie	26	2	0	-	-	2	0
MCVICAR, Sean	33	31	9	4	0	35	9
MOONEY, Ben	24	2 (9)	1	(2)	0	2 (11)	1
MUDIE, Blair	33	2	0	-	-	2	0
NESS, Bryce	21	10 (1)	0	1 (1)	0	11 (2)	0
OGILVIE, Sam	18	14 (8)	0	4	0	18 (8)	0
RILEY, Matthew	18	30	3	4	2	34	5
RITCHIE, Reece	32	4	0	-	-	4	0
ROBERTSON, Gary	37	17	3	3	1	20	4
ROY, Richard	36	6	4	-	-	6	4
SLATER, Finlay	18	11 (5)	1	2	0	13 (5)	1
STURROCK, Fraser	33	21 (5)	1	4	0	25 (5)	1
SWEENEY, Thomas	22	21	0	2	0	23	0
WILSON, Fraser	29	26 (2)	0	2	0	28 (2)	0
YUNNISSI, Gino	28	6	0	1	0	7	0

MATCH RESULTS 2022/23

Date	Opponent	Comp	Score	Scorers
Jul 23	Dundee North End (A)	LGE	1-2	Low
Jul 27	Forfar West End (A)	LGE	1-2	Low
Jul 30	Letham (A)	LGE	1-1	Robertson
Aug 3	Scone Thistle (A)	LGE	2-0	Buik, Robertson
Aug 10	Coupar Angus (A)	LGE	1-2	Affleck
Aug 13	Tayport (A)	LGE	1-3	Black
Aug 17	Arbroath Victoria (A)	LGE	0-2	
Aug 20	Dundee Violet (A)	LGE	0-3	
Aug 24	Carnoustie Panmure (A)	LGE	1-4	McVicar
Aug 27	Newmachar United (H)	SJC R1	0-1	
Sep 3	East Craigie (H)	LGE	1-10	Gray
Sep 17	Forfar United (A)	LGE	1-2	Sturrock
Oct 1	Kirriemuir Thistle (H)	LGE	3-3	Riley, Robertson, Gray
Oct 8	Letham (H)	IRC R1	2-1	L Allan o.g., Robertson
Oct 15	Blairgowrie (H)	LGE	4-1	McVicar, Slater, Gray, Hart
Oct 22	Brechin Victoria (A)	LGE	2-2	Flynn (2)
Oct 29	Coupar Angus (A)	IRC R2	1-1p	Flynn
Nov 5	Broughty Athletic (H)	LGE	1-3	McVicar
Nov 12	Lochee United (A)	LGE	1-5	Flynn
Nov 19	Dundee St James (H)	LGE	1-1	Flynn
Nov 26	Dundee North End (H)	LGE	0-4	
Dec 3	Downfield (A)	LGE	1-2	Davidson
Dec 10	Forfar West End (H)	LGE	7-0	Davidson (2), Brown, McVicar, I Zinko o.g., A Conway (2)
Jan 7	Letham (H)	LGE	1-1	McVicar
Jan 14	Blairgowrie (A)	LGE	4-2	Flynn, McVicar, Davidson (2)
Jan 21	Coupar Angus (H)	LGE	0-2	
Jan 28	Brechin Victoria (H)	LGE	2-3	Riley, McVicar
Feb 4	Dundee St James (A)	LGE	1-3	Gray
Feb 11	Rothie Rovers (H)	IRC R3	2-1	Davidson, Riley
Feb 18	Carnoustie Panmure (H)	LGE	2-7	McVicar, Mooney
Feb 25	Dundee Violet (H)	LGE	2-5	Davidson, Riley
Mar 4	East Craigie (A)	LGE	1-5	Flynn
Mar 11	Forfar United (H)	LGE	3-1	Davidson, Flynn, McVicar
Mar 18	Carnoustie Panmure (H)	IRC QF	1-6	Riley
Mar 25	Downfield (H)	LGE	1-6	Flynn
Apr 8	Tayport (H)	LGE	4-5	Low (2), Roy, Hopkins
Apr 15	Scone Thistle (H)	LGE	1-3	Roy
Apr 19	Lochee United (H)	LGE	2-4	Roy, Davidson
Apr 22	Broughty Athletic (A)	LGE	1-4	Kolo
Apr 29	Arbroath Victoria (H)	LGE	1-3	Roy
May 6	Kirriemuir Thistle (A)	LGE	1-2	Davidson

LOCHEE UNITED J.F.C.
Thomson Park, Dundee

		LEAGUE		CUPS		ALL	
	Age	Apps	Goals	Apps	Goals	Apps	Goals
ASARE, Prince	20	7 (5)	1	-	-	7 (5)	1
BALLANTINE, Andy	42	21	1	1 (1)	0	22 (1)	1
BUCHAN, Kevin	29	4 (2)	0	3 (1)	0	7 (3)	0
CAVANAGH, Danny	29	21 (3)	14	3 (1)	0	24 (4)	14
COLQUHOUN, Calvin	27	12	1	3	0	15	1
CORD, Jamie	-	2 (6)	0	-	-	2 (6)	0
DAVIE, Logan	25	34	10	6	2	40	12
FOTHERINGHAM, Mark	37	1	0	-	-	1	0
GALLACHER, Ross	33	8 (1)	0	1	0	9 (1)	0
GORTON, Josh (GK)	28	24 (2)	0	3	0	27 (2)	0
HAY, Kerr	27	30 (3)	22	5 (1)	1	35 (4)	23
HIGGINS, Dylan	21	22 (1)	0	4	0	26 (1)	0
JOHNSTON, George	22	18 (8)	4	4 (2)	1	22 (10)	5
KERRIGAN, Jacob (GK)	18	10 (1)	0	1	0	11 (1)	0
KIRK, Greg	37	19 (7)	3	5	1	24 (7)	4
LAWSON, Grant	36	17 (4)	3	4 (1)	0	21 (5)	3
LUNAN, Owen	-	(5)	0	-	-	(5)	0
LUNAN, Paul	41	22	2	2 (1)	0	24 (1)	2
MCCONVILLE, Josh	21	26 (2)	1	4	0	30 (2)	1
MCINNES, Ryan	18	1	1	-	-	1	1
MCLELLAN, Paul	28	(5)	1	(1)	0	(6)	1
MCPAKE, Liam	19	18 (16)	3	1 (3)	0	19 (19)	3
MILNE, Kevin	33	7 (3)	4	2 (3)	1	9 (6)	5
PATERSON, Ryan	21	16	17	1	0	17	17
SCOBIE, Paul	28	28 (3)	6	5	0	33 (3)	6
SMITH, Craig	29	2	0	1	0	3	0
SUTHERLAND, Gary	39	23 (7)	17	5 (1)	2	28 (8)	19
TRISTAN, Mitchell da Costa (GK)	23	1	0	2	0	3	0
WEBSTER, Scott	30	2 (2)	0	(1)	0	2 (3)	0

Date	Opponent	Comp	Score	Scorers
Jul 23	Arbroath Victoria (H)	LGE	1-1	Davie
Jul 27	Tayport (A)	LGE	1-0	Hay
Jul 30	Dundee Violet (H)	LGE	0-0	
Aug 3	Carnoustie Panmure (H)	LGE	2-0	Cavanagh, McConville
Aug 6	East Craigie (H)	LGE	5-3	Davie, Johnston (2), Colquhoun, Milne
Aug 10	Forfar United (A)	LGE	0-1	
Aug 13	Downfield (A)	LGE	0-0	
Aug 17	Kirriemuir Thistle (H)	LGE	5-5	Sutherland (2), Cavanagh (2), Lawson
Aug 20	Brechin Victoria (A)	LGE	5-0	Sutherland, McInnes, Milne, McLellan, Hay
Aug 22	Blairgowrie (H)	LGE	8-1	Sutherland (2), Hay (3), Davie, Milne (2)
Aug 27	Dalkeith Thistle (A)	SC PR.	3-1	Kirk, Hay, Johnston
Sep 3	Broughty Athletic (H)	LGE	2-2	Kirk, Sutherland
Sep 17	Wick Academy (A)	SC R1	1-5	Davie
Sep 24	St Rochs (H)	SJC R2	1-2	Davie
Oct 1	Dundee St James (A)	LGE	3-1	Cavanagh, Hay, Lawson
Oct 8	Arbroath Victoria (H)	IRC R1	3-0	Sutherland (2), Milne
Oct 15	Forfar West End (A)	LGE	2-1	Sutherland, Davie
Oct 22	Scone Thistle (H)	LGE	6-0	Sutherland (2), Lawson, Cavanagh, Hay (2)
Oct 29	Dundee North End (H)	IRC R2	3-4	Unknown
Nov 5	Letham (A)	LGE	7-0	Cavanagh (2), Hay (3), Davie (2)
Nov 12	Lochee Harp (H)	LGE	5-1	Hay, Sutherland, Cavanagh (3)
Nov 26	Arbroath Victoria (A)	LGE	0-0	
Dec 3	Dundee North End (H)	LGE	3-1	Cavanagh, Kirk, Davie
Jan 14	East Craigie (A)	LGE	2-1	Scobie, Asare
Jan 21	Forfar United (H)	LGE	2-0	P Lunan, Scobie
Feb 4	Downfield (H)	LGE	1-3	Scobie
Feb 11	Coupar Angus (A)	LGE	4-1	Hay, Sutherland (2), McPake
Feb 18	Blairgowrie (A)	LGE	5-1	Paterson (3), J Simpson o.g., Hay
Feb 25	Brechin Victoria (H)	LGE	3-0	Kirk, Sutherland, Cavanagh
Mar 4	Broughty Athletic (A)	LGE	3-5	McPake, Paterson, Hay
Mar 18	Dundee St James (H)	LGE	4-2	Sutherland (2), Ballantine, Paterson
Mar 25	Dundee North End (A)	LGE	1-4	Paterson
Apr 1	Forfar West End (H)	LGE	5-0	Cavanagh (2), Davie, Hay, McPake
Apr 8	Scone Thistle (A)	LGE	2-3	Hay, Davie
Apr 15	Kirriemuir Thistle (A)	LGE	4-0	Johnston, Paterson (2), Scobie
Apr 19	Lochee Harp (A)	LGE	4-2	Hay (3), Scobie
Apr 22	Tayport (H)	LGE	5-1	Paterson (3), Scobie, Sutherland
Apr 26	Coupar Angus (H)	LGE	4-1	Sutherland, Paterson (2), P Lunan
Apr 29	Letham (H)	LGE	3-2	Paterson, Hay (2)
May 3	Dundee North End (A)	ELC R2	0-2	
May 6	Dundee Violet (A)	LGE	3-1	Paterson, Johnston, Davie
May 13	Carnoustie Panmure (A)	LGE	2-1	Paterson (2)

SCONE THISTLE J.F.C.
Farquharson Park, Scone

		LEAGUE		CUPS		ALL	
	Age	Apps	Goals	Apps	Goals	Apps	Goals
ALCORN, Ally	20	9 (9)	2	1 (1)	0	10 (10)	2
ANDERSON, Euan	20	12 (8)	0	2	0	14 (8)	0
ANTONIEWICZ, Ronan	20	17 (1)	0	-	-	17 (1)	0
BATEMAN, Cody	19	20 (6)	5	1	0	21 (6)	5
BLACK, Calum	23	27 (1)	0	1	0	28 (1)	0
BRAND, Kairn	20	32	3	2	0	34	3
CAMERON, Ross	20	2	0	-	-	2	0
CARTER, Andrew	23	(2)	0	-	-	(2)	0
CLARK, Jon	20	6	0	1	0	7	0
DEWAR, Cole	-	6 (6)	0	(1)	0	6 (7)	0
EMMETT, David	18	10 (8)	1	(1)	0	10 (9)	1
FINNIE, Lewis	20	9 (1)	0	1	0	10 (1)	0
FORBER, Ethan	18	5 (8)	0	-	-	5 (8)	0
FORBER, Kieran	20	9 (6)	1	1	0	10 (6)	1
FORBES, Cameron	20	12 (5)	0	2	0	14 (5)	0
FRASER, Ben	22	(3)	1	-	-	(3)	1
FYFE, Jamie	28	(2)	0	-	-	(2)	0
HASTIE, Sean	21	31 (1)	22	2	0	33 (1)	22
HENDERSON, Jack	33	2	0	-	-	2	0
HEPBURN, Owen	24	2 (1)	0	-	-	2 (1)	0
JASSIM, Omar	19	9 (11)	1	(2)	0	9 (13)	1
JENKINS, Ross	23	4 (1)	0	-	-	4 (1)	0
KINNEAR, James	27	1 (2)	0	(1)	0	1 (3)	0
KINNEAR, Ryan	28	23 (6)	0	1 (1)	0	24 (7)	0
LAING, Willie	38	13	0	1	0	14	0
LEASK, Paul	28	22 (8)	8	1 (1)	0	23 (9)	8
LOUDON, Ross	21	28	1	2	0	30	1
MACINTYRE, Rory (GK)	21	5	0	-	-	5	0
MARTIN, Sean (GK)	19	12	0	2	0	14	0
MCWILLIAM, Keiran	22	(4)	0	-	-	(4)	0
PEEBLES, Scott	20	25 (3)	0	1	0	26 (3)	0
REOCH, Rory	23	1 (7)	0	(1)	0	1 (8)	0
RICE, David (GK)	40	2	0	-	-	2	0
RODGER, Elliot	28	5 (5)	0	-	-	5 (5)	0
SCOTT, Elliott	20	7	0	-	-	7	0
SORLEY, Gavin (GK)	35	10	0	-	-	10	0
STAMP, Jonathan (GK)	30	5 (1)	0	-	-	5 (1)	0
URQUHART, Campbell	-	(2)	0	-	-	(2)	0

* Players with less than 2 appearances not displayed due to size of squad.

MATCH RESULTS 2022/23

Date	Opponent	Comp	Score	Scorers
Jul 27	Letham (A)	LGE	1-5	Leask
Jul 30	Coupar Angus (A)	LGE	4-2	Hastie (2), Leask, Alcorn
Aug 3	Lochee Harp (H)	LGE	0-2	
Aug 6	Arbroath Victoria (H)	LGE	2-1	Bateman, Loudon
Aug 10	Tayport (A)	LGE	0-2	
Aug 13	Dundee Violet (A)	LGE	0-1	
Aug 17	Carnoustie Panmure (H)	LGE	0-4	
Aug 20	Forfar United (A)	LGE	2-4	Hastie (2)
Aug 24	East Craigie (H)	LGE	0-2	
Aug 27	New Elgin (H)	SJC R1	5-2	Unknown
Sep 3	Kirriemuir Thistle (H)	LGE	0-4	
Sep 17	Downfield (A)	LGE	1-3	Hastie
Sep 24	Livingston United (A)	SJC R2	1-4	Unknown
Oct 1	Blairgowrie (H)	LGE	0-1	
Oct 8	Dundee Violet (A)	IRC R2	3-6	Unknown
Oct 15	Broughty Athletic (H)	LGE	0-4	
Oct 22	Lochee United (A)	LGE	0-6	
Oct 29	Brechin Victoria (A)	LGE	3-3	Brand, Leask, Hastie
Nov 5	Dundee St James (H)	LGE	3-1	Hastie (2), Emmett
Nov 12	Dundee North End (A)	LGE	3-11	Hastie, K Forber, Jassim
Dec 3	Brechin Victoria (H)	ELC R2	0-3	
Jan 14	Arbroath Victoria (A)	LGE	0-3	
Jan 28	Carnoustie Panmure (A)	LGE	1-5	Hastie
Feb 4	Dundee Violet (H)	LGE	1-3	Alcorn
Feb 11	Forfar West End (H)	LGE	4-1	Bateman (2), R Hoon o.g., Leask
Feb 18	Dundee St James (A)	LGE	2-2	Bateman, Hastie
Mar 4	Kirriemuir Thistle (A)	LGE	1-3	Hastie
Mar 11	Downfield (H)	LGE	1-5	Hastie
Mar 25	Brechin Victoria (H)	LGE	1-1	Brand
Apr 8	Lochee United (H)	LGE	3-2	Hastie (3)
Apr 15	Lochee Harp (A)	LGE	3-1	Hastie, Brand, Leask
Apr 19	Coupar Angus (H)	LGE	1-2	Leask
Apr 22	Dundee North End (H)	LGE	2-1	Hastie (2)
Apr 29	Forfar United (H)	LGE	1-1	Hastie
May 6	Forfar West End (A)	LGE	1-0	Leask
May 10	East Craigie (A)	LGE	2-2	Hastie, Leask
May 13	Letham (H)	LGE	0-2	
May 20	Tayport (H)	LGE	2-1	Bateman, Fraser
May 27	Broughty Athletic (A)	LGE	2-5	G McNaughton o.g., Hastie

TAYPORT J.F.C.
The Canniepairt, Tayport

		LEAGUE		CUPS		ALL	
	Age	Apps	Goals	Apps	Goals	Apps	Goals
ADDO, Caleb	25	(10)	0	-	-	(10)	0
ARMSTRONG, Lewis	23	(2)	1	-	-	(2)	1
BARBOUR, Innes	18	13 (11)	5	3 (1)	0	16 (12)	5
BAXTER, Tristan	18	5 (4)	0	1	0	6 (4)	0
BROWN, Darren (GK)	35	13 (1)	0	4	0	17 (1)	0
BURNS, Darryl (GK)	31	4	0	-	-	4	0
CAMERON, Ross	20	(4)	0	-	-	(4)	0
DEBEMBE, Bruno	19	5 (7)	0	(1)	0	5 (8)	0
EDWARDS, Nik	18	5 (9)	1	3 (1)	1	8 (10)	2
FRASER, Adam	28	3 (6)	0	(3)	0	3 (9)	0
GILLESPIE, Rikki	30	10	4	2	0	12	4
HEGGIE, Bradie	27	14	0	1 (1)	0	15 (1)	0
HUME, Jamie	29	27 (1)	6	3	0	30 (1)	6
KENNEDY, Charlie (GK)	22	2	0	-	-	2	0
LEIPER, Arran	19	3 (5)	0	1	0	4 (5)	0
LOWE, Nairn	-	3	0	-	-	3	0
MALONE, Jim	26	9	1	1 (1)	0	10 (1)	1
MCCOLM, Greg	23	30	2	4	0	34	2
MCDONALD, Ross	27	18 (4)	1	4	0	22 (4)	1
MCDOUGALL, Aiden	18	12 (4)	2	1	0	13 (4)	2
MCINNES, Ryan	18	3	0	-	-	3	0
MCKELVIE, Aidan	19	6 (1)	0	1	0	7 (1)	0
MCKENZIE, Daryl	38	25 (3)	0	4 (1)	1	29 (4)	1
MCMULKIN, Kyle	-	8 (19)	1	1 (2)	1	9 (21)	2
MIDDLETON, Kyle	21	(1)	0	-	-	(1)	0
NAGLIK, Dominic	19	7 (5)	1	1	0	8 (5)	1
O'BRIEN, Luke	24	10 (1)	2	(1)	0	10 (2)	2
PATERSON, Ryan	21	18	4	4	2	22	6
PETRIE, Callum	27	3 (1)	0	-	-	3 (1)	0
ROBERTSON, D	-	(1)	0	-	-	(1)	0
ROBERTSON, Gary	37	15 (2)	2	-	-	15 (2)	2
SAMSON, Ethan	21	19 (2)	7	4 (1)	1	23 (3)	8
SLUDDEN, Paul	33	17	8	1	0	18	8
STEWART, Paul	31	(1)	0	-	-	(1)	0
STURROCK, Craig	35	13	1	3 (1)	0	16 (1)	1
STURROCK, Keiran	27	28 (1)	24	3 (1)	4	31 (2)	28
WALLS, Andy	30	17 (2)	0	-	-	17 (2)	0
WALLS, Callum	25	14 (8)	0	4 (1)	0	18 (9)	0
WELSH, Thomas (GK)	19	17	0	1	0	18	0

MATCH RESULTS 2022/23

Date	Opponent	Comp	Score	Scorers
Jul 23	Broughty Athletic (A)	LGE	0-2	
Jul 27	Lochee United (H)	LGE	0-1	
Jul 30	Dundee North End (H)	LGE	1-2	Hume
Aug 3	Dundee St James (A)	LGE	3-0	K Sturrock (2), Malone
Aug 6	Forfar West End (A)	LGE	3-0	Hume, Paterson, O'Brien
Aug 10	Scone Thistle (H)	LGE	2-0	R Loudon o.g., Armstrong
Aug 13	Lochee Harp (H)	LGE	3-1	O'Brien, K Sturrock (2)
Aug 17	Letham (A)	LGE	1-0	Paterson
Aug 20	Arbroath Victoria (H)	LGE	3-1	Hume, McColm, K Sturrock
Aug 24	Coupar Angus (A)	LGE	2-0	Edwards, Naglik
Aug 27	Dundonald Bluebell (A)	SC PR.	1-3	McKenzie
Sep 3	Arbroath Victoria (A)	LGE	2-2	Hume, K Sturrock
Sep 24	Ardeer Thistle (H)	SJC R2	7-1	K Sturrock (3), Edwards, Paterson (2), McMulkin
Oct 1	Dundee Violet (H)	LGE	2-2	K Sturrock, Barbour
Oct 8	Dundee North End (A)	LGE	0-1	
Oct 15	Forfar United (H)	LGE	8-0	K Sturrock (3), Samson (2), Barbour, Paterson (2)
Oct 22	Kirriemuir Thistle (A)	LGE	1-4	Samson
Oct 29	Rutherglen Glencairn (H)	SJC R3	0-4	
Nov 5	Downfield (H)	LGE	0-4	
Nov 12	Blairgowrie (A)	LGE	2-0	Gillespie, Samson
Nov 26	Broughty Athletic (H)	LGE	0-3	
Dec 3	Broughty Athletic (A)	IRC R2	2-4	K Sturrock, Samson
Jan 14	Forfar West End (H)	LGE	4-1	C Sturrock, Sludden, Gillespie, K Sturrock
Jan 28	Letham (H)	LGE	1-0	K Sturrock
Feb 4	East Craigie (H)	LGE	0-1	
Feb 11	Brechin Victoria (A)	LGE	3-1	K Sturrock, Gillespie, Hume
Feb 18	Coupar Angus (H)	LGE	5-1	McDonald, Barbour, Gillespie, McDougall, G Robertson
Feb 25	Forfar United (A)	ELC R1	0-1	
Mar 11	Carnoustie Panmure (H)	LGE	0-3	
Mar 25	Kirriemuir Thistle (H)	LGE	3-2	Barbour, Sludden (2)
Apr 1	Forfar United (A)	LGE	4-2	K Sturrock (2), Sludden, Samson
Apr 8	Lochee Harp (A)	LGE	5-4	K Sturrock (3), Sludden (2)
Apr 15	Carnoustie Panmure (A)	LGE	2-4	G Robertson, Hume
Apr 19	Dundee St James (H)	LGE	0-1	
Apr 22	Lochee United (A)	LGE	1-5	Sludden
Apr 26	East Craigie (A)	LGE	0-4	
Apr 29	Brechin Victoria (H)	LGE	1-0	K Sturrock
May 6	Downfield (A)	LGE	3-1	Samson (2), K Sturrock
May 13	Blairgowrie (H)	LGE	5-0	McColm, K Sturrock (3), McDougall
May 20	Scone Thistle (A)	LGE	1-2	K Sturrock
May 27	Dundee Violet (A)	LGE	3-3	Barbour, Sludden, McMulkin

THORNTON'S PROPERTY EAST REGION LEAGUE CUP

GoWFERS AT THE DoUBLE

League winners Carnoustie Panmure made it a double-winning season with a penalty-shoot out win over Broughty Ferry in Dundee.   Photo: Matthew Anderson (Fitba AM Photography)

The beginnings of the East Region Midlands Football League shall tell a story of dominance in its earliest years, with Carnoustie Panmure top of the bill.

Having already retained the league championship for a second season, the Gowfers made it a double winning season with a penalty shoot-out win over Broughty Athletic at Glenesk Park in the Thornton's Property East Region Cup final.

A three-minute spell saw each side notch a goal, with Panmure taking the lead through Pat Smith on 16 minutes. Craig Tosh quickly levelled for Broughty Athletic.

It was left to Brian Clark on 39 minutes to score the only other goal of the first half to give Carnoustie a half-time advantage, scoring six minutes before the interval.

Josh Skelly brought Athletic back into the game just before the hour mark at 2-2, but for the third time in the game, Carnoustie retook the lead when top scorer Dale Reid found the net on 78 minutes.

It seemed as though the trophy would be heading back to Laing Park with a win in normal time, but a sting in the tail saw Tosh nodded home to score Broughty's third, forcing a penalty shoot-out.

In the end though, Panmure's perseverance paid off as they emerged winners by 5 kicks to 3.

CARNOUSTIE PANMURE............3 (2)
Smith 16, Clark 39, Reid 78
BROUGHTY ATHLETIC.................3 (1)
Tosh 18, 90, Skelly 59
Carnoustie: Clarkson, Warwick, Steel, Stephen, Fraser, Millar, Clark (Winter 85), Reid, MacDonald, Smith, Joyce. Not used: Roche, Martin, Conway, Chalmers, Robertson

Broughty: Diamond, Winter (Sivewright), Ferguson (Findlay), McNaughton (Boylen), Middleton, Reid, Tosh, Kesson, Skelly, Smith, Henry (Fraser). Not used: Anderson, Buchanan, Burnett

NORTH END'S QUEST FOR CUP GLORY PAYS OFF

Dundee North End overcame the odds to lift the Quest Engineering Cup with a 4-1 win over Carnoustie Panmure.
Photo: Dundee North End Facebook

The cross-region cup pitting the north half of the pyramid's junior sides against each other ended in an emphatic win for Dundee North End in May, defeating Midlands Football League champions Carnoustie Panmure in the final.

After going a goal down to a MacDonald strike in the first half, Jordan Garden fired back for the Dokens with the finishing touch on a ball across the face of goal.

Brian Rice made it 2-1 in the second half, with a tight finish after North End broke on the counter.

The third came via Owen McCabe soon after with a spectacular drive from 30 yards, looped over Clarkson and into the net.

McLaughlin put the game beyond doubt with North End's fourth.

DUNDEE NORTH END....................4 (1)
McLaughlin
CARNOUSTIE PANMURE..............1 (1)
MacDonald
North End: Thain, Gibb, Rice, Allan, Jamieson, Montgomery (McCabe 76), Garden (Smith), Devine (McLaughlin), Richardson (Britton), McCord, Bollan. Not used: Law, Ferrie
Carnoustie: Clarkson, Steel, Roche, Winter (Stephen 52), Millar, Clark (Simpson 52), Reid, MacDonald (Martin 69), Suttie, Smith (Fraser 69), Joyce. Not used: McWalter, Leiper, Dorovic

SENIOR CLUB DIRECTORY (2023-24)

ALNESS UNITED FOOTBALL CLUB

Formed:	1925 approx
Ground:	Dalmore Park
Address:	Alness Leisure Centre
	Dalmore Road
	Alness
	IV17 0UY
Chairman:	Thomas Regan
Club Secretary:	Fiona Sutherland
Team Manager:	Robert Mitchell
Email:	alnessunitedfc@outlook.com
Web:	facebook.com/Alnessunited

BANKS O' DEE FOOTBALL CLUB

Also known as:	"The Dee"
Formed:	1902
Ground:	Spain Park
Capacity:	876 (100 seated)
Address:	Abbotswell Road
	Aberdeen
	IV3 6DR
President:	Gordon Christie
Chairman:	Brian Winton
Director of Football:	Paul Bain
Team Managers:	Josh Winton
	Paul Lawson
Email:	banksodeefc
	@highlandleague.com
Web:	pitchero.com/clubs/
	banksodeefootballclub

BONAR BRIDGE FOOTBALL CLUB

Also known as:	"The Bridge"
Formed:	1968
Ground:	Migdale Playing Fields
Address:	Matheson Road
	Bonar Bridge
	IV24 3AG
Chairman:	Iain Maclean
Club Secretary:	Carrie Vetters
Team Manager:	Bobby Breen
Email:	bonarbridgefc@gmail.com
Web:	bonarbridgefc.co.uk

BRECHIN CITY FOOTBALL CLUB

Also known as:	"The City, The Hedgemen"
Formed:	1879
Ground:	Carnegie Fuels Stadium
	Glebe Park
Capacity:	4123 (1519 seated)
Address:	Trinity Road
	Brechin
	DD9 6BJ
Chairman:	Kevin Mackie
Club Secretary:	Gary Robertson
Team Manager:	Gavin Price
Email:	secretary@brechincityfc.com
Web:	brechincity.com

BRORA RANGERS FOOTBALL CLUB

Also known as:	"The Cattachs"
Formed:	1879
Ground:	Dudgeon Park
Capacity:	4000 (200 seated)
Address:	Brora
	Sutherland
	KW9 6QN
Chairman:	Scott Mackay
Club Secretary:	Kevin Mackay
Director of Football:	Kevin Munro
Team Manager:	Ally MacDonald
Email:	brorarangersfc
	@highlandleague.com
Web:	brorarangers.football

Brora Rangers director of football, Kevin Munro.

BUCKIE THISTLE FOOTBALL CLUB

Also known as:	"The Jags"
Formed:	1889
Ground:	Victoria Park
Capacity:	5000 (400 seated)
Address:	Midmar Street
	Buckie
	AB56 1BJ
President:	Garry Farquhar
General Manager:	Stephen Shand
Club Secretary:	David Pirie
Team Manager:	Graeme Stewart
Email:	buckiethistlefc
	@highlandleague.com
Web:	buckiethistlefc.co.uk

CLACHNACUDDIN FOOTBALL CLUB

Also known as:	"The Lilywhites"
Formed:	1885
Ground:	Grant Street Park
Capacity:	3000 (154 seated)
Address:	Wyvis Place
	Inverness
	IV3 6DR
Chairman:	Alex Chisholm
Club Secretary:	Scott Dowling
Team Manager:	Conor Gethins
Email:	info@clachfc.co.uk
Web:	clachfc.co.uk

DEVERONVALE FOOTBALL CLUB

Also known as:	"The Vale"
Formed:	1938
Ground:	Princess Royal Park
Capacity:	2651 (360 seated)
Address:	56 Airlie Gardens
	Banff
	AB45 1AZ
Chairman:	Jim Mair
Team Manager:	Craig Stewart
Email:	deveronvalefc
	@highlandleague.com
Web:	deveronvale.co.uk

FORMARTINE UNITED FOOTBALL CLUB

Formed:	1948
Ground:	North Lodge Park
Capacity:	1800 (300 seated)
Address:	Old Meldrum Road
	Pitmedden
	AB41 7PA
Chairman:	Atholl Cadger
Club Secretary:	Bryan Braidwood
Team Manager:	Stuart Anderson
Email:	formartineunitedfc

	@highlandleague.com
Web:	formartineunitedfc.co.uk

FORRES MECHANICS FOOTBALL CLUB

Also known as:	"The Can Cans"
Formed:	1884
Ground:	Mosset Park
Capacity:	2700 (502 seated)
Address:	Lea Road
	Forres
	IV36 1AU
Chairman:	David MacKintosh
Club Secretary:	Tony Broadhurst
Team Manager:	Steven MacDonald
Email:	forresmechanicsfc
	@highlandleague.com
Web:	forresmechanics.net

FORT WILLIAM FOOTBALL CLUB

Also known as:	"The Fort"
Formed:	1974
Ground:	Claggan Park
Address:	Achintee Road
	Fort William
	PH33 6TE
Chairman:	Robert Coull
Team Manager:	Alan Gray
Email:	info@fortwilliamfc.com
Web:	fortwilliamfc.com

FRASERURGH FOOTBALL CLUB

Also known as:	"The Broch"
Formed:	1910
Ground:	Bellslea Park
Capacity:	3000 (480 seated)
Address:	21 Seaforth Street
	Fraserburgh
	AB43 9BB
Chairman/Secretary:	Finlay Noble
Team Manager:	Mark Cowie
Email:	fraserburghfc
	@highlandleague.com
Web:	thebroch.online

GOLSPIE SUTHERLAND FOOTBALL CLUB

Formed:	1877
Ground:	King George V Park
Address:	Alistair Road
	Golspie
	KW10 6SW
Chairman:	Ewen Campbell
Club Secretary:	James Urquhart
Team Manager:	Andrew Banks
Email:	email@jamesurquhart.co.uk
Web:	facebook.com/golspie.sutherlandfc

Keith football club chairman, Andy Troup

HALKIRK UNITED FOOTBALL CLUB

Also known as:	"The Anglers"
Formed:	1993
Ground:	Morrison Park
Address:	Bridge Street
	Halkirk
	KW12 6XF
Chairman:	Robbie Macleod
Club Secretary:	Willie Campbell
Team Manager:	Ewan McElroy
Email:	williecam09@icloud.com
Web:	facebook.com/HalkirkUnitedFC

HUNTLY FOOTBALL CLUB

Also known as:	"The Black and Golds"
Formed:	1928
Ground:	Christie Park
Capacity:	2200 (270 seated)
Address:	East Park Street
	Huntly
	AB54 8JE
Chairman:	Gordon Carter
Club Secretary:	Alix Turner
Match Secretary:	Grant Turner
Team Manager:	Allan Hale
Email:	huntlyfc@highlandleague.com
Web:	huntlyfc.co.uk

INVERGORDON FOOTBALL CLUB

Formed:	1870s
Ground:	Recreation Grounds
Address:	Castle Avenue
	Invergordon
	IV18 0AZ
Chairman:	Edwin Skinner

Club Secretary:	Mandy MacKenzie
Team Manager:	Gary Campbell
Email:	mandy.mackenzie123
	@btinternet.com

INVERNESS ATHLETIC FOOTBALL CLUB

Formed:	2016
Ground:	Ferry Brae Park
Address:	North Kessock
	IV1 3YH
Chairman:	Sandy Stephen
Club Secretary:	Grant Donald
Team Manager:	Stuart Ross
Email:	info@invernessathleticfc.co.uk
Web:	invernessathleticfc.co.uk

INVERURIE LOCO WORKS FOOTBALL CLUB

Also known as:	"The Locos, The Railwaymen"
Formed:	1902
Ground:	Harlaw Park
Capacity:	2500 (175 seated)
Address:	Harlaw Road
	Inverurie
	AB51 4SF
Chairman:	Mike Macaulay
Secretary:	Billy Thompson
Football Operations:	Scott Buchan
Team Manager:	Dean Donaldson
Email:	inverurielocoworksfc
	@highlandleague.com
Web:	inverurielocos.com

KEITH FOOTBALL CLUB

Also known as:	"The Maroons"
Formed:	1910
Ground:	Kynoch Park
Capacity:	2362 (370 seated)
Address:	Balloch Road
	Keith
	AB55 5EN
Chairman:	Andrew Troup
Director of Football:	Michael Brown
Team Manager:	Craig Ewen
Email:	keithfc@highlandleague.com
Web:	keithfc.com

LOCH NESS FOOTBALL CLUB

Formed:	1999
Ground:	King George V Playing Fields
Address:	Ness Road
	Fortrose
	IV10 8TZ
Chair/Team Manager:	Shane Carling
Email:	lochnessfc@gmail.com
Web:	lochnessfc.com

LOSSIEMOUTH FOOTBALL CLUB

Also known as:	"The Coasters"
Formed:	1946
Ground:	Grant Park
Capacity:	3250 (250 seated)
Address:	Kellas Avenue
	Lossiemouth
	IV31 6JG
Chairman:	Alan McIntosh
Club Secretary:	Kevan McIntosh
Team Manager:	Frank McGettrick
Email:	lossiemouthfc
	@highlandleague.com
Web:	lossiemouthfc.co.uk

NAIRN COUNTY FOOTBALL CLUB

Also known as:	"The Wee County"
Formed:	1914
Ground:	Station Park
Capacity:	2250 (250 seated)
Address:	Balblair Road
	Nairn
	IV12 5LT
President:	Donald Matheson
Chairman:	Mark Kelman
Club Secretary:	Ian Finlayson
Director of Football:	Graeme Macleod
Team Manager:	Steven Mackay
Email:	nairncountyfc
	@highlandleague.com
Web:	nairncountyfc.co.uk

ORKNEY FOOTBALL CLUB

Also known as:	"The Orcadians"
Formed:	2012
Ground:	KGS Sports Centre
Address:	The Meadows
	Kirkwall
	Orkney
	KW15 1QN
Chairman:	Edgar Balfour
Club Secretary:	Inga Foubister
Team Manager:	Charlie Alway
Email:	inga.foubister@btinternet.com
Web:	orkneyfc.co.uk

ROTHES FOOTBALL CLUB

Also known as:	"The Speysiders"
Formed:	1938
Ground:	MacKessack Park
Capacity:	1731 (167 seated)
Address:	36 Provost Christie Drive
	Rothes
	AB38 7BX
Chairman:	Iain Paul
Club Secretary:	Andrew G Simpson
Head of Football:	Derek Thomson
Team Manager:	Ross Jack
Email:	rothesfc@highlandleague.com
Web:	rothesfc.co.uk

ST DUTHUS FOOTBALL CLUB

Also known as:	"The Saints"
Formed:	1884
Ground:	Grant Park
Address:	Shore Road
	Tain
	IV19 1EH
Chairman:	Niall Harkiss
Team Manager:	Alan Geegan
Email:	committee@stduthusfc.co.uk
Web:	stduthusfc.co.uk

STRATHSPEY THISTLE FOOTBALL CLUB

Also known as:	"The Strathy Jags"
Formed:	1993
Ground:	Seafield Park
Capacity:	1600 (150 seated)
Address:	Heathfield Road
	Grantown-on-spey
	PH26 3HY
Chairman:	Donly Mcleod

Team manager of St Duthus FC, Alan Geegan.

Club Secretary:	Clive Wolstenholme		Turriff
Team Manager:	Robert MacCormack		AB53 4EF
Email:	strathspeythistlefc	Chairman:	Gairn Ritchie
	@highlandleague.com	Club Secretary:	Philip Napier
Web:	strathspeythistlefc.com	Team Manager:	Warren Cummings
		Email:	turriffunitedfc

Club Secretary: Clive Wolstenholme
Team Manager: Robert MacCormack
Email: strathspeythistlefc
@highlandleague.com
Web: strathspeythistlefc.com

THURSO FOOTBALL CLUB

Also known as: "The Vikings"
Formed: 1998
Ground: Sir George's Park (The Dammies)
Address: Thurso
KW14 8HN
Chairman: Ewan Scott
Club Secretary: Iain Grant
Team Manager: Scott Davidson
Email: imgrant9@gmail.com
Web: thursofc.info

TURRIFF UNITED FOOTBALL CLUB

Also known as: "Turra"
Formed: 1954
Ground: The Haughs
Capacity: 2135 (135 seated)
Address: Bridge of Turriff

Turriff
AB53 4EF
Chairman: Gairn Ritchie
Club Secretary: Philip Napier
Team Manager: Warren Cummings
Email: turriffunitedfc
@highlandleague.com
Web: turriffunitedfc.co.uk

WICK ACADEMY FOOTBALL CLUB

Also known as: "The Scorries"
Formed: 1893
Ground: Harmsworth Park
Capacity: 2412 (102 seated)
Address: South Road
Wick
KW1 5NH
President: Clair Harper
Chairman: Pat Miller
Club Secretary: Melanie Roger
Team Manager: Gary Manson
Email: wickacademyfc
@highlandleague.com
Web: wick-academy.co.uk

Bumper crowd for the Scottish Cup at Harmsworth Park – home of Wick Academy FC.

BUCKIE SUCCESS PROOF OF GROWING STRENGTH

The Buckie Ladies squad celebrate the double as they are presented with the league trophy.   Photo: Daniel Forsyth

SWL HIGHLAND AND ISLAND LEAGUE

		Pl	W	D	L	F	A	GD	Pts	PPG
1.	Buckie Ladies	12	10	2	0	40	8	+32	**32**	2.67
2.	Orkney Women	12	9	1	2	49	16	+33	**28**	2.33
3.	Caithness	12	7	1	4	47	21	+26	**22**	1.83
4.	Sutherland	12	6	2	4	41	23	+18	**20**	1.67
5.	Clach Women	11	2	2	7	20	41	-21	**8**	0.73
6.	Ross & Cromarty	12	1	1	10	16	51	-35	**4**	0.33
7.	Nairn Ladies	11	1	1	9	13	66	-53	**4**	0.33

SCOTTISH Women's Football believes the Highland and Island League is continuing to grow all the time – with a new title sponsor **in place and at least one new team set to enter the division in 2024.**

The league had something of a false start, only completing one season before Covid-19 brought a halt to the competition. Even in that first year, a Western Isles team looked on course to become the inaugural champions only to pull out half way through the year for logistical reasons.

Since returning in 2021, though, progress has been much smoother. There are still challenges, like the withdrawal of Brora Rangers part-way through the 2023 season, but SWF chief executive officer Aileen Campbell is confident things are moving in the right direction.

"I think the big thing is that there is lots of growth and optimism, but there is still a need to find resilience and sustainability in the game – not just in the Highlands, but across the whole country," Campbell said.

"We're really pleased that with a new sponsor and with new clubs looking to join the league, it will strengthen that league and help grow the game across the Highlands.

"They will enable us to dedicate more time and resources to help, and we will work with clubs to increase their profile and visibility, because we want to make sure that girls across the Highlands know that football is absolutely a sport for them.

"We're really keen and pleased as an organisation within that wider football landscape that we're dedicated to ensuring there are opportunities across the country – regardless of where you live.

"The game that we run in Scottish Women's Football has that geographic spread and reach that others don't currently have, so we're really proud to deliver that and pleased that we have a first-time league sponsor for the Highlands and Islands League in Scottish Power. Hopefully that will leave a lasting legacy."

Goalkeepers Sophia Golebiewski and Dana Hahmann with the club's two trophies.   Photo: Daniel Forsyth

While some teams have left the Highlands and Islands League, others have joined.

Buckie are one of them, dropping down from the SWFL to win back-to-back doubles over the last two seasons.

Campbell believes that has been part of the teething process in early years, with clubs figuring out which path and level is right for them.

"They have absolutely found the level for them," she added.

"There have been some changes to the regional football leagues as well, where we have shifted that back to align with our two top leagues which means there are promotion opportunities.

"The regional football leagues also offer that chance for women to gather and play football in a space that's right for them.

"If they have higher aspirations and want to progress as a club, there is a route for them to do that.

"As a result of that, those leagues have grown. We have an extra regional league this season, with more teams taking part and more teams coming and using that as the entry level to progress. Hopefully we see that continue.

"There are also other gaps geographically. We could have a similar conversation about the south of Scotland, where there are fewer teams as well.

"There's a lot of work to do, and a lot of

Buckie's Emily McAuslan thought she had a second half double against Caithness Ladies in their title decider, but the goal was disallowed.
Photo: Daniel Forsyth

Buckie Ladies celebrate Rheo Laurensen's equaliser against Caithness Ladies.   Photo: Daniel Forsyth

way to go, but we're really pleased that what we've got at the moment is on an upwards trajectory."

Title sponsor Scottish Power's director of engagement, Hazel Gulliver, knows first hand why it is so important to back opportunities for women and girls to play sport.

She had to move abroad to play football on a regular basis, and says Scottish Power are committed to inclusion in and out of the work place.

"I was that wee girl at school who was in the headmaster's office demanding to play in the boys' team, because there was no girls' team," Gulliver explained.

"I never actually played in Scotland, it was only when I moved to Belgium that I discovered every village has a women's football team! I played there for 10 years and absolutely loved it.

"We started off getting trounced, but we made it to the first division of the women's amateur league, so we were really quite proud of ourselves.

"It's a shame I had to move abroad to get that opportunity, but that's why I'm so passionate about giving girls and women the opportunity I never had. I'm a little jealous, but also very proud to be able to support it at the same time.

"My partner's daughter has just started playing at Ross County, she's 11 and lives up at Bonar Bridge, and she's getting opportunities now through this partnership by complete coincidence that she would never have had otherwise.

"That would have been the best thing in my life, so I'm living through the girls of this generation, it's just fantastic.

"We have a whole plan about working and supporting the communities we operate in, so it's really important to us to give people those opportunities where we can. This is the perfect chance to do that – it's number one value for us basically."

Report by Andrew Henderson
Highland News & Media

NORTH TRIUMPH IS THE 'PINNACLE' FOR ALNESS

Highland League Under-18 North champions Alness United won the division for the first time in 2022-23.
Photo: Alan Cruickshank

Alness United secured this year's Highland Football League under-18 north championship without kicking a ball in April.

A 4-6 defeat for nearest rivals Inverness Athletic at home to Clachnacuddin confirmed that this season's title would be awarded to the Easter Ross youngsters, who sit at the top of the league table with nine points to spare.h a 3-0 win over Inverurie Locos on February 20th.

Forres Mechanics, who finished third,

HIGHLAND FOOTBALL LEAGUE UNDER-18 - NORTH

		Pl	W	D	L	F	A	GD	Pts	PPG
1.	Alness United	20	15	1	4	67	24	+43	46	2.30
2.	Inverness Ath	20	12	1	7	69	41	+28	37	1.85
3.	Forres Mech	20	12	0	8	56	33	+23	36	1.80
4.	Wick Academy	20	10	3	7	46	25	+21	33	1.65
5.	Lossiemouth	20	11	0	9	42	42	0	33	1.65
6.	Clachnacuddin	20	10	2	8	58	43	+15	32	1.60
7.	Nairn County	20	10	1	9	36	45	-9	31	1.55
8.	Rothes	20	9	3	8	46	48	-2	30	1.50
9.	Keith	20	8	2	10	43	51	-8	26	1.30
10.	St Duthus	20	5	0	15	41	73	-32	15	0.75
11.	Buckie Thistle	20	1	1	18	13	92	-79	4	0.20

did all they could to push for the runners-up spot by beating Keith away from home, but fell just one point short.

Led by coaches Liam Mackenzie and Sean Kelman, it is the first time the Alness club have secured the top youth honour under the Highland League north banner, having first competed in 2001.

Chairman Tommy Regan, who has overseen the club's rise over the years, said: "We have made ourselves a team who are capable of winning this league in recent years, and have fallen short.

"This season we have managed to win it and to me, a little surprisingly. I thought we would be up there competing, but never expected to win it – so that is a nice surprise, and I am absolutely delighted.

"I am delighted especially for our under-18 coaches, Liam and Sean, and all of our coaches who have worked hard throughout the year at all of our age levels. This is the pinnacle for us as a club.

"Winning the league, as I say to our kids, is the ultimate achievement, but sometimes just participating in these leagues is a reward. For us to have been competing for over 20 years at these age levels is great achievement."

It was a slow start to the campaign for United, who stuttered to begin with, drawing with Rothes and losing 3–0 to new boys Inverness Athletic.

But an up-turn in form throughout September and October saw them race back into contention with big wins over St Duthus, Buckie and Clachnacuddin.

They stumbled against Nairn County and Rothes in November, but they would go on to win their next eight games to secure the title in style – with some big victories against Wick Academy and Keith.

They hit their biggest win of the season at the end of March, beating bottom-placed Buckie Thistle by 9 goals to nil.

The goalscoring feats of Arran Thain and Cameron Grant, have been a particular highlight, netting 16 and 12 goals, respectively. Grant, in particular, grabbed the spotlight after he hit the net four times against defending champions Clachnacuddin in February.

Aaron Skinner, too, hit a rich vein of scoring form in the second half of the season, netting an impressive hat-trick against closest rivals Inverness.

Alness United scored their biggest win of the season against bottom-placed Buckie Thistle. Photo: Alan Cruickshank

LOCOS STARLETS ARE BEST IN THE HIGHLANDS

Highland League Under-18 champions Inverurie Loco Works won the North v East playoff at Rothes with a win over Alness United.   Photo: Kevin Taylor Photography

Under-18 East champions Inverurie Locos may have had a shorter campaign than their North counterparts, Alness United – but it proved to be no factor when the teams met to decide the Highland League under-18 championship in April.

The young Railwaymen prevailed thanks to a 4-2 win over United at MacKessack Park in Rothes, and were

HIGHLAND FOOTBALL LEAGUE UNDER-18 - EAST

		Pl	W	D	L	F	A	GD	Pts	PPG
1	Inverurie Locos	14	9	4	1	37	18	19	31	2.21
2	Dyce	14	9	1	4	42	31	11	28	2.00
3	Formartine Utd	14	9	1	4	39	28	11	28	2.00
4	Fraserburgh	14	8	0	6	32	23	9	24	1.71
5	Huntly	14	6	2	6	23	23	0	20	1.43
6	Deveronvale	14	5	1	8	21	27	-6	16	1.14
7	Turriff United	14	3	2	9	31	46	-15	11	0.79
8	Hermes	14	1	1	12	18	47	-29	4	0.29

dominant throughout.

Going 3-1 up in the first half thanks to goals from Liam Cowie and Taylor Mason (2), the Locos were as good as out of sight at the interval.

A fourth goal came courtesy of Anton

The playoff between Alness United and Inverurie Locos was played at Rothes.   Photo: Kevin Taylor Photography

Chauvin, and atlhough Alness were able to reduce the deficit, they could not prevent the Inverurie side from lifting the championship.

Locos' campaign in the East division was completed with their closest competition coming from close neighbours Dyce and Formartine United.

They secured the league title back in the middle of March with a 5-3 win over Hermes, having drawn with Dyce and Turriff United in February as it seemed like they may be about to trip before the finish line.

But an impressive record of just one league defeat - at the hands of Formartine in November - is what ultimately won them the division title.

Locos saved a penalty to deny Alness United a late chance to reduce the deficit.   Photo: Kevin Taylor Photography

BRUCH'S U21 STARLETS CLAIM LEAGUE HONOURS

Fraserburgh U21s with the GPH Builders Merchants Aberdeenshire League trophy. Photo: David Bartlett

INST. 1887

		Pl	W	D	L	F	A	GD	Pts	PPG
1	Fraserburgh	9	7	1	1	30	15	+15	22	2.44
2	Turriff United	9	6	2	1	36	10	+26	20	2.22
3	Deveronvale	9	6	1	2	22	18	+4	19	2.11
4	Dyce	9	5	2	2	36	23	+13	17	1.89
5	Formartine Utd	9	4	1	4	14	19	-5	13	1.44
6	Inverurie Locos	9	3	2	4	16	21	-5	11	1.22
7	Keith	9	2	3	4	26	26	0	9	1.00
8	Stonehaven	9	3	0	6	15	25	-10	9	1.00
9	Huntly	9	2	2	5	24	34	-10	8	0.89
10	Hermes	9	0	0	9	10	38	-28	0	0.00

8 AUGUST 2022

Deveronvale 5 Stonehaven 1
Turriff United 14 Huntly 2
Keith 4 Dyce 4
Inverurie 2 Fraserburgh 4
Hermes 0 Formartine 1

22 AUGUST 2022

Huntly 1 Deveronvale 2
Dyce 8 Stonehaven 1
Fraserburgh 3 Turriff United 2
Formartine 3 Keith 2
Hermes 2 Inverurie 4

12 SEPTEMBER 2022

Deveronvale 7 Dyce 6
Huntly 4 Fraserburgh 4
Stonehaven 2 Formartine 4
Turriff United 3 Hermes 0
Keith 1 Inverurie 3

26 SEPTEMBER 2022

Fraserburgh 4 Deveronvale 1
Formartine 1 Dyce 2
Inverurie 0 Stonehaven 1

10 OCTOBER 2022

Dyce 5 Inverurie 0
Stonehaven 0 Turriff United 1

13 OCTOBER 2022

Fraserburgh 8 Hermes 1

24 OCTOBER 2022

Keith 1 Fraserburgh 2
Turriff United 2 Dyce 2
Stonehaven 2 Huntly 1

7 NOVEMBER 2022

Deveronvale 0 Inverurie 0
Hermes 2 Keith 7
Formartine 1 Turriff United 5

21 NOVEMBER 2022

Stonehaven 5 Hermes 1

5 DECEMBER 2022

Deveronvale 0 Turriff United 4
Keith 3 Stonehaven 2
Inverurie 5 Huntly 3
Hermes 3 Dyce 6

9 JANUARY 2023

Deveronvale 3 Formartine 1
Hermes 1 Huntly 3

23 JANUARY 2023

Fraserburgh 2 Stonehaven 1
Keith 2 Turriff United 2
Inverurie 2 Formartine 2

6 FEBRUARY 2023

Formartine 0 Fraserburgh 3
Hermes 0 Deveronvale 1
Dyce 0 Huntly 5

20 FEBRUARY 2023

Keith 1 Deveronvale 3
Turriff United 3 Inverurie 0
Stonehaven 5 Hermes 1
Huntly 0 Formartine 1
Dyce 3 Fraserburgh 0

30 MARCH 2023

Huntly 5 Keith 5

The destination of this season's Aberdeenshire & District League Championship has been determined after fixtures in the competition were completed in March 2023.

Despite falling to a 3-0 defeat away to Dyce on February 20th, the season-long efforts of Fraserburgh's under-21 combination saw them lift the trophy, which was presented to them by Mike Macaulay of sponsors, GPH Builders Merchants.

Led by coaches Dean Cowie and Graham Johnston, it is the first time Fraserburgh have won the league since 1997-98, and is the eighth time overall as winners since the trophy's introduction in 1919. They are now the competition's second most successful club, just behind Buckie Thistle on 11 wins.

The defeat to Dyce was their first and only defeat of the nine game campaign, having won seven and drawn one other fixture.

The Broch's closest rivals Turriff United secured second place with a 3-0 win over Inverurie Locos on February 20th.

Deveronvale, who finished third, did all they could to push for the runners-up spot by beating Keith away from home, but fell just one point short.

ABERDEENSHIRE & DISTRICT (2022/23)

ABERDEEN & DISTRICT AFA

PREMIER DIVISION

	Pl	W	D	L	F	A	Pt
Kincorth	26	21	3	2	85	27	66
Cowie Thistle	26	17	2	7	79	31	53
Woodside *	26	15	6	5	75	42	53
Echt	26	14	4	8	69	43	46
Nicolls Amateurs	26	13	2	11	43	56	41
Insch	26	10	7	9	53	52	37
St Laurence	26	10	5	11	37	38	35
Tarves	26	9	8	9	59	59	35
Alford	26	8	4	14	45	55	28
Cove Thistle *	26	10	4	12	51	52	27
Banchory Am	26	6	9	11	46	56	27
Rattrays XI	26	7	2	17	35	72	23
Beacon Rangers	26	4	4	18	39	97	16
Tolbooth *	26	6	4	16	35	71	13

DIVISION ONE (NORTH)

	Pl	W	D	L	F	A	Pt
Kaimhill United	26	21	1	4	86	41	64
Bervie Caley	26	20	3	3	107	29	63
Great Western Utd	26	19	1	6	97	53	58
Stonehaven Ath	26	15	4	7	69	61	49
JS XI	26	14	4	8	66	55	46
Feughside	26	12	3	11	58	56	39
Auchnagatt Bar	26	12	2	12	75	57	38
Bridge of Don	26	12	2	12	60	62	38
AC Mill Inn	26	7	8	11	62	61	29
S'wood PV Am	26	9	1	16	47	57	28
Burghmuir	26	8	4	14	70	84	28
Kintore	26	5	2	19	53	99	17
FC Polska	26	4	4	18	49	98	16
Huntly Am *	26	4	1	21	38	124	10

DIVISION TWO (NORTH)

	Pl	W	D	L	F	A	Pt
University *	21	17	1	3	87	27	46
Kemnay Youth	21	14	1	6	57	27	43
Postal ALC	21	11	6	4	53	36	39
Newmachar U	21	9	5	7	31	29	32
AC Mill Acad	21	7	7	7	27	33	28
Halliburton	21	7	5	9	29	29	26
Byron SC	21	5	3	13	30	58	18
West End Utd *	21	0	0	21	13	88	-3

DIVISION ONE (EAST)

	Pl	W	D	L	F	A	
Westdyke	24	18	2	4	76	36	56
Kemnay Ams	24	17	4	3	91	23	55
St Mamans	24	12	10	2	47	18	46
Newburgh Th	24	12	4	8	52	35	40
Fyvie	24	10	8	6	45	32	38
BSFC	24	11	4	9	47	43	37
Turriff Thistle	24	10	7	7	55	44	37
Cammachmore	24	10	0	14	46	66	30
Glendale *	24	7	7	10	39	47	25
Lads Club Ams	24	6	3	15	30	58	21
Aboyne	24	6	1	17	36	64	19
Jesus House *	24	7	2	15	29	60	17
Continental *	24	3	2	19	33	100	8

DIVISION TWO (EAST)

	Pl	W	D	L	F	A	
Bon Acc City	24	21	1	2	123	35	64
Ellon Thistle	24	19	1	4	106	28	58
Glentanar Reflex *	24	16	2	6	95	59	44
Monymusk	24	13	1	10	87	43	40
Uni Colts *	24	10	3	11	75	70	29
Ellon Ams *	24	10	0	14	53	60	24
Theologians	24	7	2	15	48	79	23
Ferryhill	24	4	2	18	36	131	14
Blackburn *	24	1	2	21	26	144	2

CUP FINALS

ASSOCIATION TROPHY FINAL

Kemnay 5 Woodside 1
Balmoral Stadium, Aberdeen

ABERDEEN F.C. TROPHY FINAL

Kincorth 2 Woodside 1
Balmoral Stadium, Aberdeen

EDMOND TROPHY FINAL

Winners - Cove Thistle

PREMIER LEAGUE TROPHY FINAL

Woodside 1 Alford 0
Denmore Park, Bridge of Don

NORTH OF SCOTLAND AMATEUR CUP FINAL

Kincorth 6 Beacon Rangers 1
New Advocates Park, Aberdeen

WHITE CUP FINAL
Westdyke 2 Kemnay 1
Rothienorman

BARCLAY COOK CUP FINAL
Monymusk 0 Ellon Thistle 1
Rothienorman

BOWIE CUP FINAL
Great Western United 1 Tarves 2
Balmoral Stadium, Aberdeen

CASTLE ROVERS CUP FINAL
Halliburton 0 Kemnay Youth 0 (aet)
(Halliburton win 6-5 on pens)
Balmoral Stadium, Aberdeen

STEPHEN SHIELD FINAL
Feughside 1 Kaimhill United 2
New Advocates Park, Aberdeen

DICKIE TROPHY FINAL
University 3 Ellon United 3 (aet)
(University win 7-6 on pens)
Rothienorman

HANS FYFE TROPHY FINAL
Bon Accord City 2 AC Mill Inn Academy 5
Lochside Park, Bridge of Don

IAN NAPIER SHIELD FINAL
Alford 5 Nicolls Amateurs 0
Glenury Park, Stonehaven

Ian Napier Shield winners, Alford. Photo: Alford AFC

Kincorth AFC celebrated a treble winning season in June after winning the Premier League, North of Scotland Cup and Aberdeen F.C. Trophy.
Photo: Kincorth FC

AVOCH SECURE SEVENTH HIGHLAND AMATEUR CUP

Inverness & District Amateur side Avoch lifted the Highland Amateur Cup for a seventh time with a 1-0 win over Caithness champions Wick Groats. Photo: James Gunn Photography

Manager Martyn MacAllister said he reckoned the celebrations could last for up to a week after Avoch lifted the Highland Amateur Cup for the seventh time in their history.

A second-half strike by Stuart Leslie gave the Black Isle outfit a 1-0 win against old rivals Wick Groats in a scrappy, bruising final on Saturday.

It was tetchy at times and chances were at a premium – but MacAllister admitted he "couldn't really care less" about the lack of flowing football on show at Wick's Harmsworth Park as Avoch landed the trophy for the first time since 2017.

"I can't believe it – it's going to take a while to sink in," MacAllister said after the trophy presentation. "I'm absolutely delighted for the lads.

"It has been a tough cup run to get here but they've been brilliant, they've been absolutely excellent, and they deserved it today.

"I thought we were the better team. I didn't think it was the best of games, far from it, but I couldn't really care less – it's all about winning the trophy and that's all that matters to me.

"I don't think I've been involved in many cup finals that have been pretty. There was a lot of nerves involved in it too, but I thought we dealt with it better and I thought we deserved to win the game.

"All credit to Kevin [Anderson, Wick Groats manager] and his boys – they're always there or thereabouts. I've got a lot of time for them.

"They're a good group of lads and they'll be back again next year as well, no doubt about it."

Avoch are the second most successful club in terms of Highland Amateur Cup wins. Saturday's success means they are now just one behind eight-time winners Pentland United.

"I saw a stat that it's 12 finals out of the last 18 years we've been involved in, since 2004," MacAllister said.

"Pentland United are obviously in front. At the start of the competition the three teams that are bandied about are ourselves, Pentland United and Groats, and there's a reason for that.

"But we're just going to enjoy the next day or two, or week maybe, however long the celebrations go on for."

When the decisive moment came, after 53 minutes, there was more than a touch of fortune about it as Leslie sent a high ball into the danger zone from the left edge of the penalty box.

It looked more like an attempted cross than a shot, but either way it looped over the diving Kieran Macleod and went in at the far post.

Leslie admitted: "I think I'd be lying if I said it was intended as a goal, but it was put into the right area and if you don't buy a ticket you don't get a chance to win it.

"It is as a bit fortunate but I think we deserved it in the end. It was a proper final. It probably wasn't the best for the neutral to watch, but on the balance of play we won the battle and came away with the win."

Groats had to make an early change when Alan Mathieson hobbled off after eight minutes.

The first clear chance of the match fell to Groats about 10 minutes before half-time when Jonah Martens picked out Steven Anderson in space on the edge of the box, but keeper Neil Hastie reacted quickly and was able to smother the striker's shot.

Avoch broke downfield immediately and a hooked effort by Ian Penwright bounced off the top of the bar.

Avoch had an opportunity to put the issue beyond doubt in the closing stages when Leslie picked out the unmarked Dean Wallace but the newly introduced substitute knocked the ball over the top.

Wick Groats manager Kevin Anderson said: "There wasn't much in the game.

"We had a great chance in the first half that fell to Steven Anderson. It was a good save from the keeper but Steven was a bit gutted with himself, he thought he could have done better.

"I thought it was quite a scrappy game from both teams. There weren't many chances either way."

Commenting on the goal, Anderson said: "Sometimes you get them, sometimes you don't. It goes for you or it goes against you, but it was probably a cross-cum-shot that has ended up in the back of the net. There are fine lines in football.

"We're obviously disappointed but it has been a great season. At the end of the day we can be proud of what we've done this year – we've won three out of five trophies.

"The league title was the number one priority at the start of the season and we've got that in the bag.

"Of course we would have wanted to win today. Of course we're disappointed. But you use days like today to fuel you going forward.

"We'll just need to take it on the chin."

Report by Alan Hendry
Highland News & Media

HIGHLAND AMATEUR CUP 2023

FIRST ROUND - NORTH

Saturday May 14

Castletown 2 Lairg Rovers 2
(Castletown win on pens)
Golspie Stafford 7 Invergordon Social Club 3
Helmsdale United 1 Staxigoe United 2
High Ormlie Hotspur 3 Thurso Academicals 1
Inver 3 Lochinver 2
Lochbroom 0 Wick Groats 5
Thurso Pentlands 2 Keiss 8
Wick Thistle 3 Top Joes 0

FIRST ROUND - SOUTH

Saturday May 14

Ardersier 7 G16 United 1
Auctioneers 0 Mallaig 3
Avoch 7 Contin 2
Black Rock Rovers 5 Portree 2 (aet)
Black Isle United 3 Loch Ness 5
Clachnacuddin Res 3 Ness City 0
Conon Bridge 6 Slackbuie Rovers 0
Ferrybache 5 Sleat & Strath 4 (aet)

Fortrose Union 4 Hill Rovers 1
Inverness Athletic w/o Muir of Ord Rovers
North West Skye 7 Glenurquhart 1
Stratton 1 Gellions 6

FIRST ROUND - WESTERN ISLES

Friday May 13

Barra 2 Westside 1
Eriskay 1 Iochdar Saints 3
Harris 7 Stornoway United 1
Lochs 0 Carloway 5
Ness 1 Back 2
Stornoway Athletic 4 Benbecula 0

FIRST ROUND - NORTHERN ISLES

Saturday May 14

Kirkwall Accies 1 Dounby Athletic 2
Kirkwall Hotspurs 1 Rendall 0
Lerwick Celtic 5 Firth 1
Lerwick Thistle 1 Lerwick Spurs 6
Ness United 2 East United 0
Stromness Athletic w/o Orphir

The young reserve combination of Clachnacuddin FC reached the semi-final of this year's competition, losing to eventual winners Avoch. Photo: Clach FC Reserves Facebook

Golspie Stafford were the last club flying the flag for the county of Sutherland at the quarter final stage of this year's Highland Amateur Cup.   Photo: Golspie Stafford Facebook

SECOND ROUND

Saturday June 3

Ardersier 0 Avoch 2

Barra 2 Stromness Athletic 3

Black Rock Rovers 0 Back 2

Castletown 1 Lerwick Celtic 3

Clachnacuddin Res 4 Stornoway Athletic 2

Dounby 1 Harris 3

Ferrybache 1 Inver 2

Fortrose Union 2 Conon Bridge 1

Golspie Stafford 4 Ness Utd 0

Keiss 1 Carloway 5

Kirkwall Hotspurs 1 High Ormlie Hotspur 3

Lerwick Spurs w/o Gellions

Loch Ness 4 Iochdar Saints 0

Mallaig 2 North West Skye 1

Staxigoe Utd w/o Inverness Athletic

Wick Groats 3 Wick Thistle 1

THIRD ROUND

Saturday June 24

Back 0 Avoch 2

Carloway 2 Golspie Stafford 4

Clachnacuddin Res 3 Inver 2

Harris 1 Lerwick Celtic 3

Lerwick Spurs 2 High Ormlie Hotspur 1

Mallaig 2 Loch Ness 4

Stromness Athletic 2 Staxigoe United 2

(Stromness win 5-4 on pens)

Wick Groats 3 Fortrose Union 2

QUARTER FINALS

Saturday July 22

Stromness Athletic 4 Lerwick Spurs 3

Saturday July 15

Avoch 1 Loch Ness 0

Clachnacuddin Res 5 Golspie Stafford 5

(Clach win 5-4 on pens)

Wick Groats w/o Lerwick Celtic

SEMI FINALS

Saturday August 5

Wick Groats 1 Stromness Athletic 0

Clachnacuddin Res 0 Avoch 7

CUP FINAL

Saturday August 19

Wick Groats 0 Avoch 1

Harmsworth Park, Wick

SUMMER IN THE HIGHLANDS

Wick Groats completed a league and David Allan Shield/Colin Macleod Cup treble in 2023.   Photo: James Gunn

CAITHNESS AFA

LEAGUE 1

	Pl	W	D	L	F	A	Pt
Wick Groats	14	11	2	1	48	11	**35**
Pentland United	14	10	3	1	49	15	**33**
High Ormlie Hotspur	14	7	2	5	28	27	**23**
Staxigoe United	14	6	3	5	27	26	**21**
Wick Thistle	14	5	3	6	30	31	**18**
John O'Groats	14	4	1	9	16	31	**13**
Castletown	14	3	3	8	22	34	**12**
Thurso Acks	14	1	1	12	12	57	**4**

2ND DIVISION

	Pl	W	D	L	F	A	Pt
Lybster	15	11	2	2	77	19	**35**
Keiss	15	10	3	2	51	17	**33**
Thurso Swifts	15	10	2	3	49	22	**32**
Top Joes	15	4	4	7	29	35	**16**
Watten	15	3	3	9	21	50	**12**
Thurso Pentland	15	0	0	15	13	97	**0**

DAVID ALLAN SHIELD FINAL

High Ormlie Hotspur 1 Wick Groats 4
Back Park, Castletown

EAIN MACKINTOSH CUP FINAL

High Ormlie Hotspur 6 Wick Groats 0
Recreation Park, Halkirk

COLIN MACLEOD CUP FINAL

Wick Groats 1 Wick Thistle 0
Back Park, Castletown

STEVEN CUP FINAL

Lybster 0 Thurso Swifts 3
Cow Park, Lybster

FAIR PLAY WINNERS

1st Division - Pentland United
2nd Division - Top Joes

INVERNESS & DISTRICT AFA

PREMIER DIVISION

	Pl	W	D	L	F	A	Pt
Maryburgh	16	16	0	0	79	11	**48**
Avoch	16	12	1	3	69	22	**37**
Loch Ness	16	10	1	5	51	39	**31**
Inverness Ath	16	7	3	6	55	37	**24**
Ardersier	16	6	5	5	41	29	**23**
Black Isle United	16	5	1	10	36	85	**16**
Clach Amateur	16	3	2	11	21	40	**11**
Conon Bridge	16	2	3	11	32	68	**9**
Blackrock Rov.	16	2	2	12	23	76	**8**

1ST DIVISION

	Pl	W	D	L	F	A	Pt
Culloden B'smiths	18	15	0	3	70	25	**45**
Ferrybache	18	13	3	2	69	30	**42**
Hospice	18	12	4	2	56	25	**40**
Tomatin	18	12	1	5	40	26	**38**
Gellions	18	7	3	8	45	43	**24**
Tomatin United	18	6	2	10	40	60	**20**
Fortrose Union	18	6	2	10	35	58	**20**
Ness City	18	3	4	11	28	50	**13**
Gilham Flooring	18	2	3	13	29	61	**9**
Highland Athletic	18	2	3	13	26	60	**9**